HOW TO Supercha[rge] & Turbocharge GM LS-Series Engines

D1003765

Barry Kluczyk

CarTech®

CarTech®

CarTech®, Inc.
39966 Grand Avenue
North Branch, MN 55056
Phone: 651-277-1200 or 800-551-4754
Fax: 651-277-1203
www.cartechbooks.com

Edit by Paul Johnson and Scott Parkhurst
Layout by Sue Luehring

ISBN 978-1-934709-12-2
Item No. SA180

Library of Congress Cataloging-in-Publication Data

Kluczyk, Barry
  How to supercharge and turbocharge GM LS-Series engines / by Barry Kluczyk.
     p. cm
  ISBN 978-1-934709-12-2
1. General Motors automobiles—Motors—Superchargers. 2. General Motors automobiles—Motors—Superchargers. I. Title

TL215.G4K58 2010
629.25'040288–dc22

                                             2010001680

Printed in China
10 9 8 7 6 5 4 3 2

Front Cover:
Whether it's provided by a belt-driven supercharger (as on the engine on the left) or a pair of exhaust-driven superchargers (as on the engine on the right), boost equates to increased power output for your LS-based engine.

Title Page:
Whether a supercharger or turbo system, the GM family of LS engines responds well to forced induction, delivering horsepower for street vehicles that, only a few years ago, was the domain of race cars.

Back Cover Photos

Top Left: *Forced induction has been used to boost the power of engines for decades. Hot rodders made it a common practice after World War II, with engine-driven supercharging becoming popular on street and drag racing cars.*

Top Right: *A couple of the biggest advantages of a supercharger for a primarily street-driven vehicle are comparatively easy installation and a lower labor investment. Bolt-on kits—particularly Roots/screw-type systems that essentially swap out the original intake manifold—can be installed relatively quickly, with little impact on the rest of the vehicle's components or systems. The quicker the installation, the lower the labor cost at a professional shop.*

Middle Left: *Here's a typical bolt-on ProCharger system on a fifth-generation Camaro SS. As with Vortech superchargers, ProCharger's larger compressors are mostly interchangeable with the bracketry, allowing custom combinations. Proper tuning is paramount when using a high-boost, large-displacement compressor, as is the durability of factory engine parts.*

Middle Right: *Looking up at the chassis, with the left-rear tire on the right side of the photo, this image shows STS's mounting location for the turbocharger. It's the location of the original muffler, which is eliminated with this system (although that is not true for all STS kits). A benefit of this mounting position is the factory heat shield that was originally designed for the muffler.*

Bottom Left: *There is an almost endless list of possibilities when it comes to boost-friendly cylinder heads for LS engines. The excellent port design and large capacity runners allow for easy and efficient cylinder filling. Ensuring intake manifold compatibility with the heads' intake ports is the only major caveat when selecting them for a supercharged or turbocharged combination.*

Bottom Right: *Based on the LSX cylinder block and using a smaller, 400-ci displacement, this Thomson Automotive-built twin-turbo engine consistently delivers more than 2,000 earth-shaking horsepower—with nearly 30 pounds of boost.*

OVERSEAS DISTRIBUTION BY:

Brooklands Books Ltd.
P.O. Box 146, Cobham, Surrey, KT11 1LG, England
Phone: 01932 865051 • Fax: 01932 868803
www.brooklands-books.com

Renniks Publications Ltd.
3/37-39 Green Street, Banksmeadow, NSW 2109, Australia
Phone: 2 9695 7055 • Fax: 2 9695 7355

CONTENTS

Dedication..4
Acknowledgments...4
Introduction 5

Chapter 1: LS Engines and Forced Induction 6
LS Family Tree 7
Gen III Automotive Engines 8
Gen IV Automotive Engines 8
Gen III/IV Vortec Truck Engines 9
Supercharging vs. Turbocharging 9
Understanding Boost—Including PSI vs. Bar 12
Drag Racing 13
LS Performance Potential 13
Cast Rotating Parts: Pushing the Factory Parts' Envelope 14
Compression Ratio and Recommended Boost Limits 14
Importance of Tuning and Avoiding Detonation 15
Charge Cooling/Intercooling 15
Forced-Induction Terms 16
Real-World Project:
    Steve Gilliland's 1,000-hp Twin-Turbo Z06 17

Chapter 2: Supercharger Types and Selection 18
Positive-Displacement Superchargers 18
Centrifugal Superchargers 22
Kit and Cost Considerations 24
Positive-Displacement vs. Centrifugal Blowers 26
How Much "Blower" Do You Need? 26
Music to the Ears? 27
The Importance of a Charge Cooler 27
Surge Protection 27
Pulley Size and Performance 27
Belt Wrap and Belt Size 28
GM Factory-Supercharged LS9 and LSA Engines 29
Real-World Project: Pratt & Miller's LS9.RS—The Ultimate
    Supercharged LS Street Engine 31

Chapter 3: Turbocharger Types and Selection 34
LS-Powered Production Vehicles 35
Turbocharger Component Terms 36
Operation Basics 36
Selecting the Right Size Turbocharger 40
Turbocharger Aspect Ratio 40
Pitfalls of Mixing Turbines and Compressors 41
Elements of a Turbo System 41
Boost Controller and Turbo Timer 42
Single- vs. Twin-Turbo Systems 42
Bolt-On Turbo Kits and Tuner Systems 44

Chapter 4: Kit Pre-Installation 46
Body and Chassis Component Removal 46
Engine Preparation 47
Fuel-Pressure Relief 48
Oil-Pan/Oil-System Modifications 49
"Pinning" the Crankshaft 49
Fuel Pump 51
Fuel Injectors 52
Spark Plugs 53
Real-World Project: Camshaft and Valvesprings Swap 54

Chapter 5: Supercharger Installation Projects 60
Project 1: Roots/Screw-Type Supercharger Kit 60
Project 2: Centrifugal Supercharger Kit 68

Chapter 6: Turbocharger Installation Projects 72
Real-World Project: Lingenfelter System 72
Custom Turbo System Fabrication 78
The STS Option 81
Building a Racing Car around a Turbo System 83

**Chapter 7: Tuning for Supercharged and
    Turbocharged Engines 87**
Air + Fuel = Horsepower 87
Mass Airflow vs. Speed Density 88
Map Sensors 89
GM Controllers 90
Pre-Packaged Programming 91
Aftermarket Flash Software 91
Livernois Motorsports' X-Treme Cal Tuning System 93
Standalone Control Systems 94
Chassis Dyno Tuning 95
Wideband Tuning 96
Electronic Throttle 97
Methanol Injection 98
The Martin SS 427 Package 99

**Chapter 8: Building an LS Engine: Cylinder Block and
    Rotating Assembly 100**
Cylinder Block 100
Rotating Assembly 104

**Chapter 9: Building an LS Engine: Heads, Cam
    and Induction 116**
Cylinder Heads 116
Valves 120
Valvetrain Components 120
Cylinder-Head Gaskets 121
Camshaft 121
Turbocharger Camshaft 123
Ignition and Ignition Controller 126
Intake Manifold 127
Throttle Body 128
Real-World Project:
    Building a 2,000-hp Twin-Turbo LS Engine 129

**Chapter 10: Forced-Induction Support and Auxiliary
    Components 134**
Headers and Exhaust System 134
Real-World Project: Installing a Cat-Back Exhaust System 135
Cooling System 137
Transmissions 137
Axle Upgrades 139
Real-World Project: F-Car Axle Swap 140
Auxiliary Instruments 142

Source Guide..144

DEDICATION

To Mary Kluczyk

ACKNOWLEDGMENTS

I wish to acknowledge and thank the following for their assistance and support during the creation of this book: Brian Thomson and the technicians at Thomson Automotive; Joe Borschke at Stenod Performance; Dan Millen and the technicians at Livernois Motorsports; Shari McCullough-Arfons and Sunpro; and Aaron Schoen.

A longtime cliché of the automotive world is the phrase, "they don't build 'em like they used to." When it comes to the performance capability of the General Motors Gen III/Gen IV engines (commonly known as "LS" engines), that old adage couldn't be more true—but not in the traditional sense.

The LS engine isn't built like the old small-blocks, and that's a good thing. They've proven to be very durable and, with their exceptional airflow capabilities, they make tremendous power with comparatively little work. Throw a supercharger or turbo system on one of these compact powerhouses and the dyno numbers go through the roof. In fact, the only factor that holds back an LS engine from making astronomical horsepower is the amount of boost that can be safely shoved through it.

I first encountered the LS engine when the rest of the performance public did, in the late 1990s. I was shooting stories at a variety of tuning shops and was, frankly, suspicious of the chassis dyno numbers that were being generated by LS1-powered F-body cars and Corvettes with bolt-on superchargers. Compared to what the previous GM LT1 engines produced and the amount of time and money the Mustang guys were spending to get power out of their 4.6-liter pony cars, the ease at

which 500 rear-wheel horsepower was spitting out of the LS-powered vehicles raised more than a few eyebrows. But, as time progressed and GM increased the displacement and performance range of its well-engineered new engine family, big power has become the norm. In fact, street cars pushing 900 hp and more are not hard to find.

Of course, there's more than one key required to unlock such supercharged performance. The high-flow attributes of the cylinder heads are tailor-made for big power, but it wouldn't be possible without easily adjustable factory controllers that enable tuning that are the envy of the Mustang and Hemi camps. The controllers, however, are mostly limited to the fuel they can direct into the engine and, in most cases, that ceiling is around the 1,000-hp level. After that, special injector requirements typically mean a stand-alone aftermarket controller that can handle them. But even then, the engine can still be tuned for streetable, pump-gas drivability.

This book outlines the basics of supercharging and turbocharging, as they're applied to LS engines. It doesn't suggest either method of forced induction is better than the other, but points out the performance differences, installation challenges, and cost implications between them. There are also great

tips for building an engine to support higher-boost combinations.

Whether you're looking for a simple bolt-on blower kit on an otherwise-stock fifth-generation Camaro or a custom-fabricated twin-turbo system for a Corvette Z06, you'll find plenty of ideas to ponder within these pages. And you'll see everything from a $46,000 turbo-kit installation to a homemade turbo system built with cast-off and salvage-yard parts.

If you're new to the performance world or, more specifically, the corner of it that involves forced induction, do yourself a favor and start browsing the online message boards and forums for ideas, and ask around for recommendations on knowledgeable and reputable tuning shops. Before you spend what will minimally be several thousand dollars on a blower or turbo system for your vehicle(s), you'll want to know unequivocally that it's going to deliver the performance you're seeking.

There's another old automotive saying: "Speed costs money; how fast do you want to go?" I believe that can be re-written for the LS engine this way: Horsepower requires boost; how much can you afford?

Whatever your answer, a little forethought and some careful planning will ensure you'll come away satisfied when that boost-gauge needle swings into positive-manifold-pressure territory.

LS ENGINES AND FORCED INDUCTION

In general terms, and assuming everything else is equal, an internal combustion engine with larger displacement flows more air than a smaller-displacement engine. The engine with the greater airflow makes more power.

Forcing more air into an engine than it naturally draws can substantially increase the output of a smaller engine and give it the power of a larger engine. The forced or ambient air is delivered to the intake manifold at a pressure greater than the outside. It is denser, delivering more oxygen to the combustion chamber. When mixed with the appropriate ratio of additional fuel, the result is a more powerful combustion. That's the essence of supercharging; whether through an engine-driven supercharger or exhaust-driven turbocharger.

The technology for forced induction supercharging and turbocharging internal combustion engines has been around since the early twentieth century, with automotive manufacturers employing the power-boosting effects for more than 80 years. Both supercharging and turbocharging are

Forced induction has been used to boost the power of engines for decades. Hot rodders made it a common practice after World War II, with engine-driven supercharging becoming popular on street and drag racing cars.

General Motors experimented with turbocharging in the early 1960s, and perfected it in the mid-1980s by combining it with electronic fuel injection. The turbocharged and intercooled V-6 engine of the 1986–1987 Buick Grand National outperformed most V-8s when new.

In the early 1990s, GM adopted supercharging for a number of V-6-powered midsize and large passenger cars, including the Pontiac Grand Prix. GM used a Roots-blown 3.8-liter engine, with the supercharger supplied by Eaton. The engines proved exceptionally robust and powerful, spawning a cult of enthusiasts who continue to modify and race the vehicles.

currently used on dozens of regular production automobiles, and they have been staples of the high-performance world since the close of World War II.

One of the most popular performance engines of today is GM's "LS" family. As technology progresses, it continues to become an increasingly popular choice for forced induction. Since its introduction in the late 1990s, the GM Gen III/Gen IV engine family (commonly known as LS) has proven itself a capable foundation for high-performance engines. By relying on a conventional, cam-in-block configuration with the benefit of exceptionally high flowing cylinder heads, the LS engine delivers tremendous torque at low RPM and great power at the upper rev range.

Forced induction was attempted with early LS engines, but often with mixed results. Early adopters of supercharging and turbocharging typically encountered tuning trouble when they tried to work around the factory engine-control system and crank-triggered ignition system. That, and the greater airflow capability of the LS heads, made it difficult to match a supercharger or turbocharger to the engine. Often, the "blowers" ran out of breath.

But much has changed in the years since tuners first experimented with supercharging the LS engine. Properly sized superchargers and turbochargers, relatively easy tuning, and other elements have made supercharging or turbocharging an LS-powered vehicle a simple, yet highly effective method of generating a dramatic increase in power.

Of course, GM itself has adopted supercharging as a regular production method of building big power. The Corvette ZR1's LS9 engine and

GM's relationship with Eaton superchargers reached its zenith in 2009, with the introduction of the factory-blown Corvette ZR1. With its sixth-generation supercharger atop its 6.2-liter V-8, the ZR1 is rated at 638 hp. It is the most powerful production car ever produced by General Motors. (Photo courtesy General Motors)

Along with the Corvette ZR1, GM launched another factory-supercharged car in 2009: the Cadillac CTS-V. Like the ZR1, it featured a sixth-generation Eaton supercharger on a 6.2-liter engine, but the supercharger was smaller—resulting in "only" 556 hp. (Photo courtesy General Motors)

the Cadillac CTS-V's LSA engine use Roots-type superchargers to make 638 hp and 556 hp, respectively. The engines are designed with specific components to support forced induction.

LS Family Tree

Although all engines in the family are referred to as LS series, GM has manufactured two generations within that family. The first generation was called Gen III and includes, from an automotive standpoint, the LS1 and LS6 engines.

The biggest differences between Gen III/IV engines are larger bores in the cylinder blocks of Gen IVs, and Gen IV cylinder heads in general.

There are also different camshaft-position-sensor locations: front timing-cover area on Gen IV blocks and top-rear position on Gen III blocks. On most Gen IV blocks, there are cast-in provisions for GM's Active Fuel Management cylinder-deactivation system.

Also, many Gen IV engines made from around 2006 and later are equipped with electronically controlled (wireless) throttle systems.

Those engines also feature a 58X timing system that includes a different engine controller and 58-tooth reluctor wheel on the crankshaft (also known as a 60-minus-2 wheel), rather than the 24X system used with earlier LS engines (mostly those with cable-operated throttles).

There is great interchangeability between LS engines, including the Gen III and Gen IV versions. Cylinder heads, crankshafts, intake manifolds, and more can be mixed and matched, but there is not *absolute* compatibility. Not every head matches every intake manifold and not every crankshaft works with every engine combination. (See Chapters 8 and 9 for more information on parts interchangeability and building a forced-induction LS engine.)

What follows here is a quick primer on production LS engines and their notable features.

Gen III Automotive Engines

The Gen III LS engine is defined by its 3.90-ci (99 mm) cylinder bore. Like later LS engines, it carries the basic design attributes and good-flowing heads, but the bore dimension ultimately limits the type of cylinder head that can be used on it. Later, larger-bore engines can use almost all LS-style heads, while the Gen III is limited to the heads from LS1, LS6, and Gen IV LS2 engines.

LS1

LS1 5.7-liter (346 ci) engines were installed between the 1997 and 2004 model years in North America (Corvette, Camaro, and Firebird, as well as the GTO in the United States only) and encompassing some 2005 models in other markets (primarily Australia).

LS1 5.7-liter Gen III. (Photo courtesy General Motors)

LS6

The LS6 was introduced in 2001 in the Corvette Z06 and was manufactured through 2005, when it was also installed in the first-generation Cadillac CTS-V. The LS6 shared the LS1's 5.7-liter displacement, but used a unique block casting with enhanced strength, greater bay-to-bay breathing capability, and other minor differences. The heads, intake manifolds, and camshaft are unique LS6 parts, but fit the LS1 block.

Gen IV Automotive Engines

In automotive applications, the Gen IV introduced a larger, 4.00-ci (101.6 mm) bore dimension that enables heads of larger-displacement Gen IV engines to be used with it. The Gen IV engines also introduced electronic throttle control, while the Gen III LS1 and LS6 engines only used cable-operated throttles. It is possible to adapt either throttle style, although the proper controller must be used.

LS2

In 2005, the LS2 6.0-liter (364 ci) engine and the Gen IV design changes made their debut. In GM performance vehicles, it was offered in the Corvette, GTO, and even the heritage-styled SSR roadster. It is the standard engine in the Pontiac G8 GT. Its larger displacement brought greater power. The LS2 is one of the most adaptable engines, as LS1, LS6, LS3, and L92 cylinder heads work well on it.

LS3/L99

Introduced on the 2008 Corvette, the LS3 brought LS base performance to an unprecedented level: 430 hp from 6.2-liter (376 ci), making it the most powerful base Corvette engine in history.

The LS3 block not only has larger bores than the LS2, but a strengthened casting to support more-powerful 6.2-liter engines, including the LS9 supercharged engine of the Corvette ZR1. The LS3 is offered in the Pontiac G8 GXP and is the standard V-8 engine in the 2010 Camaro SS.

The L99 is essentially the same as the LS3, but it is equipped with GM's fuel-saving Active Fuel Management cylinder-deactivation system. It is standard on 2010 Camaro SS models equipped with an automatic transmission.

LS3 6.2-liter Gen IV. (Photo courtesy General Motors)

LS4

Perhaps the most unique application of the LS engine in a car, the LS4 is a 5.3-liter version used in the front-wheel-drive Chevrolet Impala SS and Pontiac Grand Prix GXP. The LS4 has an aluminum block and unique, low-profile front-end accessory system, including a "flattened" water pump, to accommodate the transverse-mounting position in the Impala and Grand Prix. It is rated at 303 hp and 323 ft-lbs of torque.

LS7

The LS7 is the standard engine in the Corvette Z06 and its 7.0-liter displacement (427 ci) makes it the largest LS engine offered in a production car. Unlike the LS1/LS6, LS2, and LS3 engines, the LS7 uses a Siamese-bore cylinder-block design—required for its big, 4.125-inch bores. Competition-proven heads and lightweight components, such as titanium rods and intake valves, make the LS7 a street tuned racing engine, with 505 hp.

LS9

The most powerful production engine ever from GM, the LS9 is the 6.2-liter supercharged and charge-cooled engine of the Corvette ZR1. It is rated at an astonishing 638 hp. The LS9 uses the strengthened 6.2-liter block with stronger, roto-cast cylinder heads and a sixth-generation 2.3-liter Roots-type supercharger. Like the LS7,

it uses a dry-sump oiling system. It is the ultimate production LS engine.

LSA

A detuned version of the LS9, this supercharged 6.2-liter engine is standard in the 2009 Cadillac CTS-V. It is built with several differences compared to the LS9, including hypereutectic pistons versus the LS9's forged pistons; and a smaller, 1.9-liter supercharger. The LSA also has a different charge-cooler design on top of the supercharger. Horsepower is rated at 556.

Gen III/IV Vortec Truck Engines

Although performance car engines have typically carried "LS" designations, truck engines built on this platform have been dubbed Vortec. They are generally distinguished by iron cylinder blocks and smaller displacements than car engines. Interestingly, a 5.7L Vortec LS engine has never been offered. Here's a quick rundown of the previous and current production LS truck engines.

4.8-liter: The smallest displacement LS engine (293 ci); it uses an iron block with 3.78-inch bores and aluminum heads.

5.3-liter: The most common LS truck engine, it uses the same iron block with 3.78-inch bore as the 4.8-liter, but with a larger, 3.62-inch stroke (327 ci). Later versions came equipped for Active Fuel Management. They were manufactured with iron and aluminum cylinder blocks.

6.0-liter: Used primarily in 3/4 and 1-ton trucks, the 6.0-liter (364 ci) uses an iron block (LY6) or aluminum block (L76) and aluminum heads, with provisions for Active Fuel Management; some are equipped with variable valve timing.

6.2-liter: Commonly referred to by its L92 or L94 engine codes, the Vortec 6.2-liter (376 ci) engine uses an aluminum block and aluminum heads, and incorporates advanced technology including variable valve timing. The 6.2-liter is used primarily as a high-performance engine for the Cadillac Escalade and GMC Yukon Denali, but also in some Silverado and Sierra pickup models. In 2010, some 6.2-liter engines took the L9H name to reflect changes that included E85 fuel compatibility.

Supercharging vs. Turbocharging

At their most basic, turbochargers and superchargers are air pumps, but with different pumping characteristics. The turbocharger is an exhaust-driven pump that saps no engine power when not making boost. A supercharger is an engine-driven pump that is essentially another component on the accessory drive system that requires a modicum of power to drive, even when it's not producing much boost.

The thermal efficiency (the amount of combustion energy that is converted to power) is greater with

LSA 6.2-liter supercharged Gen IV. (Photo courtesy General Motors)

L94 Vortec 6.2-liter Gen IV. (Photo courtesy General Motors)

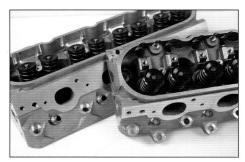

Excellent airflow characteristics of the basic LS cylinder head design greatly exploit the benefits of forced induction, as air is easily and quickly moved through the engine. Because of this, a higher-capacity supercharger or larger turbo is often used, when compared to older, previous-generation Chevy small-block designs, to fulfill the airflow capability of the free-flowing LS engine.

Superchargers (particularly Roots and screw-type blowers) are excellent at delivering low-RPM power, as they are always making at least a minimal amount of boost when the engine is running. That's because the supercharger is directly linked to the crankshaft via the drive belt. That connection also requires a small amount of horsepower to simply turn the supercharger.

Turbochargers require no engine power to drive, and therefore are considerably more efficient than an engine-driven supercharger. However, boost only occurs when the engine RPM rises. At low speeds, particularly off idle, the turbocharger provides no power increase.

a turbocharger system than a supercharger, because it recycles a significant amount of exhaust energy to spin the compressor. That exhaust energy is lost to the exhaust system in normally aspirated and supercharged engines. That said, centrifugal and Lysholm (screw-type) superchargers are up to 85 percent efficient.

In general terms, superchargers deliver greater power and torque at low- and mid-range RPM levels, with nearly full boost available immediately at wide-open throttle (WOT). A supercharger's effectiveness tends to trail off at higher RPM, while turbochargers typically deliver their greatest power contribution at mid- to high-RPM levels, with boost building progressively in line with an increase of engine speed. Turbochargers are also very good at building mid-range torque, and when properly sized, can deliver excellent low-end power, too.

Below are a number of factors to consider before purchasing a bolt-on

system. The performance requirements and engine demands for custom combinations and racing applications are different, but for the enthusiast seeking to add a forced induction system to his or her vehicle, the following points are the most relevant.

Horsepower and Power Adjustability

Although supercharger and turbocharger kits deliver approximately the performance their manufacturers advertise, turbocharging generally delivers more power for the equivalent dollar spent on a supercharger kit. Turbo systems also offer almost unlimited upgrade potential.

Apart from the capacity to change the drive pulley on some superchargers, the output of a blower is pretty much determined by the size of the compressor. With a turbo system, a number of elements are easily manipulated to increase power. In fact, the almost infinite adjustability of turbo systems is one of their primary appeals.

The advantage of turbocharging in a racing application is clearly illustrated in this partially constructed fourth-generation Firebird, as two very large turbochargers have been adapted to an LS engine. Except for the older, "71"-series superchargers used in Top Fuel, Top Alcohol, and some Pro Mod-type drag racing classes, there aren't Roots and screw-type superchargers capable of delivering the airflow of a pair of extra-large turbos. Even large centrifugal blowers are typically limited to only one per engine. With a pair of turbos, each driven by half of the cylinders, the only real limit is keeping the engine itself together under maximum boost.

Modern Roots and screw superchargers make excellent choices for street-driven performance vehicles, as they deliver instant power at low-engine speeds. They're also quieter and offer greater drivability than ever before. And when compared to custom or bolt-on turbo kits, they are very cost effective.

Performance Range

As noted earlier, superchargers—particularly Roots/screw types—generally deliver gobs of low-end power and become less efficient at higher RPM. The opposite is generally true for turbochargers; they tend to deliver their greatest performance as maximum boost is delivered with higher engine speed.

Drivability

Because an engine-driven supercharger is "on," it tends to give a street-driven vehicle an abundance of off-the-line/low-speed pull—to the point where it is difficult to manage part-throttle driving in some instances, as tire spin becomes an issue. The higher-RPM power application of turbo systems typically makes them more tractable at low speeds. The enthusiast wishing for supremacy off the line at stoplights with the instant application of full boost will probably enjoy a super-

charger; while the enthusiast seeking a wider performance range will likely find a turbo system more rewarding.

Noise

Generally speaking, the compressors of most supercharger and turbocharger systems are very quiet these days. Turbos are essentially silent until they start spinning at high RPM, and the same is true for most Roots/screw-type blowers. Centrifugal superchargers are much quieter than they used to be, but at idle, they're not as quiet as turbos or Roots/screw-type superchargers.

Tuning

There's no real advantage between tuning a supercharged or turbocharged engine, as the need to maintain an adequate air/fuel ratio and optimal spark to avoid detonation is paramount with both methods. Both types of systems have unique needs for delivering safe, optimal per-

formance, but the basic approach to tuning is similar. There's no clear advantage to either system.

Maintenance and Reliability

When installed and used properly, supercharger and turbocharger kits are very reliable, with the compressors for both lubricated with engine oil—although some Roots/screw-type blowers feature self-contained lubrication systems. Over time, the drive belt for a supercharger must be inspected just like the engine's standard accessory belt, and after a few years, the compressor may require an inspection to ensure the tolerances and clearances are within specification limits for the rotors. Turbochargers are very susceptible to heat and even with adequate lubrication, the internal seals and turbine can wear and allow oil blow-by. This requires the turbo to be rebuilt.

System Cost

Because of the myriad of extra equipment—from the wastegate to the exhaust manifolds—turbocharger bolt-on kits generally cost two to three times more more than supercharger kits. Additionally, turbocharger systems generally take longer to install than supercharger kits. This adds up when outsourcing the project to a professional shop.

Installation Impact on the Vehicle

Assuming all turbocharger and supercharger systems employ an intercooler, the Roots/screw-type supercharger systems generally require the fewest compromises and/or fabrication modifications during installation. Because they install in place of the intake manifold, few changes are required at the front of the engine or in the engine compartment.

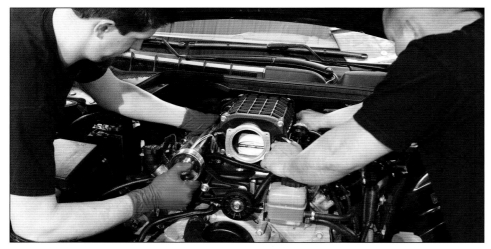

A couple of the biggest advantages of a supercharger for a primarily street-driven vehicle are comparatively easy installation and a lower labor investment. Bolt-on kits (particularly Roots/screw-type systems that essentially swap out the original intake manifold) can be installed relatively quickly, with little impact on the rest of the vehicle's components or systems. The quicker the installation, the lower the labor cost at a professional shop.

Consequently, they offer the most integrated, "factory-looking" appearance under the hood. Centrifugal superchargers require a mounting bracket on the front of the engine that can require moderate modification, removal, or relocation of factory components.

With bolt-on turbocharger systems, the installation of the exhaust manifolds, turbochargers, and associated plumbing typically require considerably more fabrication, modification, and relocation of stock parts than supercharger systems.

Installation Cost

Again, because of the extra equipment associated with them, turbocharger kits are generally more time consuming to install, and therefore, more labor costs.

So, while a turbo kit offers greater performance potential, the cost involved with this investment may steer some toward a supercharger. In fact, there are other fac-

tors to consider before ordering a system for your car.

For one, the tight confines of the engine compartments in Corvettes, Camaros/Firebirds, and GTOs/Monaros make packaging and installing a turbo kit very difficult. This not only makes the installation a painstaking and difficult procedure, but can make future servicing all but impossible without an extensive teardown of the vehicle's front end.

There is more room in the engine compartments of full-size trucks SUVs, and TrailBlazer SSs; but stuffing a turbo system—excluding the STS-type rear-mount system—can be a challenge in a regular street car.

My opinion is that turbocharging is great for vehicles destined to spend most of their time on the drag strip; but for typical, street-driven vehicles, a supercharger system is the easier and more economical method to build power. Many tuners and manufacturers who fall on the turbo side of the argument will undoubt-

edly disagree; but when it comes to bolt-on, forced-induction kits, superchargers are easier and cheaper to implement, with less maintenance.

Understanding Boost Including PSI vs. Bar

Whether it is a supercharger or turbocharger system, the measure of pressurized air fed into the engine is referred to as "boost." It is the difference between the ambient air pressure and the increased air pressure the boost-producing device generates at the intake manifold. Boost is the opposite of vacuum, which is what a non-boosted engine makes during normal operation.

When an engine isn't running, it generates no vacuum or boost (negative pressure), meaning the pressure in the intake manifold is the same as the ambient air pressure—about 14.7 pounds per square inch (psi). At idle and low-throttle conditions, an engine generates vacuum, indicating the pressure in the intake manifold is lower than the ambient pressure.

In a supercharged or turbocharged engine, boost is created as more throttle is applied and the boost-generating device forces air into the intake manifold at a higher pressure than ambient (positive) pressure. The air pressure at the intake manifold swings from negative to positive—that's why high-performance boost gauges indicate both vacuum and boost measurements.

In North America, boost is generally measured in psi, while bar is more common in other countries. When measuring in psi, the ambient air pressure is regarded as the base, or 0 pounds of boost. The positive pressure builds on that base, with 1

The adjustability and boost capability of turbocharging has made it the power adder of choice for most professional and semi-professional drag racers in the Fastest Street Car series. One of the quickest competitors has been Tom Kempf, whose red, single-turbo Camaro was capable of mid-7-second ETs.

Boost is generated when the super-charger or turbocharger creates air pressure greater than ambient when it is introduced to the engine (at the throttle body). Supercharged engines generate a small amount of boost whenever the engine is running—even at idle. Turbocharged engines require higher RPM to generate boost.

pound of boost indicating 1 psi greater than ambient pressure.

With bar measurements, bar is roughly the equivalent of ambient air pressure. Technically, 1 bar is equivalent to 14.7 psi, not 14.5 psi, but many enthusiasts equate it to the normal atmospheric pressure, so a .5-bar pressure reading is roughly 7.25 pounds of boost. A full, 1-bar reading would indicate 14.5 pounds of boost.

Drag Racing

An inspection of the competitors at any outlaw-type drag racing event shows more turbochargers than superchargers and there's a reason for it: Turbos make more power. More specifically, there aren't superchargers that have the capability to match the performance of very large turbochargers. That is changing with the advent of larger centrifugal supercharger compressors from ProCharger, but at the time this book was published, even ProCharger's largest compressors didn't quite

match the maximum boost from the largest turbo systems.

That's not to say that turbocharging is the optimal power adder for a drag car. Dan Millen, a longtime championship drag racer and proprietor of the renowned tuning shop Livernois Motorsports in Dearborn Heights, Michigan, has been driving single-turbo race cars since 2001.

"Right now, turbos make more power than superchargers—with twin-turbo combinations making more than single turbos—and that's why I use them," Millen says. "I like the simplicity of blowers and the relative ease of tuning with them, but superchargers just don't match turbos yet on the drag strip. Also, there is comparatively little parasitic loss with a turbo, whereas a blower requires a lot of power just to turn the compressor."

LS Performance Potential

In a word, the performance potential of a boosted LS engine is almost unlimited. Whether you're simply adding a bolt-on kit to an otherwise unmodified engine, or building an engine from the ground up to support a larger horsepower goal, the parts are available to do it

all—including dedicated performance cylinder blocks designed to withstand nearly 30 psi of turbocharged boost and more than 2,000 hp.

Realistically, most enthusiasts and builders are aiming for something more modest in a street-driven or street/strip car. But the already high power levels of stock LS-powered vehicles—from the 305 hp of the 1998–2002 LS1-powered F-cars to the 505 hp of the LS7-powered Corvette Z06—means the return on a supercharger or turbocharger investment will be impressive.

In most cases, a standard street-based bolt-on supercharger or turbocharger kit adds approximately 100 to 125 hp. Bolt-on twin-turbo systems can approach or exceed 200-hp gains, but extreme care must be taken with tuning on an engine with a stock rotating assembly, as factory-installed cast pistons and rods don't stand up long if detonation occurs, or even if there is excessive heat from a slightly lean air/fuel mixture.

In fact, when a forced-induction system is planned to exceed the stock engine's output by more than about 150 hp, the builder should consider fortifying the engine with forged rotating parts and lower compression pistons.

When building a forced-induction combination that's planned to exceed the performance level of a bolt-on kit with relatively mild boost, the investment in stronger rotating parts must be made. Most LS production engines don't come with a forged crankshaft, rods, or pistons. They're must-haves for ensuring engine strength and durability.

Perhaps the ultimate demonstration of forced-induction LS power is the twin-turbocharged 1996 Impala SS built by GM Performance Parts. Its 400-ci LSX iron-block engine produces more than 2,000 hp, with help from a pair of 88-mm turbos. (See Chapter 9 for a complete look at the engine, including the components and dyno testing.)

Cast Rotating Parts: Pushing the Factory Parts' Envelope

To put it simply, production LS engines—except the ZR1's LS9 and CTS-V's LSA—weren't designed for supercharging. And while the basic engine design has proven to be remarkably durable, the cylinder pressure generated by a supercharger or turbocharger takes its toll on the engine's internal components.

The only LS engine from the factory to come with forged pistons is the LS9. All of the rest (the LS7 and LSA included) use hypereutectic (cast) aluminum pistons. Powdered metal rods and a mix of cast and forged crankshafts are used, too, but the bottom line is the basic rotating assembly was *not* designed for the rigors of forced induction.

That's not to say the factory parts don't withstand forced induction. In fact, typical bolt-on blower and turbo kits survive very well with otherwise-stock engines. Generally speaking, however, bolt-on kits deliver less than 15 pounds of boost and vehicles that are primarily street driven don't see extended use at wide-open throttle. When tuned properly, stock engines survive admirably. It's when the boost level is turned up and the vehicle's use sees increased racing duty that the longevity of the factory internal components is reduced. (See Chapters 8 and 9 for engine-building guidelines, including the use of forged rotating components.)

Compression Ratio and Recommended Boost Limits

Another performance limitation when using forced induction on an LS engine with stock internal components is the high compression ratio. The engines in most popular LS-powered performance vehicles, from the LS1-powered F-bodies to the

Because production LS engines have relatively high compression ratios, extreme care must be taken to avoid detonation with superchargers and turbo systems. Bolt-on kits can be tuned to minimize the risk, but lower-compression pistons should be used when building an engine for greater power and higher boost levels.

LS7-powered Corvette Z06 have comparatively high compression ratios that range from 9.0:1 to 11.0:1.

A high compression ratio increases the tendency for the engine damaging conditions of detonation and pre-ignition. Those conditions can be especially hard on the factory-installed cast pistons. As a result, the boost pressure on otherwise-stock engines should be limited to prevent damage and ensure performance longevity.

Most intercooled/charge-cooled, street-intended bolt-on supercharger and turbo kits deliver between 5 and 8 pounds of boost—and that's sufficient for stock-engine vehicles. Some kits push toward 10 pounds, with turbo kits easily tuned to deliver much more, but anything more than about 12 pounds is pushing the boundary of engine safety. Enthusiasts and builders seeking more than 12 pounds of boost from an LS engine should consider rebuilding it with forged rotating parts and a lower compression ratio of approximately 9.0:1 to 9.5:1.

Importance of Tuning and Avoiding Detonation

The previous sections that described boost levels, compression ratios, and forged engine components are all tied together by the importance of proper tuning of a forced-induction engine. Without it, even the strongest engine parts don't last long under pressure if the air/fuel ratio is too lean or the engine is prone to detonation.

Detonation is the uncontrolled combustion that is typically caused by excessive heat in the cylinders, whether through a too-lean air/fuel mixture or other factors. The added heat generated by a blower or turbo system makes forced-induction engines extremely susceptible to detonation, particularly under high load and higher boost levels.

A high compression ratio can also contribute to detonation, making it important that an otherwise-stock engine—especially an LS engine with its comparatively high compression ratio—is tuned properly

PRODUCTION ENGINE COMPRESSION RATIOS	
Gen III Engines	
LS1 5.7L	10.1:1
LS6 5.7L	10.5:1
Vortec 5.3-liter (early trucks, including SSR)	9.5:1
Vortec 5.3-liter (later trucks)	9.9:1
Vortec 4.8-liter (truck applications)	9.1:1
Gen IV Engines	
LS2 6.0-liter	10.9:1
LS3 6.2-liter	10.7:1
L99 6.2-liter (2010+ Camaro SS with Active Fuel Management)	10.4:1
LS4 (front-drive application)	10.1:1
LS7 7.0-liter	11.0:1
LS9 6.2-liter	9.1:1
LSA 6.2-liter	9.0:1
L92/L94/L9H 6.2-liter	10.5:1
Vortec 6.0-liter (various truck applications)	9.4:1, 9.6:1, and 10.8:1

to prevent detonation at all costs. Many builders are adept at installing the hardware of a turbocharger or supercharger system, but don't have the knowledge to upload the proper software when it comes to the engine controller. Anyone who isn't proficient at tuning should leave it to someone who is (see Chapter 7 for more tuning details).

Charge Cooling/Intercooling

To put it simply, compressing air, as superchargers and turbochargers do, generates heat. In the engine, that means an increase in the inlet-air temperature—the boosted air that enters the engine—of up to 200 degrees F at 8 pounds of boost.

Hotter inlet air significantly reduces the effectiveness of the boosted air charge, because it is less dense than cooler air. It also makes the engine more susceptible to detonation. A charge-cooling system, commonly called an intercooler, combats the effects of a hotter cooling system by forcing the air charge through a radiator-like device to reduce its temperature before it enters the engine at the throttle body. Because of the concern for detonation on LS engines with their relatively high compression ratios, almost all bolt-on supercharger and turbocharger kits include a charge cooler.

There are two basic types of charge coolers: air-to-air and liquid-to-air (also known as water-to-air). With an air-to-air intercooler, the boosted air charge simply blows through a "radiator," where air rushing over the fins provides the cooling effect. A liquid-to-air system is more like a conventional radiator

A charge-cooling system not only helps deliver more power through a denser intake charge, but it is especially important on street-driven cars to stave off the engine-damaging effects of detonation with the high compression ratio of internally stock engines.

and includes a dedicated circuit of coolant (typically a 50/50 mix of anti-freeze and water, just as in the engine's radiator).

Generally speaking, a liquid-to-air charge-cooling system is more effective on higher powered street-engine combinations and racing combinations. It requires a separate cooling circuit, a coolant reservoir and an electric-driven water pump.

Forced-Induction Terms

Throughout this book, a number of terms are used to describe or support specific characteristics, components, and performance related to forced induction. Reviewing them through the definitions below will enhance your comprehension of the following chapters.

Adiabatic Efficiency: The amount of heat generated when air is compressed by the supercharger or turbocharger in relation to the amount of the air compressed. Superchargers and turbochargers typically have adiabatic efficiency ratings of 50 to 75 percent. A 100-percent efficiency rate equals no heat generated during compression.

Air Compressor: With either a supercharger or turbocharger, it is the fan-like device that blows pressurized air into the engine's air inlet.

Air Density Ratio: The difference between the denser air under boost and the outside air.

Air/Fuel Ratio: The mass difference between air and fuel during the combustion process. For gasoline engines, the optimal (see Stoichiometric) air/fuel ratio is 14.7:1, or 14.7 times the mass in air to fuel. A higher number indicates a leaner mix, or lower fuel content in the mix. A lower air/fuel ratio number indicates a richer mix, or one with greater fuel content. A lean mixture—one with a higher air/fuel ratio—can lead to detonation.

Blow-off Valve: A vacuum-actuated valve that releases excess boost pressure in the intake system of a supercharged or turbocharged engine when the throttle is lifted or closed. The excess air pressure is released to the atmosphere.

Boost: The pressure of compressed air at the intake manifold that is generated by the supercharger or turbocharger. It is generally measured in pounds per square inch (psi) or bar. A 1-bar measure is equal to 14.7 psi.

Boost Controller: A device used to limit the air pressure that acts upon a turbocharger's wastegate actuator in order to control the maximum boost at the engine. It can be a mechanically or electronically controlled device.

Bypass Valve: Similar to a blow-off valve, it is a vacuum-actuated valve designed to release excess boost pressure in the intake system of a turbocharged car when the throttle is lifted or closed. The air pressure is re-circulated back into the non-pressurized end of the intake (before the turbo) but after the mass airflow sensor.

Charge Cooler: A radiator-like device that is used to dissipate or reduce some of the heat generated by the compression of the boosted air charge, enabling greater power and/or helping reduce or eliminate the tendency for detonation.

Detonation: Abnormal and uncontrolled flame activity in the combustion chamber that can cause engine damage, typically due to excessive heat. In a forced-induction engine, detonation is generally caused by a lean fuel mixture, too-high compression, improper tuning, or a combination of all three.

Heat Exchanger: The radiator-like part of a charge-cooling system.

Intercooler: See Charge Cooler.

Pre-ignition: Similar to detonation, pre-ignition is a potentially catastrophic condition whereby heat retained in the cylinder causes the spark plug to act like a diesel engine's glow plug, igniting incoming fuel charge before the piston reaches the top of its stroke. A cooler air charge can reduce the chance of pre-ignition.

Stoichiometric Combustion: The ideal combustion process that completely burns the air/fuel mixture. Generally speaking, an air/fuel ratio of 14.7:1 in a gasoline engine delivers stoichiometric combustion (see Air/Fuel Ratio).

Turbine: The part of a turbocharger that is acted upon by the engine's exhaust gases. Hot exhaust gases flow into the turbine, spinning it. In turn, the turbine spins the corresponding air compressor that blows fresh air into the engine.

Turbo Lag: The time difference between the application of the throttle and the power boost delivered by the turbocharger.

Wastegate: A boost-pressure-activated valve that allows excessive exhaust gas to bypass the turbo-charger's turbine. It is used to control boost pressure.

Real-World Project: Steve Gilliland's 1,000-hp Twin-Turbo Z06

Out on the windswept plains of Oklahoma, Steve Gilliland's Millenium Yellow Corvette Z06 must seem like a UFO, with the locals sometimes glimpsing a fast-moving, strange-sounding object that seems to defy the laws of physics. And while the car may have seemingly unearthly capability, it's the result of decidedly earth-based technology.

Gilliland sent his Z06 to Katech Performance in Detroit. There, the stock LS7 engine was reinforced with Katech's Air Attack 7.0-liter engine package and fitted with an APS twin-turbo kit. On Katech's engine dyno, this combination made a staggering 1,008 hp and 827 ft-lbs of torque.

Of course, there's more to the engine than a collection of parts and a pair of turbochargers. Here's a closer look at the combination.

Rotating Assembly

Because the factory LS7 uses cast pistons, the engine's rotating assembly was completely replaced with racing-spec parts to withstand the pressure and heat applied by the twin-turbo system. A Callies Dragonslayer forged-steel crankshaft anchors the assembly, with a set of Carrillo forged-steel H-beam connecting rods and Katech's forged-aluminum pistons. The pistons are dished slightly to reduce the engine's compression ratio from a high 11.0:1 to a more boost-friendly 9.0:1.

Heads and Camshaft

The engine uses the factory LS7

Steve Gilliland's twin-turbo Corvette Z06 makes more than 1,000 reliable horsepower.

heads, but the exhaust valves were swapped for Inconel units that better withstand high heat. Also, higher rate valvesprings were added to withstand the greatly increased cylinder pressure that can make it difficult to close the valves. Racing-spec ARP head studs and fasteners along with premium head gaskets have provided a leak-free seal of the heads against the block.

As for the camshafts, it's a custom grind designed especially for this engine combination, with .615-inch-intake and .613-inch-exhaust lift specs; duration of 220 degrees on the intake valve and 229 degrees on the exhaust; and a lobe separation angle of 116 degrees. (That compares with .591/.591-inch lift, 211/230-degrees duration, and 121-degree lobe-separation angle on the stock LS7 cam.)

Turbo System

Katech fitted the reinforced LS7 with APS' Z06 intercooled twin-turbo kit. It uses a pair of Garrett GT3582R ball-bearing turbochargers, featuring 61.4-mm inlets and 82-mm outlets on the compressor and a 68-mm turbine. The turbochargers mount very low on the engine—essentially in the transmission tunnel—because of the

Mounted low and out of sight on the LS7 engine, the APS twin-turbo kit on Steve Gilliland's Corvette works with additional components from Katech Performance to produce more than 1,000 hp; and it's a completely streetable, easy-driving combination.

space restrictions and proclivity for heat buildup under the Corvette's hood. Gilliland wasn't concerned about pump-gas compatibility, so the system was tuned to push 12 pounds of boost on 100-octane gas and 15 pounds of boost on 105-octane racing fuel. An A'PEXi AVC-R boost controller is used to maintain boost at predetermined RPM levels as Gilliland shifts through the gears.

Beyond the engine compartment, the drivetrain was upgraded with a strengthened transaxle from RPM, a stronger triple-plate carbon clutch from Exedy, a Quaife differential, and stronger, 300M alloy axleshafts.

SUPERCHARGER TYPES AND SELECTION

Superchargers come in many different shapes and sizes, but they are related by a common attribute: They generate boost pressure via an engine-driven mechanism. Typically, superchargers are driven by a belt connected to the crankshaft.

When it comes to the commercially available superchargers for LS engines, there are two basic types: positive displacement and centrifugal.

Positive-Displacement Superchargers

Positive-displacement superchargers are those that spin a pair of multi-lobe rotors that mesh tightly to squeeze air through an outlet under high pressure. The displacement is derived from the amount of air delivered with each revolution of the supercharger. Typically, the larger the rotors, the more air the supercharger displaces.

Within the spectrum of positive-displacement superchargers are Roots types and Lysholm types. Following are design details and operational differences of the various supercharger types.

Most enthusiasts and hot rodders were introduced to street supercharging with the large, "Jimmy"-style Roots superchargers that originated on large truck and bus GMC diesel engines, but were adapted to automotive powerplants. Although impressive looking and sounding, these blowers are pretty inefficient, but they're guaranteed to draw a crowd on cruise night.

Roots Type

The Roots-type supercharger is an engine-driven air pump that contains a pair of long rotors that are twisted somewhat like pretzel sticks. As they spin around each other, incoming air is squeezed between the rotors and pushed under pressure into the engine—forcing more air into the engine than it could draw under "natural" aspiration. The rotors are driven by a pulley and belt that are connected to the engine's accessory drive system.

With a Roots blower, a discharge hole is located at one end of the supercharger case. As the rotors mesh and squeeze air, it is forced at high pressure through the discharge hole. It is relatively efficient, particularly in the later designs refined by OEM supplier Eaton.

The Roots blower was used on a variety of high-end automobiles in the early twentieth century, including the Cords, Bentleys, and Mercedes, but it really made its mark on the aftermarket performance world when it was used on GMC-built transit buses of the 1930s and later. The buses used large superchargers to pump up the horsepower of their

General Motors helped kick off the new era of efficient street supercharging with the introduction of the 3800 Series II Supercharged V-6. It powered the popular Pontiac Grand Prix GTP (seen here), the Buick Regal GS and, later, the Chevy Monte Carlo SS and Impala SS. (Photo courtesy General Motors)

Earlier Eaton-based supercharger systems, such as those found on the 3800 V-6 and larger V-8-size compressor, make excellent, usable power and absolutely help lower a vehicle's elapsed time at the drag strip. A comparatively limited power range and a tendency for the compressor to soak up engine heat, however, make them better suited to vehicles used primarily on the street and occasionally at the track. Also, they feature drive pulleys that are pressed onto the drive gear. Swapping them to adjust boost pressure is very difficult and almost impossible to do with the supercharger installed on the engine and in the vehicle. Only specialized pulling tools designed for the job should be used; and even then, there's no guarantee damage won't occur to the supercharger's nose section.

diesel engines. By the 1950s, enterprising drag racers began attaching GMC (also known as "Jimmy") blowers to automotive gasoline engines, and the rest is history.

The "71"-series GMC blowers were adapted to street cars, too, and those are the iconic superchargers seen reaching through the hoods of so many vintage street machines and Pro Street hot rods.

To the generation of late-model performance enthusiasts, Roots blowers are synonymous with Eaton superchargers. That company pioneered the use of smaller-displacement, low-profile Roots blowers on everything from Jaguars to the Pontiac Grand Prix GTP. The Corvette ZR1 uses an Eaton supercharger, too.

Although Blower Drive Service offers manifolds to adapt the classic, tall 71-style blower to LS engines, those considering a Roots-type supercharger system for their vehicle are selecting one with an Eaton compressor.

Refinements to Eaton superchargers' rotor design over the years has made them quieter and more capable

of greater airflow and boost; the packaging size and rotor speed is the biggest restriction to making tremendous power with them. Look around at professional and semi-professional drag racers who rely on superchargers or turbochargers for power adders and you see virtually none use an Eaton-type blower. They just don't generate the boost necessary to support a very large displacement or the high-RPM power needs.

That said, Eaton blowers are exceptionally durable, dependable, and on the street, make reasonably good power at lower RPM—especially when compared with centrifugal superchargers and turbochargers. The OEM quality of Eaton systems makes them nearly bulletproof and delivers exceptional drivability. They're not loud at low RPM and don't have on/off performance characteristics—the power comes on smoothly and firmly.

And while the hardware (including a custom-intake manifold) can make Eaton-based kits somewhat expensive, their installation is clean,

unobtrusive, and as close to a factory-style installation found in aftermarket kits. Generally, most Eaton-based bolt-on kits are offered through California-based Magna Charger, which has developed a number of very popular kits for many LS-powered vehicles. Indeed, many of Magna Charger's kits represent the easiest-to-install systems and have earned a reputation for excellent reliability.

Eaton's TVS

The Twin Vortices System (TVS) represents the sixth generation of

For those building an LS engine for a street rod, muscle car, or other older vehicle and appreciate the look of the old-school "71"-style Jimmy blowers, Blower Drive Service offers supercharger kits for engines that use LS cathedral-port heads. This example was built by Martin Motorsports to be installed in a vintage Nova. Note the custom, marine-style intercooler sandwiched between the blower case and the intake manifold. It was the best solution in order to maintain the vintage drag racing look of the engine, with its classic "bug catcher" intake.

This is the Nova for which Martin Motorsports built the classic blower combination. The engine is shown test fitted in the chassis, but it doesn't have the intercooler installed yet. That will add about another 4 inches to the blower's height, pushing it even higher out of the hood. There's no reason a similar, retro-style setup couldn't be adapted to, say, a fifth-generation Camaro—giving it a classic street-machine look with modern drivability and performance.

Although hidden under the lid of its integral intercooling systems, GM's LSA (CTS-V) and LS9 (Corvette ZR1) supercharged engines use an Eaton TVS supercharger. An LSA engine is shown here.

The large displacement of the 2.3-liter TVS compressor helps generate truly impressive performance. In the application seen here, a Harrop-supplied TVS blower was used on a 7.0-liter LS engine to make nearly 900 daily drivable horsepower on readily available pump gas. The engine was then stuffed into a Pontiac Solstice roadster by Thomson Automotive.

This photo shows the unique, four-lobe rotors of the Eaton TVS blower. The quartet of lobes, combined with the high helix (rotor angle) design, gives the blower a quasi-twin-screw look. That's intentional, because like a twin-screw design, the TVS delivers greater performance at low and high RPM. (Photo courtesy General Motors)

The Eaton compressor-based Magna Charger bolt-on kits are very popular for C5/C6 Corvettes, Pontiac G8s, fifth-generation Camaros, and trucks/SUVs—and for good reason. They are relatively easy to install, deliver an excellent return on investment when it comes to horsepower, and have proven to be very durable. Corvette applications, however, have underhood clearance problems, and an aftermarket or modified stock hood is typically required.

In late 2009, Edelbrock introduced a new, OEM-style supercharger system for a number of LS2- and LS3-powered C6 Corvettes and the 2010+ Camaro SS. Carrying the E-Force brand name, Edelbrock's supercharger kits use Eaton's four-rotor, 2.3-liter TVS compressor at their cores. Like the factory LSA and LS9 engines, the E-Force systems feature air-to-water intercooling systems with dual brick-style heat exchangers mounted on top of the supercharger assembly. Design features of the E-Force system include a front-driven compressor and long, 12-inch intake runners that optimize low-RPM torque. For C6 Corvette owners, the advantage of the E-Force kit is that it mounts under the stock hood. Currently, the popular Magna Charger kit requires a replacement or modified stock hood with increased clearance.

Eaton's ubiquitous Roots supercharger design and it blends elements of a twin-screw compressor, including a four-lobe, high-helix (160-degree twist angle) rotor design. Previous Eaton superchargers featured a conventional three-lobe design.

As with the twin-screw design, the TVS supercharger was developed to expand the efficiency range of the supercharger to deliver more power at lower RPM and sustained boost at higher RPM, while requiring less engine power to drive. And when compared with previous three-rotor designs, the TVS represents a night-and-day difference in overall performance. Wherever possible, the use of the TVS compressor is recommended. It is currently manufactured in 1.9-liter (MP1900) and 2.3-liter (MP2300) displacements. The design also features an internal bypass valve.

The TVS blower was designed primarily for OEM applications. In fact, it was driven by GM's performance and efficiency requirements for the LS9/LSA engines, which represent the first production applications for this new compressor (see page 29, "GM Factory-Supercharged LS9 and LSA Engines."

Since appearing under the hood of the Corvette ZR1 and the Cadillac CTS-V models, the TVS supercharger has grown into the aftermarket, with Eaton's Magna Charger outlet offering a number of bolt-on kits for engines that have either cathedral- or rectangular-port heads. Additionally, Australia-based Harrop Engineering offers TVS-based kits (1.9-liter and 2.3-liter versions) for the 6.0-liter Pontiac GTO/G8 GT, as well as the VE-series Holden Commodore.

Lysholm/Twin-Screw Types

The Lysholm-type or twin-screw supercharger is similar in design and function to the Roots type—including squeezing air through a discharge hole in the case to deliver boosted air pressure to the engine.

Rather than using the intermesh-ing lobes of the Roots type, the Lysholm uses a pair of worm screw-type rotors that squeeze air together in order to generate boost. It also generates internal compression, meaning it develops pressure progressively as the air is continually squeezed by the screws on its way to the discharge hole. This can help build more low-end power and deliver more boost at lower RPM. The relative efficiency of twin-screw superchargers is greater than a conventional Roots type. They also enable generally higher boost levels than Roots or centrifugal superchargers, providing 20 pounds or more with some compressors.

Sweden-based Lysholm Technologies AB (a company that has undergone several corporate changes in recent years) is the name behind the technology and manufactures many sizes of twin-screw compressors, ranging from 1.2 to 3.3 liters in displacement. Rather than offering retail systems, the company licenses its product to other manufacturers, including OEM companies such as Ford, which used a Lysholm

Whipple Industries offers bolt-on kits for a variety of 1999–2006 GM trucks with 4.8-, 5.3-, and 6.0-liter engines. Tuner kits (non-emissions legal) are available for many automotive applications with Gen III cathedral-port cylinder heads (LS1, LS2, LS6). In late 2009, Whipple announced a kit for the 2010-later Camaro SS that features the company's large, 2.9-liter W175AX compressor.

Vortech's twin-screw supercharger system for 5.3-liter LS-powered GM trucks includes an integral bypass valve within the supercharger housing. The kit also includes a charge-cooler/intake-manifold assembly (with fuel rail mounts), higher-rate fuel injectors, pump system for the intercooler, and cold-air-style intake system. Tuning calibration is provided through a DiabloSport Predator programmer. Similar systems are expected for a variety of other LS-powered vehicles.

supercharger on the 2003–2006 GT sports car (through a licensing agreement with Eaton that essentially made them Eaton superchargers).

In the performance aftermarket, Whipple Industries is just about the most recognizable name in twin-screw technology, with Lysholm-type blowers derived from industrial air compressors that were adapted to automotive use. For years, Whipple relied on the twin-screw compressors from the company currently known as Lysholm Technologies AB, but since 2005 has used a twin-screw compressor of its own design.

In 2009, Vortech joined the twin-screw blower fray with the addition of a Lysholm-based supercharger of its own. Rather than manufacturing its own blowers, Vortech has licensed the compressors from Lysholm Technologies AB and developed its own installation kits. Vortech offers 2.3- and 3.3-liter superchargers. Currently, the only dedicated twin-screw kit for LS engines from Vortech is for 5.3-liter truck engines. The company also offers "tuner" kits that can be adapted to a variety of LS engines—as long as a suitable manifold is available to match the ports on the cylinder heads.

Another player in the twin-screw market is Kenne Bell. Known primarily for its systems for Ford vehicles, the company offers bolt-on kits for 1997–2004 Corvettes equipped with the LS1, LS2, or LS6 engine. No applications for later Gen IV engines with rectangular-port heads are offered.

Centrifugal Superchargers

Although engine-driven and not exhaust-driven, a centrifugal supercharger generates boost much like a turbocharger, with an impeller (similar to a turbine) that spins upward of 40,000 rpm to draw air into the compressor and blow pressurized air into the engine.

The impeller is the engine-driven part of the supercharger, as it is linked via a pulley and belt to the crankshaft. After the impeller draws air into the compressor head unit, it is squeezed and forced into the supercharger's scroll (a chamber within the head unit that funnels the compressed air charge out of a discharge tube and toward the engine's throttle body). The scroll has a progressive shape that gets larger the farther it is from the center of the head unit. That design feature reduces airflow while simultaneously increasing the air charge's pressure.

Air is compressed in the head unit when it leaves the impeller and is forced into the scroll. A venturi-like outlet, through which the air is forced, creates boost pressure, so the greater the impeller speed and the faster the air moves through the venturi, the higher the boost pressure.

A centrifugal supercharger is comparatively efficient, requiring relatively little engine power to drive, but its downside is the need for very high impeller speed to make horsepower-building boost. That's why centrifugal blowers are known mostly as mid- and higher-range power adders; the impeller speed at lower RPM doesn't make sufficient boost, and once the maximum impeller speed is achieved—usually around the peak horsepower mark—boost levels trail off at higher RPM.

A change to a smaller-diameter drive pulley can add a few extra pounds of boost, but matching a properly sized compressor head unit with the displacement and airflow capabilities of the engine is the key to sustaining power throughout the middle and upper ranges of the RPM band.

The two main players in the centrifugal supercharger business are Vortech Superchargers and ATI ProCharger. Another centrifugal blower manufacturer is Rotrex, but currently, there were no direct applications for LS engines. The following is a closer look at the offerings from Vortech and ProCharger.

Vortech centrifugal superchargers typically make 6 to 8 pounds of boost in most bolt-on kits, but a range of higher-performing, racing-oriented compressors can supply more than 30 pounds of boost. Most of Vortech's compressors are interchangeable with the company's brackets, allowing you to swap compressors to better suit your engine combination. (See Chapter 5 for installation details on a Vortech-based bolt-on system.)

Vortech Superchargers

Vortech centrifugal superchargers have been mainstays of both the street and racing worlds. Typically, Vortech blowers are known for their relatively quiet performance and engine-oil-fed lubrication system (except for the V-3 compressor). Vortech has also been at the forefront of developing bolt-on kits, which are available for most popular LS-powered vehicles, including the fifth-generation Camaro. Several aftermarket companies, such as A&A Corvette, use Vortech compressors as the basis for tailored supercharger systems (see Chapter 5 for details on installation).

Vortech offers a number of different compressors designed for a wide variety of performance requirements. They're also subdivided among "trim" types—X trim, F trim, SCi trim, etc. Here's a quick rundown on them.

V-1 Series: a high-performance compressor with high-speed ball bearings that makes it compatible for high-boost, cog-belt racing applications. Depending on the trim, a V-1 is capable of up to 26 pounds of boost and 1,200 cfm of airflow.

V-2 Series: lower maximum boost (17 to 22 pounds, depending on the trim) and slightly lower maximum airflow than the V-1, but designed as a direct replacement. V-2 SQ trim is known for exceptionally quiet operation.

V-3 Series: the only internally lubricated compressor in Vortech's portfolio. A V-3 compressor fills the mounting brackets for V-1, V-2, V-4, V-5, and V-7 compressors. Maximum boost and airflow is similar to V-2 compressor trims.

V-4 Series: a racing-intended compressor that Vortech claims is twice as efficient as a Roots blower at 12 pounds of boost. Depending on the trim, a V-4 can produce up to 32 pounds of boost and flow 2,000 cfm.

V-5 Series: designed for smaller-displacement engines, typically four- and six-cylinders, the V-5 is not well-suited to the airflow capabilities of LS V-8 engines.

V-7 Series: a high-flow, racing-intended compressor designed for modified engines built to accommodate high boost levels. Depending on the trim, a V-7 can flow more than 1,400 cfm and generate 30 pounds of boost.

V-9 Series: this more compact compressor is designed for engine compartments with little room, such as the fourth-generation F-bodies. They're also designed for smaller displacement V-8s (smaller than 400 ci). Maximum boost is about 14 pounds and maximum airflow is 750 cfm.

V-20 Series: designed purely for the rigors of drag racing, these compressors, in V-24 and V-27 forms, can flow up to 2,000 cfm and produce more than 30 pounds of boost.

An excellent reference chart of Vortech's various compressors, trims and boost/airflow capacities is available at www.vortechsuperchargers.com.

ATI ProCharger

Unlike Vortech blowers, most ProCharger compressors have a self-contained lubrication system, meaning there's no need to tap the oil pan for the oil feed source. Some of ATI's ProCharger compressors are relatively loud, especially at idle, but

PROCHARGER COMPRESSOR COMPARISON CHART		
Compressor	Maximum Airflow (cfm)	Maximum Boost
P600B	1,200	24
P-1SC	1,200	30
P-1SC-1	1,200	32
P-1SC-2	1,200	30
D-1	1,400	32
D-1SC	1,400	32
F-1	1,525	38
F-1A	1,650	38
F-1C	1,850	38
D-1R	2,000	32
F-1R	2,000	38
F-2M	2,250	40
F-2	2,700	38
F-2R	2,750	38
F-3A-117	2,800	40
F-3A-123	3,100	40
F-3R-131	3,600	45
F-3R-139	4,000	45

Here's a typical bolt-on ProCharger system on a fifth-generation Camaro SS. As with Vortech superchargers, ProCharger's larger compressors are mostly interchangeable with the bracketry, allowing custom combinations. Proper tuning is paramount when using a high-boost, large-displacement compressor, as is the durability of factory engine parts.

ProCharger's large compressors and cog-style belt-drive systems are designed for racing applications, with several compressors capable of 40 pounds of boost or more. It is these big blowers that are giving some turbo systems a run for the money in drag racing. This is ProCharger's F3R compressor.

their street-based blowers have become admirably quiet in recent years. Like Vortech, there are numerous compressors in the ProCharger portfolio, with several designed specifically for racing applications. In fact, ATI offers the largest centrifugal superchargers, with some capable of more than 40 pounds of boost and up to 4,000 cfm.

Kit and Cost Considerations

Unlike turbocharger systems, there is a great number of bolt-on blower kits designed to work on stock LS engines. The number of kits changes constantly as new vehicle models are introduced and supercharger manufacturers and other aftermarket companies develop kits for them. For Roots-type systems, Magnuson's Magna Charger kits cover most popular LS-powered vehicles. When it comes to twin-screw systems, there are few choices for vehicles with rectangular-port heads; most are designed for earlier, cathedral-port engines (LS1, LS2, and LS6). Vortech's new twin-screw blower is offered in kit form for the rectangular-port LS3 engine of the Camaro and G8 GXP, with more applications expected.

To ensure pump-gas compatibility and to lower the risk of detonation, bolt-on kits typically make less than 10 pounds of boost and deliver around 80 to 125 additional horsepower with preprogrammed tuning. Greater performance is attainable with custom tuning, smaller-diameter pulleys, and the like, but such changes increase the risk of detonation on stock engines with high compression ratios and cast rotating parts.

Of course, cost is an important factor for any enthusiast selecting a supercharger kit. One of the important factors in the centrifugal supercharger's favor is generally a lower purchase cost in kit form when compared with Roots/screw kits. That's

SUPERCHARGER COMPARISON CHART

Manufacturer/ Retailer	Compressor	Cathedral Port Kits	Rectangular Port Kits	Notes
A&A Corvette	centrifugal	N/A	N/A	Uses Vortech compressors
ATI ProCharger	centrifugal	N/A	N/A	Systems not dependent on cylinder head design
Blower Drive Service	Roots	yes	no	Old-school, 6-71-type blower case does not fit under the hood
Edelbrock	Roots	yes	yes	Uses Eaton TVS compressor; kits for fifth-generation Camaro, LS2-powered C6 Corvette and LS3-powered C6 Corvette
Harrop	Roots (Eaton TVS)	yes	yes	Kits for GTO/Monaro and G8 GT/Commodore; and 2010+ Camaros
Kenne Bell	twin-screw	yes	no	Kits for 1997-2004 Corvettes only
Magna Charger	Roots (Eaton, including TVS)	yes	yes	Kits for most popular LS vehicles; easy and quick bolt-on installation
Rotrex	centrifugal	no	no	No LS applications at press time, but they've been long-promised
Vortech	centrifugal	N/A	N/A	Systems not dependent on cylinder head design
Vortech	twin-screw	yes	no	Systems not dependent on cylinder head design
Whipple Industries	twin-screw	yes	yes	Various truck kits and bolt-on kit for the 2010+ Camaro SS

Here's the 550-hp engine of the Berger Camaro. It uses nothing more than a Magna Charger kit (non-TVS compressor) and the kit's supplied tuning upgrade. It is a simple upgrade that delivers a huge increase in performance.

because the ability to mount the compressor head unit almost anywhere allows manufacturers to bundle most of the kits with universal components. Typically, only relatively inexpensive mounting brackets and other related components separate, say, a 2006 GTO kit from a 2002 Camaro Z28 system.

The Roots/screw-type systems generally require a dedicated intake manifold that must be matched to the heads—and casting an entire intake manifold is a lot more expensive than laser cutting a steel mounting bracket for a centrifugal blower.

Where Roots/screw blowers can narrow the price gap with centrifugal kits is in the installation labor

The relative ease of installation and tuning, as well as the limited impact on other factory vehicle systems, makes a bolt-on supercharger an increasingly cost-effective alternative to a custom-built engine. That's exactly what Berger Chevrolet did with the latest versions of its limited-production Berger Camaros. On its fourth-generation models, the dealership sourced custom, 500-hp, naturally aspirated engines that cost much more to build and install than the Magna Charger kits used on its fifth-generation cars.

charge. Typically, it takes less time to install a Roots/screw-type system on most vehicles, as centrifugals typically require more extensive modification of the accessory drive system.

Positive-Displacement vs. Centrifugal Blowers

When it comes to supercharged horsepower, positive-displacement superchargers and centrifugal blowers produce it differently. In simple terms, a centrifugal supercharger's boost increases exponentially with engine speed, while a positive-displacement supercharger's airflow is linear—with maximum boost occurring at very low in the RPM band. That means a Roots or twin-screw blower that delivers, for example, 500 cfm of air at 2,500 rpm pushes 1,000 cfm at 5,000 rpm.

With a centrifugal supercharger, boost builds in a non-linear way, much like a turbocharger. As RPM increases, the airflow from the compressor increases at a faster rate. Because of that, maximum boost is not achieved until the engine's redline, or maximum RPM level.

The differences in airflow delivery create very different performance curves and driving experiences. In general terms, a positive-displacement supercharger has a flatter power curve, with more low-RPM power. The centrifugal delivers a greater feeling of increasing power as the revs climb. On the street, and all other things being as equal as possible, a positive-displacement blower feels stronger on the low end, especially directly off idle. A Roots or twin-screw blower makes a small amount of boost whenever the engine is running. The centrifugal, on the other hand, "rolls" into its boost and

Unlike a Roots or twin-screw blower, which delivers maximum boost at relatively low RPM, a centrifugal, like this ProCharger D1SC, increases its airflow with the RPM, much like a turbo. Maximum boost comes at the engine's maximum RPM.

is generally easier to launch, with a stronger feel through the mid- and upper-range RPM levels.

The non-linear airflow delivery also makes the centrifugal supercharger better suited for drag racing, because the graduated boost application enables an easier launch, with greater power coming on as the RPM increases. Of course, with peak boost not occurring until redline, the blower's effectiveness is not fully realized at lower RPM.

In general terms, a street vehicle with a positive displacement blower feels the effects of the blower immediately and at all low-RPM levels, while a centrifugally blown car feels more like stock until around the 3,000-rpm level. There is also a more pronounced application of the power with a centrifugal blower, but not the "on/off" feeling of a turbocharger.

How Much "Blower" Do You Need?

Unless you are adapting a GMC/71-series-style Roots blower, which is offered in tremendous size increments

for drag racing, there is a limit to the effectiveness of many bolt-on, under-hood-type superchargers. Unlike a turbocharger that generates more boost as the engine speed increases, the boost level with a supercharger plateaus relatively quickly in the RPM band. If the supercharger—be it a positive displacement or centrifugal—can't flow enough air to support the engine's high-RPM requirements, horsepower falls off, and the effectiveness of the supercharger is greatly diminished. Increasing the boost pressure increases the effectiveness to a certain degree, but in the end a supercharger with a larger compressor is the best way to optimize the blower's performance across the RPM band.

The great airflow capability of LS engines and the larger displacements offered in production and aftermarket versions of the engine make sizing a supercharger particularly important, as the smaller-displacement superchargers that were common on a street car only a few years ago simply don't flow enough to support later and larger-displacement LS combinations.

At the time of this writing, the 3.3-liter Lysholm twin-screw supercharger from Vortech is the largest positive-displacement supercharger offered in bolt-on kits, although the Eaton 2.3-liter TVS blower is offered in more kits—and even it can struggle to keep up with some large-displacement combinations. Whipple offers 3.3-, 4.0-, and 5.0-liter compressors, but none had been adapted to LS engines.

When it comes to centrifugal superchargers, both Vortech and ProCharger offer a number of large compressors to suit high-powered street engines and dedicated racing combinations.

Getting the most from a super-charger, regardless of the compressor design, is dependent on flowing enough air to satisfy the airflow capability of the engine. A blower's maximum boost will not be realized on a large-displacement engine that isn't matched with a commensurately sized compressor.

Music to the Ears?

For many contemplating a supercharger, the sound, or lack thereof, is an important consideration. Whether it's the whir of a centrifugal's impeller or the meshing of a set of rotors, superchargers generate sound during operation. Some think it's noise, while others think it's music to their ears.

Generally speaking, centrifugal superchargers are noisier. At least, they make more sound than Roots and screw-type blowers at idle and low RPM. The Roots/screw-type compressors are, for the most part, silent at idle.

Companies, such as Vortech, have worked hard to reduce the low-speed sound of their centrifugal units, while others, like Power-dyne, use quieter, belt-driven impellers rather than gear-driven ones. But for the most part, the sound hasn't been eliminated. If a subtler, stealthier approach is desired, the Roots/screw blower is the way to go. For those who don't mind rolling up to a stoplight and having all eyes focus at the hood area of their vehicle, a centrifugal does the trick.

The Importance of a Charge Cooler

Almost every supercharger and turbocharger kit for LS-powered vehicles includes some type of charge cooler or intercooler to reduce the inlet temperature of the boosted air before it enters the engine through the throttle body. It's necessary to ward off the engine-damaging effects of detonation and/or pre-ignition—conditions LS engines are particularly susceptible to because of their high-compression ratios.

In general terms, forced-induction engines are safer with compression ratios in the neighborhood of 8.5:1 to 9.5:1, but LS engines have much greater "squeeze" from the pistons. The LS7 engine of the Corvette Z06 has 11:1 compression, the LS3 is at 10.7:1, and even the original LS1 engine had a 10.25:1 compression ratio. By comparison, the factory-supercharged Corvette ZR1's LS9 engine has a blower-friendly 9.1:1 compression ratio.

So, routing the boosted air charge through the cooler reduces the maximum boost level, but it typically enhances horsepower because the cooler air charge is denser than a heat-soaked charge. And it's the only option on vehicles with an otherwise-stock engine assembly.

Surge Protection

Regardless of whether it's a Roots/screw-type or centrifugal supercharger, compressor surge occurs when the blower is making boost, but the throttle suddenly closes, such as when the driver pulls his or her foot off the gas pedal. When this occurs, the blower keeps pushing air into the closed throttle body. When the pressure inside the throttle body is higher than the pressure being generated by the supercharger, air blows back toward the compressor.

In low-boost applications, this isn't a big problem, but with higher boost—more than 10 pounds or so—the comparatively great pressure can cause damage to the engine, supercharger, or both. Venting the excess pressure that builds when the throttle snaps closed is the cure, and that can be done with either a blow-off valve (which vents excess air back into the atmosphere) or a bypass valve (which vents the air back into the compressor).

Pulley Size and Performance

Sometimes not even the installation of an entire supercharger system suits some enthusiasts. They look to extract every pound of boost possible from the blower, and that usually leads to swapping the factory-installed drive pulley for a smaller-diameter pulley.

The smaller pulley typically generates more boost, because it forces the rotors to spin faster. You should explore all the performance ramifications of the swap before performing it, because the gain may be negligible

Experimentation with supercharger pulley sizes must be done carefully to prevent detonation. Even comparatively small changes in pulley size can have a dramatic effect on increasing boost and, consequently, the chances of detonation.

Even with excellent belt wrap, there are slippage issues to contend with on high-boost, high-horsepower engines that incorporate the blower drive within the factory-style accessory belt system. In the Mustang world, the Steeda company has addressed the problem with a separate, dedicated, blower-drive system, which isolates the blower drive belt from the accessory circuit (with Whipple blowers). It's a good solution that should be adapted to LS applications.

is considered, have it performed before the supercharger is installed on the vehicle.

- The greater boost of a smaller pulley can push against the engine's threshold for detonation—or exceed it—requiring revised tuning and possibly the use of higher-octane fuel.
- In many cases, the smaller pulley also requires the investment in a slightly smaller drive belt. During the swap, the tensioner and/or other idler pulleys should be inspected for wear.

Another method to increase the boost from the supercharger is a larger-diameter crankshaft pulley/balancer, which spins all of the accessories (including the supercharger) faster. The flip side to this method is that the faster rate is not necessarily healthy for the other accessories. It could affect the performance or shorten the life of the water pump, alternator, and more.

Belt Wrap and Belt Size

The drive system of a supercharger puts a tremendous amount of additional load on the belt-driven accessory system of an engine. At high RPM and under maximum boost, a supercharger belt with a production-style, cogless design can slip, robbing horsepower and possibly causing engine damage. Most blower kit manufacturers design the belt drive with a lot of belt-to-pulley contact. This higher degree of "belt wrap" helps mitigate slippage.

For bolt-on blower kits making up to about 12 pounds of boost, inserting the supercharger into the

or lead to a number of other issues that must be addressed, including the following:

- The pulleys on Eaton-based Roots superchargers, like those sold through Magnuson and

Harrop, typically have pressed-on pulleys that require special tools for removal. In fact, the procedure typically requires the removal of the supercharger if it's already been installed on the engine; so if a pulley swap

stock, six-rib accessory-drive system generally doesn't cause a problem, especially if the belt routing ensures good belt wrap. When building for a higher boost application, however, a separate, wider belt system should be considered between the blower and crankshaft pulley.

The LS9 comes from the factory with a 10-rib belt system for the entire front drive, while many aftermarket supercharger companies offer 10-rib conversion kits for systems aimed at generating more than 12 pounds of boost. A cogged belt should be used with a racing engine to maximize belt engagement.

GM Factory-Supercharged LS9 and LSA Engines

Launched in 2008, the Corvette ZR1 and Cadillac CTS-V were the first LS production engines from GM to use forced induction. Each features an Eaton-developed Roots-type supercharger blowing—via a charge cooler—into a 6.2-liter engine.

The ZR1's LS9 engine is rated at 638 hp and 604 ft-lbs of torque, while the CTS-V's LSA engine is rated at 556 hp and 551 ft-lbs of torque. Despite both engines using a similar supercharger design and 6.2-liter displacement, the LSA is not simply a

de-tuned version of the LS9. The engines are built with a number of different components.

Among the most notable differences between the engines are the superchargers. The LS9 uses a 2.3-liter compressor, while the LSA uses a smaller, 1.9-liter blower. Both superchargers are based on Eaton's sixth-generation Roots design that features four-lobe rotors for greater efficiency. The comparatively large displacement of superchargers (particularly on the LS9) helps the engines overcome two of supercharging's biggest hurdles: low-end torque and high-end horsepower.

Corvette ZR1 LS9 6.2-liter. (Photo courtesy General Motors)

Cadillac CTS-V LSA 6.2-liter. (Photo courtesy General Motors)

The LS9 is built with forged-aluminum pistons; the LSA comes from the factory with hypereutectic aluminum pistons. (Photo courtesy General Motors)

The supercharger cases of the LS9 and LSA incorporate dual brick-style heat exchangers for their respective inter-cooling systems. Here, the top section of the LSA's intercooler cover is removed, showing the triangular discharge port from the compressor. (Photo courtesy General Motors)

The LS9, for example, makes big power at lower RPM and carries it in a wide arc to 6,600 rpm. GM testing has shown the engine makes approximately 300 hp at 3,000 rpm and nearly 320 ft-lbs of torque at only 1,000 rpm. Torque tops 585 ft-lbs at about the 4,000-rpm mark, while horsepower peaks at 6,500 rpm. The engine produces 90 percent of peak torque from 2,600 to 6,000 rpm.

Both engines are offered through GM Performance Parts as complete crate engine assemblies, offering enthusiasts a ready-to-go alternative to building a supercharged engine from scratch. The PN for the LS9 engine is 19201990; the PN for the LSA is 19211708.

Below is a look at the components and processes that comprise these unique powerplants.

Cylinder Block and Rotating Assembly

Both engines feature an aluminum cylinder block with the LS-standard six-bolt main bearing caps. The LS9 uses steel main caps and the LSA uses nodular-iron caps. The block also features enlarged vent windows in the second and third bulkheads for enhanced bay-to-bay breathing. Cast-iron cylinder liners, measuring 4.06 inches in bore diameter, are inserted in the aluminum block, and they are finish-bored and honed with a deck plate installed. The deck plate simulates the pressure and slight dimensional variances applied to the block when the cylinder heads are installed, ensuring a higher degree of accuracy that promotes maximum cylinder head sealing, piston-ring fit, and overall engine performance.

A forged-steel crankshaft delivers the engines' 3.62-inch stroke. On the LS9, it features a nine-bolt flange (the outer face of the crankshaft on which the flywheel is mounted) that provides more clamping strength. The LSA uses an eight-bolt flange. Other, non-supercharged LS engines, have a six-bolt flange. A torsional damper mounted to the front of the crankshaft features a keyway and friction washer, which is designed to support the engine's high loads.

With the LS9, a set of titanium connecting rods and forged-aluminum pistons are used. The LSA uses powdered-metal rods and hypereutectic (cast) aluminum pistons. Both engines have a 9.1:1 compression ratio.

Cylinder Heads

The basic cylinder head design of the LS9 and LSA is similar to the L92-type head found on GM's LS3 V-8, but it is cast with a premium A356T6 alloy that is better at handling the heat generated by the supercharged engine—particularly in the bridge area of the cylinder head, between the intake and exhaust valves.

In addition to the special aluminum alloy, each head is created with a rotocast method. Also known as spin casting, the process involves pouring the molten alloy into a rotating mold. This makes for more even distribution of the material and virtually eliminates porosity (air bubbles or pockets trapped in the casting) for a stronger finished product.

Although the heads are based on the L92 design, they feature swirl-inducing wings that are cast into the intake ports. This improves the mixture motion of the pressurized air/fuel charge. Both engines feature 2.16-inch-diameter intake valves and 1.59-inch-diameter exhaust valves, but the LS9 uses more exotic titanium intake and hollow-stem sodium-filled exhaust valves.

Camshaft and Valvetrain

The broad power band enabled by the LS9's large, 2.3-liter supercharger allowed GM engineers to specify a camshaft with a relatively low lift of .555 inch for both the intake and exhaust valves. It is a low-overlap cam with lower lift and slower valve-closing speeds than the Z06's 505-hp LS7, giving the LS9 very smooth idle and drivability qualities.

Similarly, the LSA's camshaft delivers a relatively low .480-inch lift on the intake and exhaust sides.

The valvetrains of both engines feature many parts-bin components from the production LS3 engine, including the lifters, rocker arms, and valvesprings. However, the LS9 uses the valve-spring retainers from the LS7 engine.

Supercharger and Charge Cooler

Both engines use a sixth-generation supercharger from Eaton. Its primary improvement is a four-lobe rotor design that promotes quieter and more efficient performance. The LS9's R2300 supercharger features a case that is specific to the Corvette ZR1. Its maximum boost pressure is 1.5 psi. The LSA uses the 1.9-liter R1900 compressor and delivers up to 9 psi of boost.

Both engines employ a liquid-to-air charge-cooling system to reduce inlet-air temperature after it exits the supercharger, reducing the inlet-air temperature by up to 140 degrees F. Each charge-cooling system includes a dedicated coolant circuit with a remote-mounted pump and reservoir.

The charge-cooler design differs for each engine, because of the production packaging within the cars. The LS9 uses a "dual brick" system, with a pair of low-profile heat exchangers mounted longitudinally on either side of the supercharger. The LSA's charge cooler is mounted atop the supercharger, owing to the Cadillac's greater hood clearance. Coupled with the supercharger itself, this integrated design mounts to the intake.

Oiling System

The LS9 uses a dry-sump oiling system that is similar in design to the LS7's system, but features a higher-capacity pump to ensure adequate oil pressure at the higher cornering loads the ZR1 is capable of achieving. An oil-pan-mounted cooler is also integrated, along with piston-cooling oil squirters located in the cylinder block.

The LSA engine uses a conventional, wet-sump oiling system, but also includes oil squirters in the cylinder block.

Water Pump

To compensate for the heavier load generated by the supercharger drive system, an LS9-specific water pump with increased bearing capacity is used.

Accessory Drive System

In order to package the accessory drive system in the Corvette's engine compartment, the supercharger drive was integrated into the main drive system. This required a wider 11-rib accessory drive system to be used with the LS9 to support the load delivered by the supercharger.

Fuel System

Both engines use fuel injectors with center-feed fuel lines. The center-feed system ensures even fuel flow between the cylinders with less noise. To ensure fuel system perfor-

mance during low-speed operation and under the extreme performance requirements of WOT, a dual-pressure fuel system was developed. This system operates at 36 psi (250 kPa) at idle and low speed, and ratchets up to 87 psi (600 kPa) at higher-speed and WOT conditions. The LS9 uses 48-lb/hr injectors.

Throttle Body

An 87-mm, single-bore throttle body is used to draw air into the LSA; an 89-mm throttle body is on the LS9. Both are electronically controlled.

Real-World Project: Pratt & Miller's LS9.RS– The Ultimate Supercharged LS Street Engine

It's a logical question: What happens when you marry the 6.2-liter LS9 engine's forced-induction system with the larger, 7.0-liter displacement of the LS7? As it turns out, it's the recipe for huge horsepower. Pratt & Miller (P&M) discovered this when it designed such a combination for its premium Corvette C6RS sports car.

P&M is the racing shop that builds, maintains, and supports the factory-backed Corvette C6R racing team (and, previously, the all-conquering C5R team). Its C6RS features wider, carbon-fiber body panels, an air-adjustable suspension and, until recently, a normally aspirated 8.2-liter engine rated at 600 hp. That was before the ZR1 trumped its output at the factory.

So, for a premium product, P&M wanted an elevated performance level. The company also wanted to keep its engine project as close to OEM as possible, making the hybrid assembly of an LS7 rotating assembly and LS9 induction parts all the more logical. P&M consulted LS engine guru Thomson Automotive for some advice on the rotating assembly and airflow requirements of the engine. (Thomson Automotive also built the 2,000-hp twin-turbo engine discussed in Chapter 9.) The result is what Pratt & Miller calls the LS9.RS.

The Bottom End

The official word from GM engineers on using the smaller-bore,

The standard cylinder block for the 7.0-liter LS7 engine is the foundation for the LS9.RS. It is aluminum with pressed-in steel bore liners and forged-steel main bearing caps. Machine work prior to assembly includes deck-plate honing of the cylinders and line boring of the crankshaft main bearing surfaces.

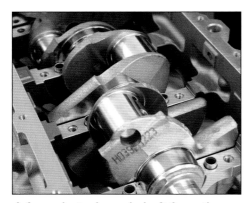

A forged-steel crankshaft from the factory LS7 engine is used, delivering a 4.000-inch stroke that combines with the 4.125-inch bores to give the engine its 427-ci displacement. The LS7 crank has a more common six-bolt flange, rather than the LS9's nine-bolt flange. Although the nine-bolt design delivers theoretically greater clamping strength, the six-bolt flange is more compatible with a variety of flywheels that may be used in the C6RS Corvettes. Premium fasteners are used to ensure the strongest possible connection.

6.2-liter platform for the LS9 is safety. The thicker cylinder walls provide a greater margin of safety for an engine designed to withstand a 100,000-mile durability standard that takes into account all manners of use, load, and abuse. That doesn't mean that using the 7.0-liter LS7 block is a recipe for a meltdown. In fact, the LS7 is commendably strong.

So, while the LS7's cylinder block wasn't a worry, its stock rods and pistons were. The featherweight titanium connecting rods from the LS7 simply weren't designed for the load, stress, and horsepower range expected of the supercharged engine. At Thomson Automotive's suggestion, they were swapped with a set of aftermarket (by Oliver) forged I-beam rods.

The hypereutectic (cast) material of the LS7 pistons may have caused concern in a supercharged application, too, but the question was rendered moot by the fact they would deliver too much squeeze in the cylinders. The LS7 has a high, 11.0:1 compression ratio—way too much for a street-driven blower engine. In their place, a set of aftermarket Diamond forged-aluminum pistons was used, each with a sizable dish to help lower the compression to a more manageable 9.0:1.

Anchoring the rods and pistons was a factory LS7 crankshaft. As a forged-steel component and one that has proved exceptionally strong and resilient, it was more than suitable for the job. For the record, the bore and stroke of this engine is 4.125 x 4.000 inches—the same as a stock LS7.

Induction Details

Curiously, one of the most significant elements of the big-inch LS7 engine that wasn't carried over was the cylinder heads. Although known for their cavernous ports and straight pathways to the combustion chambers, they simply didn't match the intake ports of the LS9 supercharger manifold. P&M had little choice but to use the factory LS9 heads; and while their intake flow is somewhat less than the LS7 heads, it isn't a detriment when the boost is up and air is being rammed through the engine with terrific velocity.

LS9 heads are based on the respected L92 design, but feature swirl-inducing wings cast into the intake ports. The valvetrain consists of 2.16-inch titanium intake valves and 1.59-inch Inconel valves (in place of the hollow-stem stock valves). Standard springs, retainers, and push rods were used. Even the

stamped-steel arms were retained, owing to the OEM parts list.

Atop the heads, of course, was mounted the LS9's supercharger/intercooler assembly. Apart from a different drive pulley (more on that below), P&M used the whole assembly without modification, along with the factory 10-rib belt system and LS9 front accessories. P&M omitted the plastic, decorative engine cover, milled off the "LS9 SUPERCHARGED" embossed letters on top of the intercooler lid, and painted the entire intercooler cover to match the car.

On the Dyno

Testing was conducted at Thomson Automotive, with the engine using an E67 controller and blowing gases through stock LS7 exhaust manifolds, which would deliver more representative results of the horsepower and torque of the engine in the vehicle. It was immediately clear the extra volume of the 7.0-liter engine was a factor to contend with. With the stock supercharger drive pulley, the blower could only deliver about 5 pounds of boost on the larger cylinders. It wasn't acceptable, but even with that, the engine spit out about the same power as a stock LS9—at only half the boost.

A new, smaller pulley was quickly milled and the testing resumed. The results were more impressive: 760 hp and 830 ft-lbs of torque. That's about 20 percent (120 hp) more power than the LS9 from an engine that is only about 13.5-percent larger in displacement. It was certainly a successful experiment, but there was more power on the table.

During the numerous test pulls on the dyno, it was noted that the air-pressure drop after the throttle body was about 1.7 psi (12 kPa). That told

The LS7's cast-aluminum pistons were replaced not so much for concern of their strength under boost, but because they delivered too much squeeze, at 11.0:1 compression. Forged-aluminum, coated pistons from Diamond were used. They are dished to lower the compression ratio to a detonation-avoiding 9.0:1. The blower-specific pistons also have a thick surface crown and reinforced pin bosses. Forged I-beam rods (in the stock, 6.067-inch length) from Oliver were used in place of the LS7's titanium rods. The lightweight titanium rods simply weren't designed for the load and power levels expected of this engine. The effect of greater mass on the rotating assembly with heavier I-beams will be quickly offset with the rise in boost pressure under load.

With a completely stock supercharger assembly, the LS9.RS delivered the power of an LS9 with only 5 pounds of boost. With the stock blower drive pulley, the 2.3-liter supercharger couldn't adequately fill the cylinders—it ran out of breath. The LS9's stock, 89-mm throttle body was swapped with the only other one available (an LS7 90-mm unit) because an aftermarket 100-mm body turned out to be smaller than the stock throttle body. With a smaller pulley and the 90-mm throttle body, the engine made 760 hp and 830 ft-lbs of torque, with 10 pounds of boost.

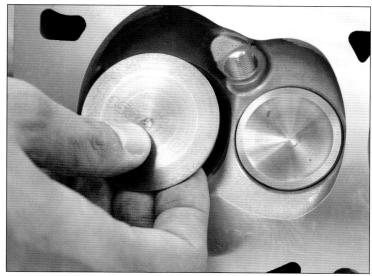

The larger-capacity LS7 cylinder heads weren't used, but only because their intake ports didn't match those of the supercharger manifold. That made the factory LS9 heads the only real choice, which is fine, because they're based on the high-flow L92 head and manufactured with a stronger alloy that helps them withstand the extra heat that comes with forced induction. The LS9.RS uses stock 2.16-inch titanium intake valves and aftermarket 1.59-inch Inconel exhaust valves (although the exhaust valves are the same size as the stock ones).

When the testing of the engine was completed, Pratt & Miller turned to the aesthetic considerations. The "hat" of the intercooler was painted to match the exterior color of the car, and the original "LS9 Supercharged" embossment was milled off. An "LS9.RS" badge or something similar will likely go in its place, but it looks nice and clean as is. Also, the valve covers were color coordinated and several other accessories were either painted or detailed to give the engine a more premium appearance.

the tuners the engine wasn't drawing enough air for maximum power. It wore an LS7 90-mm electronic throttle body (the LS9's is 89 mm in diameter), but it was determined at least a 100-mm unit was needed.

An aftermarket 100-mm throttle body (a cable-actuated unit that required "tricking" the controller to think it was electronically operated)

was ordered, but its inlet turned out to be smaller than the factory 90-mm unit. P&M tuners figure this unique engine combination is good for 800 to 820 hp with the properly sized throttle body.

Regardless of the throttle body, the LS9.RS confirms everyone's thoughts: Adding the LS9 blower to the LS7 bottom end is a *great* idea.

TURBOCHARGER TYPES AND SELECTION

Swiss engineer Dr. Alfred Buchi is credited with developing the first exhaust-driven turbocharger, sometime around 1912. By 1915, he published a proposal for employing a turbocharger on a diesel engine, but the idea was mostly ignored for the next few years. The first real-world applications were in aviation, where turbochargers helped aircraft engines build power in the thin air of higher altitudes.

Turbocharged aircraft engines became more prevalent during World War II, but were far from common. General Electric was the big supplier of turbochargers to American aircraft during the war and that's when J. C. "Cliff" Garrett entered the picture. His company supplied after-cooling systems that were used with General Electric's turbochargers on B-17 bombers.

After the war, Garrett continued manufacturing gas-turbine engines and experimenting with turbocharging. That led to the formation of a spin-off division of his company called AiResearch Industrial Division. It would later be renamed Garrett Automotive. Proving Dr. Buchi was on to something, but simply a few

decades ahead of his time, early automotive-industry uses were targeted at diesel-powered over-the-road trucks, as well as similarly powered industrial engines.

Interestingly, engine-driven supercharging had been used successfully in automobiles since the 1920s, even if it wasn't a widespread technology. Nonetheless, turbocharging didn't arrive on the North American automotive market until the early 1960s, when several import-fighting, rear-engine compacts were released by

GM. They included the Chevrolet Corvair and Oldsmobile Jetfire, but while performance was adequate, durability and reliability were not.

Turbocharging mostly disappeared for the next 15 years or so, when its use became more widespread in large trucks and racing. The technology was also revisited by mainstream auto manufacturers after the fuel crisis of the 1970s as a way to balance performance and fuel economy. Buick, Ford, and Chrysler developed turbocharged powertrains in the late

Turbocharged and intercooled 1986-1987 Buick Grand Nationals also featured electronically controlled fuel injection, ushering in the modern era of turbocharged performance for a new generation of enthusiasts.

A pair of intercooled turbos was adapted to the classic Chevy small-block V-8 to power the Callaway Twin Turbo Corvette. The system was well integrated and the base 5.7-liter engine was upgraded with lower-compression pistons and heavy-duty rotating components to support the load of the turbochargers. It was a combination that increased horsepower about 50 percent over the stock Corvette's rating.

This photo illustrates the complexities of designing and/or installing a turbo system on a street vehicle that retains all of the other factory controls, chassis and suspension elements. Note the various hard lines and hoses that snake in and out of the turbocharger (and mirrored on the opposite side of the engine compartment). Developing such a system is time intensive, and so is installation. Also, slight vehicle changes between model years can require substantial reengineering. That's why there aren't as many bolt-on turbo kits on the market, compared to blower kits.

Here's another F-body with a turbo system adapted to it. But rather than squeezing a kit around the necessary factory chassis components of a street car, this drag-race car is essentially built around the turbo system. This design simplifies many of the installation procedures for the turbo system, but (as is clear from the photo) the car won't be suitable or street-legal for the street when completed.

1970s, but it wasn't until the advent of modern-style electronic engine-control systems, electronically controlled fuel injection, and intercooling systems that turbocharging became a viable, reliable, and consistent method of building horsepower. Volkswagen and Mercedes-Benz also offered turbocharged models at that time. The intercooled turbo engine of the 1986-1987 Buick Grand National was a landmark design, not only in factory force-fed GM vehicles, but in the advancement of mainstream turbocharging. At a time when many V-8 "performance" cars struggled to offer 200 hp, the intercooled Grand National's 3.8-liter V-6 was offered with 235 hp (rising to 245 hp in 1987). And while Ford's 2.3-liter turbocharged engine was offered as a performance engine in the 1980s, the Grand National was the first turbocharged production model that offered a distinct advantage over V-8-powered competitors.

The Grand National shares nothing with the modern LS engine, but the basics of its intercooled turbo system are essentially the same as the aftermarket systems employed today.

LS-Powered Production Vehicles

There are a number of turbo kits available for production LS-powered vehicles and knowledgeable tuning shops can custom build them with the necessary components and good tube-bending skills.

With nearly unlimited performance potential, good low- and

moderate-speed driving characteristics and the undeniable aura of exoticness, there's much to like about the prospect of turbocharging a Corvette, Pontiac G8, or TrailBlazer SS. That doesn't mean, however, that it's the most practical solution to building a high-powered street car.

As mentioned in Chapter 1, the investment in kit cost and installation labor makes a turbo system typically more expensive when compared with a typical bolt-on supercharger system. There is usually more fabrication required to install a turbo system. I followed the installation of several supercharger and turbocharger systems and found a large gap in the time and special fabrication required between them, ranging from approximately 8 hours for the installation of an intercooled supercharger kit on a Pontiac G8 GT (see Chapter 5) to more than 40 hours for a turbo kit installed on a fourth-generation Trans Am.

At shop labor rates of $60 to $75 or more per hour, the installation time becomes an important and expensive consideration. On the low end of the labor rate scale, the additional time of the Trans Am's kit versus the G8's would add up to about $2,000.

With the tuning capability and driveline component strength (transmission, axle, etc.) comparatively equal between supercharged and turbocharged production vehicles, there's no clear advantage of one over the other. The performance potential with a turbo system is undeniably greater, and for the enthusiast who envisions taking his or her car's performance to higher levels in the future, a basic turbo system is an excellent foundation. System complexity and consequential installation cost, however,

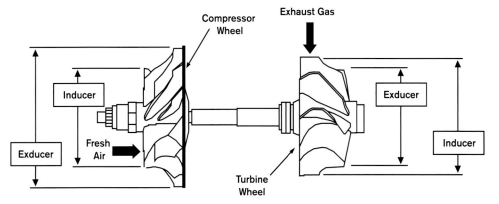

This illustration shows the internal elements of a turbocharger. When the exhaust gas spins the turbine, it simultaneously spins the compressor that is drawing in the fresh air that is forced into the engine. Exhaust gas is not fed into the engine.

should weigh heavily on the decision to invest in one.

Turbocharger Component Terms

As noted earlier, a turbocharger uses engine exhaust to spin the turbine, which is connected via the center hub shaft to the compressor side of the housing to generate boost. The basic components are defined below.

Turbine: The exhaust-driven wheel.
Compressor/Impeller: The wheel spun by the action of the turbine that compresses air and generates boost.
Center Hub Rotating Assembly: The "floating" shaft that links the turbine and compressor/impeller wheels.
Inducer Wheel: The portion of the turbine or compressor wheel where airflow enters it; on a turbine wheel, it is the "major" diameter section, while on the compressor wheel, it is the "minor" diameter section.
Exducer Wheel: The portion of the turbine or compressor wheel where airflow exits it; on a turbine wheel, it is the "minor" diameter section, while on the compressor wheel, it is the "major" diameter section.

For most manufacturers, the general size of the turbocharger is measured in millimeters across either the turbine inducer or the compressor exducer. Racers who must comply with sanctioning rules regarding turbocharger size should check the rules carefully to determine whether the size of the turbo is measured at the impeller inducer or the compressor exducer.

Operation Basics

Like a supercharger, the turbocharger helps increase engine power through increased volumetric efficiency. It does this by compressing the engine's intake air, making it denser, and forcing it into the engine at greater pressure than normal. When combined with the correct amount of additional fuel to match the denser air charge's correspondingly greater oxygen content, it is a safe and reliable method for increasing the amount of air the engine can pump at a given RPM level.

The additional air delivered by the turbocharger comes from exhaust gas that exits the engine and blows into a turbine. As the turbine spins, it spins an air compressor that blows fresh air into the engine's intake tract. The turbine and air compressor portions of the turbochargers are separate housings bolted together and linked by an interconnecting turbine shaft.

Generally speaking, the size of the turbocharger determines the volume of air it can generate, or the amount of boost it's capable of blowing into the engine; i.e., the larger the turbo, the greater the boost. That's a simplification of the theory of building horsepower with a turbocharger, but it's suitable for this portion of the discussion.

The boost level is carefully tailored in production vehicles to deliver a balance of on-demand performance and fuel efficiency, along with smoothness and quietness that is acceptable to the 99.9 percent of the car-buying public that isn't interested in running 9-second 1/4-mile ETs. In these factory applications, the size of the turbocharger is carefully selected, along with matched turbine and air-compressor sizes.

Whether a tailored factory system or high-performance aftermarket system for an LS engine, all turbocharger systems are affected by factors that influence overall performance and efficiency, including:

Heat: Turbochargers generate tremendous heat that is radiated through the engine compartment. It can elevate the inlet air temperature, reducing boost and possibly promoting detonation or pre-ignition.

Turbo Lag: The time difference between the application of the throttle and corresponding response in boost-induced power. This is typically due to the "spool-up" time it takes for the turbine to get up to

At its very basic, the turbo system channels exhaust gas via an exhaust manifold to the turbine side of the turbocharger. When the turbocharger is mounted directly to or very near the exhaust manifold, the manifold must be sufficiently thick and strong to withstand not only the heat of the turbo system, but also the reduction in temperature when the system is not under load or the engine is turned off. Thick cast-iron manifolds traditionally do the best job at this, because they resist warping.

The compressor side of the turbocharger is what sends fresh air under pressure into the engine. A common misperception about turbos is that exhaust gas is somehow part of the boosted air charge. It is not. Exhaust gas is only used to spin the turbo in order for the compressor to generate a pressurized charge of fresh air.

Like the exhaust manifolds in a turbo system, the turbine side of a turbocharger is typically constructed of thick cast iron. The mounting flange seen here reveals a thick pad to resist warping.

With this view of a basic turbocharger, it is easy to visualize its operation. Exhaust gas enters through the rectangular port on the left, which mounts on or near the exhaust manifold, and spins the turbine. When the turbine spins, it acts on a shaft that simultaneously spins the compressor on the opposite side of the unit. The spinning compressor draws in fresh air, compresses it and sends it as the boosted air charge into the engine.

Logically, the larger the size of the turbocharger, the more air it can push. However, the larger the turbo, the greater the chance for lag (the delay between the time the throttle is opened and the turbo spools enough to generate boost). Regardless of the size of the turbo, heat is a byproduct that must be dealt with to optimize performance and prevent engine damage.

Turbo systems generate a lot of heat under the hood that can damage parts and promote detonation. This twin-turbo setup uses a number of thermal barriers and wraps on the exhaust system, fuel lines, and more. Such measures are relatively cheap insurance and help ensure engine longevity.

sufficient speed to generate boost with the air compressor. Turbo lag has been a longtime detriment to turbocharging, with its tendency generally increased along with the size of the turbo.

Turbo Size: A larger turbocharger typically makes more power, but it can also induce greater turbo lag, as it takes a larger turbine more time to spool up. Conversely, a smaller turbocharger may spool up quicker, but not deliver the desired power gain or at the desired RPM level.

There is more to turbocharging than can possibly be described and explained in this single chapter. I recommend Jay K. Miller's recent book, *Turbo: Real World High-Performance Turbocharger Systems.* It offers a wealth of more-in-depth information on the theory, design, and application of turbo systems (go to www.cartechbooks.com for more information).

Dealing with the Heat

The heat generated by a turbo system is part of the price to pay for performance. It uses the already-hot exhaust gases and, rather than immediately expelling them all through the exhaust system, retains a portion to spool the turbine. The heat radiated by the turbocharger can quickly build up in closed or tightly packed engine compartments, such as the fourth-generation Camaro and Firebird or the C5/C6 Corvettes. That heat is generally absorbed by the air-intake system, heating the air charge and reducing its density.

Combating engine-compartment heat can be done with a variety of thermal wraps and thermal barriers placed on or around the affected components; a lower mounting position of the turbo(s) also helps. The innovative system designs from Utah-based Squires Turbo Systems (STS) approaches the problem by locating the turbocharger near the rear axle and removing it (and the heat it generates) from the engine compartment. (See Chapter 6 for installation details.)

The heat of a turbo system is easily absorbed by the intake system, which saps power and promotes detonation. That makes an intercooler all the more important. Its heat exchanger should be mounted in an area that receives direct, fresh air, typically in front of the radiator.

Fighting Turbo Lag

As for turbo lag, it has always been an issue with turbocharger systems and is generally more prevalent on larger turbochargers, as more inertia is required to spool up the larger, heavier turbine when compared with a smaller turbo. Ceramic roller thrust bearings are used in some lightweight turbochargers to reduce inertia, while the aspect ratio of the turbo's exhaust housing

A high-flow, restriction-free exhaust system can reduce turbo lag, although street enthusiasts have to balance low restriction with legal sound compliance. Fortunately, turbo systems can mute some of the loudness of an engine, so there's more room to play with when it comes to implementing a free-flowing exhaust system that won't draw the ire of neighbors or the ticket books of police officers.

influences lag through the affect its aspect ratio has on spool-up time (see below).

One of the more effective ways to combat turbo lag is with a high-flow exhaust system. Some backpressure is required to help the turbine spool, but a freer-flowing exhaust system minimizes the time required for it to generate boost. On engines where quick spool-up and more low-RPM power are desired, the use of a pair of smaller turbochargers rather than a larger, single unit can help.

Ball Bearing Turbos

The standard, conventional "floating" bearing in a turbocharger is what the turbine wheel rotates on during spool-up. Minimizing friction as the turbine spins on the bearing reduces inertia for quicker spool-up and enables greater maximum turbine speed.

High-performance turbo systems also undergo tremendous thrust load; the greater the boost pressure, the greater the load on the turbo's internal components. In the quest for greater turbocharger efficiency and durability, the ball-bearing-type turbo was developed by Garrett (currently a division of Honeywell). As its name suggestion, the ball bearing turbo's center section (also known as the cartridge) on which the turbine shift spins features low-friction ball bearings. The lower friction significantly reduces inertia, delivering a more immediate spool-up of the turbine. The bearings are surrounded by a film of oil that not only lubricates but acts as a vibration damper.

On the heels of the ball bearing turbo came the ceramic roller thrust bearing that was pioneered by Turbonetics. It is commonly known as the ceramic ball bearing turbo, as the bearing is made of a silicone-nitrade ceramic material. With this design, the lightweight, heat-resistant ceramic ball bearing is used on the air compressor side of the turbocharger, while the turbine side uses a conventional floating bearing.

The Garrett-style turbo uses a pair of ball bearings, while the Turbonetics design uses a single bearing. Both enable quicker spool-up through reduced friction—Turbonetics claims only half the exhaust energy is required to drive the turbine—but just as importantly, the capability to withstand substantially greater thrust load. In fact, Turbonetics claims up to 600-percent-greater thrust capacity than a conventional turbo bearing. Turbonetics also claims the builder can step up to a larger turbo size without compromising drivability on the street—thanks to the reduced turbo lag and more immediate delivery of power.

While the quicker spool-up of these low-friction turbochargers is immediately noticeable when compared with a turbo using a conventional floating bearing, the advantage is more useful with vehicles where boost is desired during driving conditions, such as primarily street driving or road racing. On a vehicle designed primarily for drag racing, the difference in spool-up on the starting line doesn't affect performance when launching under boost, but the greater thrust load capability ultimately means longer turbo life. This is due to the great load on the turbo that comes during staging, as the turbocharger is brought up to high speed in order to launch under boost. The sustained high RPM of the turbo on the starting line generates tremendous heat and load, so a ball bearing turbo pays off with performance longevity.

On a racing engine, a turbo can almost never be too large (rules permitting), but for street vehicles, there is a sweet spot between small and large that delivers effective, horsepower without lag. The minimum requirement for an engine is tied to its airflow at the maximum engine speed.

Measuring A/R Ratio

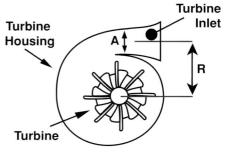

This diagram illustrates how the aspect ratio on a turbocharger is measured.

But, along with greater performance, ball bearing turbos (whether the Garrett-style or Turbonetics design) bring a significant price premium—perhaps up to double the cost of a conventional-bearing turbocharger. The performance and strength virtues of ball-bearing turbochargers are well established, but come at a price. If your budget allows, the ball-bearing turbo is the way to go.

Selecting the Right Size Turbocharger

While larger turbos generate more boost and, generally, more horsepower, there is a limit to their effectiveness. At the other end of the spectrum is the *minimum* size a turbocharger needs to be in order to effectively boost an engine. That minimum size is determined by the engine's airflow at its maximum RPM level, measured in cubic feet per minute (cfm).

Arriving at the engine airflow requirement is achieved by multiplying the displacement by the maximum RPM and volumetric effi-ciency and dividing the product by 3,456. Generally speaking, naturally aspirated engines have a volumetric efficiency of about 85 percent, so the equation would look like this:

$$\text{Displacement} \times \text{RPM} \times .85 \, / \, 3456 = \text{Minimum CFM}$$

Let's use a 6.0-liter LS2 engine as an example; it has a displacement of 364 ci and a 6,000-rpm redline:

$$364 \times 6,000 \times .85 \, / \, 3,456 = 531.157 \text{ cfm}$$

This means that a turbocharger for the LS2 must have a minimum airflow rating of at least 531 cfm. Within reason, a turbo with greater airflow capability is fine, but that's not the only consideration when selecting a turbocharger. The aspect ratio must also be considered.

Turbocharger Aspect Ratio

Another important element to turbocharger design, size and selection is the aspect ratio, which is the ratio of the area of the housing's cone to radius from the turbine or air compressor's center. Aspect ratios are measured on both the exhaust side and the air compressor side. On either side, the ratio is determined by dividing the cross section of the turbo by the distance from the center of that section to the center of the turbine wheel.

The aspect ratio should be constant throughout the housing, because the spiral-shaped housing reduces in size the closer it is to the center. The spiral shape is known as the volute; it directs airflow to the turbine. Comparing similar-size turbochargers with different aspect ratios, a greater ratio (identified by a larger number) enhances upper-RPM performance with greater airflow, but requires longer turbine spool-up time. A turbo with a smaller aspect ratio has quicker spool-up, but less upper-RPM airflow.

For turbocharged engines used primarily on the street and for road racing, a smaller aspect ratio on the exhaust side of the turbo delivers the best performance, as it promotes quicker spool-up and, consequently, more immediate power delivery. For drag racing, a larger aspect ratio helps build power at higher RPM, where it is more effective.

The size of the turbo and other factors ultimately determine the maximum airflow capability, but knowing how the aspect ratio affects performance should influence the decision when selecting similarly sized turbochargers.

Pitfalls of Mixing Turbines and Compressors

The turbine and compressor sections of a turbocharger must complement one another in order to produce strong, effective performance. Generally, turbocharger manufacturers and retailers match the exhaust-driven-turbine half of the turbo housing with an appropriate air-compressor half to generate optimal volumetric efficiency.

But in the quest to squeeze more boost from the system and generate more power, some builders experiment with different-size components, such as installing a larger turbine in the exhaust housing or bolting a larger air compressor to a smaller turbine. The changes drastically affect the turbocharger's performance and should be attempted only if you have extensive knowledge and experience with turbocharging systems. It is very easy to kill the performance advantage of a turbo system with mismatched components that generate heat and noise, but little in the way of effective boost.

If you are experimenting with a custom turbo system for the first time, consult turbo manufacturers and experienced builders prior to purchasing or bolting on a new turbocharger. A defined horsepower goal or application, such as street and/or drag racing, helps the experts size a turbocharger that is the most appropriate for the project.

The complementing engine combination must also be considered in the role of volumetric efficiency, as the cylinder-head airflow characteristics, camshaft specifications, and even the intake manifold can affect performance under boost. In other words, it's not necessary to experiment with internal turbo modifications if a camshaft swap would be a more logical and effective alternative.

Only after the as-delivered turbo has been tested and its performance parameters thoroughly understood and explored should you consider experimenting with its turbine and air-compressor components. Optimal volumetric efficiency is the goal and messing with the manufacturer's balanced turbo assembly is a good way to adversely affect it.

Elements of a Turbo System

Of course, a turbocharging system is comprised of more than the turbocharger itself. A number of supporting components go into it, each affecting performance and durability in important ways. They include the following.

Turbo Exhaust Manifolds: They replace the conventional exhaust manifolds and mount the turbochargers, positioning the turbine side within the flow stream of the exhaust.
Turbocharger(s): The exhaust-trim air compressor that generates boost to increase horsepower.
Down Pipe: The exhaust pipe located immediately after the turbocharger, which receives the exhaust after it spins the turbine, as well as the exhaust from the wastegate.
Wastegate: It is essentially a bypass valve for the turbine, whereby a portion of the exhaust gas is diverted

The flanges of the exhaust manifold need to be thick to withstand warpage caused by high heat. This is the header flange; it is 1/2-inch thick. The black appearance is the result of a heat-resistant thermal coating that helps keep down underhood temperatures.

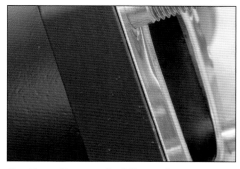

On the other end of the exhaust manifold is a mounting flange about 3/4-inch thick. The turbo bolts to it, taking the brunt of the hot exhaust gases at wide-open throttle.

around—instead blowing of into—the turbine. It is used to tune or limit boost pressure by limiting the maximum exhaust flow to the turbine. When the maximum boost level is reached, the wastegate opens to bleed off exhaust pressure and prevent the turbo boost level from increasing.
Blow-off Valve (BOV): A device mounted on the air-intake pipe, between the turbo and the throttle body, that bleeds off excessive boost, which builds after the throttle is quickly closed—a condition known as compressor surge.

Bypass Valve: Similar to a blow-off valve, the bypass valve vents excessive boost pressure; but rather than venting it to the atmosphere, as the BOV does, the bypass valve vents it back to the compressor inlet.

Intercooler: The air-charge-cooling device that reduces the inlet temperature of the boosted air charge, which serves to maximize power and reduce the chance for detonation.

Complementing the basic elements of the turbo system, of course, are the corresponding fuel and ignition system upgrades, such as the fuel injectors, fuel pump, spark plugs, etc.

Boost Controller and Turbo Timer

In addition to the basic system elements described above, a couple of accessories that optimize longevity and performance are the boost controller and turbo timer. Neither are required to enable a turbo system's operation, but they work to prevent damage and extend the operating range of the system.

The boost controller, as its name implies, is a device that controls the boost level of a turbo system, either limiting its maximum boost level or helping ensure a desired boost level at different RPM levels or throttle positions, as maximum boost can still be achieved with some systems without WOT. The boost controller works by bleeding off air pressure at the wastegate back into the intake system or venting it to the atmosphere.

Manual boost controllers are available and relatively simple to install and operate, but electronic boost controllers are better suited to an electronically controlled LS

That unmistakable "whoosh" heard with turbo systems comes when the blow-off valve opens to vent excessive air pressure. It is mounted between the intercooler and throttle body.

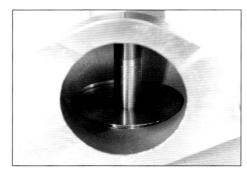

This inside view of a TiAL blow-off valve shows the vacuum-operated valve itself. As with wastegates, blow-off valves can be tuned, but their primary purpose is to prevent boost from forcing its way into the engine when the throttle closes.

engine. They can be "dialed in" to deliver prescribed boost pressure at different RPM levels for finely tuned performance. You should check with the turbocharger manufacturer for recommendations of either the most appropriate boost controller or possible hardware changes suggested for the turbocharger itself. The spring in the wastegate, as well as other turbo system components, can be very sensitive and affected adversely with an aggressive controller.

A turbo timer is an electronically controlled device that keeps the engine running for a length of time

Here's a boost controller integrated with an STS turbo system. It is an digital controller, but other electronic controllers enable the driver to dial in the desired boost from a remote control. Manual boost controllers are adjustable, much like the valve settings on adjustable shock absorbers.

to allow adequate cooling of the turbocharger after extended driving under high load. With it, the engine idles for a predetermined period, which allows the turbine to cool from extremely high exhaust temperature, with oil continuing to circulate through the system. This is a more important feature for vehicles that are routinely raced, such as drag cars, which benefit from the cool-down period in the pit area. With a street-driven vehicle, the cool-down period can be performed simply by keeping the engine's RPM low and out of boost for several minutes before turning off the engine.

Single- vs. Twin-Turbo Systems

One of the methods of generating more turbocharged power is employing a pair of smaller, parallel turbo-chargers (one turbo for each bank of cylinders) rather than a single, larger turbo. This approach generally benefits chassis and engine compartments that are mostly stock

Packaging a twin-turbo system can be challenging, even with the relatively open space of a full-size truck's engine compartment (seen here). Also, the size of the turbochargers determine the most effective mounting position. A pair of small turbos is comparatively easy to mount directly off the exhaust manifolds or slightly below them. Larger turbos (as seen here) need more room. The system seen here was designed to accommodate a pair of larger turbos.

On a street-driven vehicle, a number of inescapable details affect the design and implementation of a custom turbo system. Here, routing of the large-diameter down tube from a remotely mounted turbocharger reveals some obvious interference issues with the vehicle's brake master cylinder. A smaller-diameter tube or one with another bend in it will likely make enough room for the master cylinder, but may cause a restriction that increases turbo lag.

When the turbochargers are too large to mount directly to the manifolds on the engine, they typically end up mounted in the engine compartment. That requires a completely custom-fitted exhaust system to feed the turbine and carry away the exhaust via the down tubes. Because the turbos are located away from the exhaust manifolds, the manifolds themselves don't need to be cast iron. Here, a custom turbo exhaust system is being tacked together from conventional exhaust tubing. Such work adds complexity and cost to a turbo system.

This photo clearly illustrates the elements of the turbo system and their relationship with one another. At the bottom of the system, the exhaust tubes from the exhaust header can be seen merging into the collector that mounts on the turbine side of the turbocharger. At the left of the system, the large-diameter tube is the down tube, which carries exhaust away after it spins the turbine. Also visible is a TiAL waste gate. Note how it is integrated with the down tube, as that's where the excess pressure is vented. Finally, the compressor side of the turbo is visible on the right-hand side of the photo, with the discharge end open. Tubing will be routing from it through an intercooler and on to the engine's throttle body.

Texas-based Fastlane, Inc., offers a single-turbo bolt-on kit for the 2010+ Camaro SS. It includes a Borg Warner extended-tip turbocharger (with a large, 71.5-mm compressor wheel). The company claims the system is tuned for about 7 pounds of boost, which delivers an increase of more than 100 hp on an otherwise-stock engine.

and have limited room for a large single turbo, but many builders use twin turbos for aesthetic reasons, too.

A belief that a pair of smaller turbos spool faster and deliver more power at lower RPM isn't entirely true. Although small turbos typically spool quicker than large turbos, when they're used in a twin-turbo system, each is receiving only half the exhaust pressure as a single-turbo system. So in practical terms, the advantage of a twin-turbo system on a street car lies in the ability to package it within a tight engine compartment.

One of the most dramatic and effective examples of twin turbochargers is the Callaway Twin Turbo Corvette offered between 1987 and 1990. It used a pair of compact turbos to produce a little more than 12 pounds of boost and very little lag within the confines of the standard C4 Corvette engine compartment.

When it comes to racing engines, it is generally true that a pair of turbochargers enables more horsepower than a single-turbo system. However, the design and tuning of a twin-turbo racing engine is different from a single-turbo system to make direct comparisons not entirely accurate. Suffice it to say that, in a racing engine, more power can be had when more than one turbocharger is employed.

Bolt-On Turbo Kits and Tuner Systems

Time has proven bolt-on turbo kits to be tough to design, manufacture, and market successfully. The investment in development time, numerous special parts required for each vehicle model, and the razor-thin line those manufacturers must balance between recouping their costs and selling kits at a reasonable price often sinks them after only a few years. Consequently, the number of bolt-on kits is considerably fewer than supercharger systems.

When it comes to turbocharged LS vehicles, Australia-based APS Performance has emerged as the pre-eminent manufacturer. If offers kits for the C5 and C6 Corvettes; the Pontiac GTO and G8, the Holden Monaro and Commodore; and the 1998-2002

Camaro/Firebird. In North America, the kits are available through a number of affiliated dealers, such as Stenod Performance. APS Performance's kits have proven to be very well engineered, with inclusive kits packed with all the hardware required to install them, as well as detailed instruction manuals.

The other main turbo kit manufacturer for LS vehicles is Tacoma, Washington–based Turbo Technology. It offers a variety of intercooled kits for C5/C6 Corvettes and fourth-generation F-bodies, including:

- C6 (including Z06) street/race twin-turbo system
- C5 (including Z06) street/race twin-turbo system
- F-body street single-turbo system
- F-body race single-turbo system

Although the systems above from both APS Performance and Turbo Technology are designed specifically for various vehicles and include the correctly sized and routed mounting hardware, the term bolt-on is somewhat of a misnomer. Unlike, say, an Eaton-based supercharger kit for a Pontiac G8 that can be installed in a single working day at a tuning shop (see Chapter 5), some of the turbo kits described here require up to four times the labor time.

The tools (including a vehicle lift) and experience required to facilitate the typical installation of a bolt-on turbo kit makes professional help very advised. Assuming a professional shop handles the installation, the cost of the system increases by the number of hours the shop takes to do it. And with 20 to 40 hours of labor at typical shop rates, that could add $1,000 to $2,000 to the final cost of the system.

Currently, additional bolt-on

and/or tuner shop kits were either just introduced or planned for release by a number of other companies for the fifth-generation Camaro SS. They include:

- 2010+ Camaro SS turbo system by turbo component manufacturer Turbonetics
- 2010+ Camaro SS turbo system by Fastlane, Inc.
- 2010+ Camaro SS turbo system by Ultimate Performance and Racing.

Many turbo systems are designed and installed on an individual basis by performance tuning shops (see Chapter 6). This is typically done on vehicles that can't take advantage of a pre-engineered, bolt-on kit from an aftermarket vendor. An experienced shop can engineer a low-to-moderate-boost single- or twin-turbo system that essentially bolts onto a stock engine.

One of the tuning shops that has been particularly adept at designing and building turbo systems is Fastlane, Inc., in Houston, Texas. Proprietor Nick Field says the system complexity is what generally makes it difficult to package a bolt-on kit. "Often, the oiling systems and necessary fabrication would make a kit very complicated, especially for someone trying to install the kit in his home garage—that's why you don't see very many bolt-on turbo kits. Our kit for the 2010 Camaro is a lot more straightforward, with no fabrication required, so we're confident it will make a good bolt-on kit."

Perhaps the most unique and, in many ways, the most innovative bolt-on turbo systems are those from Utah-based Squires Turbo Systems (STS). The company has streamlined the installation process and removed

Beneath the bumper of a late-model Pontiac GTO/Holden Monaro, is a Squires Turbo Systems turbo kit. The remote-mounted turbo drastically reduces underhood temperatures and eliminates the need for a costly set of new exhaust manifolds.

the turbo-generated heat under the hood by moving the turbochargers to the rear of the vehicle chassis, near the rear axle.

In a nutshell, an STS system takes exhaust from the stock manifolds and runs it beneath the vehicle (much like a conventional exhaust system), where it meets the turbo (very close to the exhaust outlet). The traditional turbo system blows into the turbo directly from the exhaust manifold. STS claims this lowers the overall temperature of the turbo system, reducing underhood heat, as well as lowering the intake-air charge temperature.

The use of the original exhaust manifolds helps lower the cost of STS kits, relative to other turbo systems. They're still more expensive than most bolt-on supercharger systems, but the comparatively quick installation and lower component content makes them much more competitive with a blower, when installation labor is factored into the equation.

The comparative ease at which STS systems are packaged has allowed the company to offer kits for a greater number of LS-powered vehicles, including:

- C5 Corvette
- C6 Corvette
- 2010+ Camaro SS
- 1998–2002 Camaro and Firebird
- Cadillac CTS-V (2004-2007)
- Pontiac GTO/Holden Monaro (5.7-liter and 6.0-liter)
- Pontiac G8 GT/Holden Commodore
- Chevy TrailBlazer SS
- Chevy Silverado/GMC Sierra
- Chevy Tahoe/Suburban and GMC Yukon/Yukon XL
- Hummer H2

Chapter 6 illustrates the basic installation procedures of an STS kit, as well as a more conventional turbo kit.

Long regarded for exemplary engineering and extreme performance results, Indiana-based Lingenfelter Performance Engineering takes turbo systems to a unique level for LS-powered vehicles. The company offers a number of turbocharging systems, but rather than bolt-on kits, they involve completely rebuilt engines engineered to support forced induction. Its 800-hp LS7 twin-turbo system for the Corvette Z06 is the ultimate example. It uses all-new rotating parts, modified cylinder heads and a revised fuel system in conjunction with carefully tuned turbo components that include:

- Two Garrett oil-lubricated and liquid-cooled ball bearing turbochargers
- Lingenfelter-designed turbo compressor housings and exhaust housings with integral wastegates
- Air-to-air charge-cooling system
- Lingenfelter-designed stainless-steel exhaust manifolds/turbo outlets
- Belt-driven turbocharger scavenge pump and turbo oil-drain reservoir

Obviously, the Lingenfelter system is more than a bolt-on kit and its cost reflects that. The base price for the system is more than $45,000—but that includes an essentially brand-new engine engineered for the heat and stress of a high-boost turbo system. It may not be the least-expensive option, but with a three-year/36,000-mile warranty backing it, it should prove to be one of the most durable. Lingenfelter offers similar turbo packages for other LS-powered vehicles.

This is a Specter Werkes Sports' Corvette GTR equipped with a Lingenfelter Performance Engineering twin-turbocharged LS7 engine. It is a completely streetable engine combination that runs on pump gas, but delivers a stunning 800 hp. Such performance doesn't come cheaply, however. The engine package lists for more than $45,000. (See Chapter 6 for installation.)

KIT PRE-INSTALLATION

This chapter discusses peripheral modifications that are commonly performed to support them, including fuel system upgrades, spark plug selection and the process known as "pinning" the crankshaft and balancer. For the most part, the factory cooling system on LS-powered vehicles is sufficient to support bolt-on power adders. In fact, at low speeds and part-throttle conditions, the cooling needs of the engine are no greater than normal.

Removing the front fascia or bumper cover in order to install the intercooling system's heat exchanger, plumbing, and hardware typically requires the removal of the front tires in order to gain access to and adequate leverage on the fascia's fasteners.

Body and Chassis Component Removal

Systems that incorporate a charge-cooling system, typically a liquid-to-air or air-to-air system, require the installation of a radiator-style heat exchanger. It is generally mounted at the front of the vehicle to ingest air via the grille/fascia assembly, either straight through the grille or from beneath the fascia. In most cases this requires removal of the fascia, bumper cover, grille, and sometimes even the headlamps.

Although the attachment of the body/chassis components may seem obvious, read the kit instructions carefully and proceed cautiously. The plastic body parts and fasteners that typically comprise the components to be removed aren't designed for repeated installation and removal; and the fasteners can be especially fragile.

A kit with good instructions points out all of the fasteners that require removal; and even after they're removed, there will likely be press-kit/snap-fit attachments, particularly with the bumper cover. When it's clear that all other fasteners are removed, a firm tug on the fascia usually pulls it free from the chassis.

Most vehicles' fascias and other underbody plastic components are held in place not with bolts or scews, but plastic pushpins. They can be pried out with a flat-blade screwdriver, but a more efficient method (and one that won't damage the pins) is to use a dedicated trim-removal tool.

Trim removal tools like this one are available at most auto parts stores and most online tool sources. They're inexpensive and make a smart addition to any home toolbox.

There are inexpensive specialized tools that enable the removal of the factory fasteners quickly and without damaging them. Buying one is a wise investment before starting the installation project. Overpriced replacement clips/fasteners are always available at the dealer in case you damage one.

Engine Preparation

Before touching the engine or any of the vehicle's mechanical components, the power must be disconnected by removing the battery cable from the negative terminal. Most intercooled supercharger and turbocharger systems also require the draining of the engine coolant. The coolant can be reused if it is captured in a clean, contaminant-free receptacle.

Study the manufacturer's assembly manual prior to starting the project. This helps identify special tools or other necessities that need to be addressed—items that would inconveniently interrupt the installation process, because they're not in your toolbox. One of the more uncommon tools that may be required is a torque wrench with angle measures, as most of the factory fasteners on LS engines are torque-to-yield types that are final-torqued to a specific angle rather than a conventional ft-lbs measure (see page 106 for more information).

Even after the pushpins and other fasteners are removed, the bumper cover/fascia may still be held in place with locking clips. Pulling the bumper cover firmly should unhook it, but it will likely be accompanied by the sound of cracking or breaking plastic. If done correctly, no harm is done and the part snaps back into place at the conclusion of the project.

If a blower or turbo kit's instructions call for draining the coolant, it may be ultimately easier to remove the radiator as well for added clearance when pinning the crankshaft. It's also a necessary step when performing a camshaft swap in the vehicle.

Fuel-pressure relief is accomplished by accessing the Schrader valve located behind this black cap on the driver's-side fuel rail. The cap simply unscrews like the air valve on a tire.

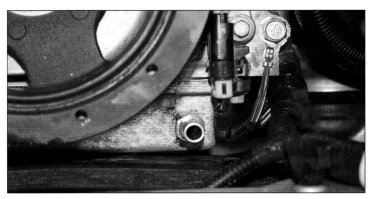

This photo shows the drilled and tapped oil-return hole at the front of the oil pan on a C6 Corvette, at the lower corner of the driver's side. Other LS vehicles requiring a return hole have them in essentially the same place. The fitting for the return line has also been installed, using a liquid sealer in addition to the torque specifications for the fitting in the pan.

The tip of a flat-blade screwdriver is pressed on the Schrader valve to relieve pressure within the fuel lines. Care must be taken (including wearing eye protection) to prevent injury from the high-pressure spray of fuel that could occur. And, obviously, the procedure shouldn't be performed near heat sources or an open flame.

Fuel-Pressure Relief

The addition of a blower or turbo system most likely comes with higher-capacity fuel injectors, which requires removal of the fuel rail to swap the injectors. Before that can be accomplished, the pressure in the fuel rails must be relieved in order to prevent fuel spraying on the installer and the vehicle when the fuel line is disconnected.

Some kits supply the necessary drill bit for modifying the oil pan. It is very important to use white lithium grease (or similar) on the end of the bit to capture material and shavings from the oil pan as they are removed. Needless to say, stray metal shavings should not enter the engine. Some builders drill the hole with oil still in the pan, to help flush out the shavings immediately.

If the vehicle has sat for a long period without starting, such as overnight, the pressure at the fuel rail shouldn't be great, but the relief procedure should still be followed for maximum safety—and it should be accomplished with eye protection. The procedure is simple. Follow these steps:

1. Make sure the engine is off; the ignition key is in the off position or removed; and the negative battery cable is disconnected.

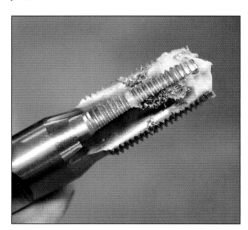

After the hole in the oil pan is drilled, it is chased with a tap to provide threads for the hose fitting. The shavings seen here in the grease on this tap illustrate the importance of protective measures, as those shavings would otherwise have fallen into the oil pan.

2. Remove the black cap from the front end of the driver's-side fuel rail, exposing the Schrader valve that is also used as a fuel-pressure test port.
3. Place a rag under the port to capture and soak up any fuel that may leak or blow out.
4. With the tip of a flat-blade screwdriver, gently and quickly press on the valve just to gauge pressure in the fuel rails.

5. Hold the screwdriver tip against the valve as necessary (similar to releasing air from a tire valve) until the pressure is eliminated.

6. With the pressure relieved, the valve cap can be reinstalled and the fuel rail/injector assembly removed.

Oil Pan/Oil System Modifications

Some superchargers, such as centrifugals and Vortech blowers, have external lubrication systems, being lubricated with oil circulated from the engine. This requires feed and return lines between the compressor and the engine. The feed line is usually routed from an unused port on the cylinder block, but connecting the return line to the engine requires drilling and tapping a hole in the oil pan.

When performed correctly, the oil pan modification is a leak-free, maintenance-free change, but it permanently alters the oil pan (even if the supercharger is removed at a future time). For some enthusiasts, the thought of drilling into the oil pan is enough to dissuade them from a particular system. If that includes you, check with the retailer or blower kit manufacturer about the compressor's lubrication.

"Pinning" the Crankshaft

The crankshaft damper/pulley on almost all production LS engines is a press-fit type, meaning it is pressed onto the front hub of the crankshaft and does not have the complementing locking feature of a traditional keyway on the hub. A large, 24-mm bolt secures the damper to the

The first step in the procedure is removal of the 24-mm bolt holding the damper against the crankshaft hub. It is a very tightly torqued bolt that typically requires the leverage of a breaker bar to break it loose—and according to General Motors' engine assembly recommendations, the bolt should not be re-used. Because it is a torque-to-yield fastener, it should be replaced with a new bolt after removal.

Supercharger systems that require pinning the crankshaft should include a template tool similar to this one. The threaded section replaces the factory damper bolt, with the thick washer serving as the pin template with a hole or tool drilled through it. This tool has a single-pin template with only one hole.

After the damper bolt is removed and the tool is installed, a drill is simply inserted through the template's hole(s) and driven into both the damper and crank hub.

Here's what a two-pin modification looks like after the holes have been drilled. Note how they straddle both the crank hub and damper.

The pins are nothing more than small, lightweight dowels similar to what is used to locate cylinder heads on the cylinder block. They're all that's necessary to provide a positive lock between the crankshaft and damper.

Here is the damper/hub assembly with the pins installed.

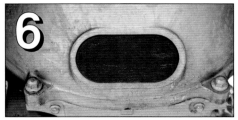

Another method of holding the damper in place is to insert a tool that holds the flywheel or flexplate. Access to the flexplate to hold it during the tightening of the damper bolt is available by removing this rubber plug at the bottom rear of the bell housing.

crankshaft after it is pressed into place, but there are no fasteners between the rear face of the damper and front edge of the crankshaft.

Although in stock and even mildly modified combinations, this isn't a problem, but there is a chance the damper could slip or spin on the crankshaft in higher-power engines, particularly supercharged and turbocharged applications that see a quick spin-up of the engine speed. A slipping damper can cause

a number of problems, including altered ignition timing.

A relatively simple method of guarding against unwanted slippage is "pinning" the damper to the crankshaft. It involves drilling a small hole through the face of the damper that interfaces with the crankshaft hub and a complementing hole into the end of the crank hub. This is performed carefully after the damper is pressed onto the crankshaft.

After the holes are drilled, one or

two dowel-type pins is inserted, providing a slip-free link between the crank and damper. The standard damper bolt is fastened, too. When this modification is performed

The final torque angle of the damper bolt is an extremely high torque spec (approximately the equivalent of 250 ft-lbs) and requires considerable leverage to hold the flywheel or flexplate to prevent the crankshaft from turning. Specialized tools are available for this job, but one of the most effective methods is to use a serpentine belt wrapped around the balancer and air-conditioning pulley, which holds the damper in place.

Inserting the pins requires nothing more than a few careful taps from a hammer to seat them. No sealer or other fasteners are required.

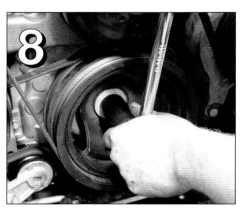

With the pins in place, a new damper bolt should be installed, per GM's assembly manual specifications. The process involves tightening the original bolt to 240 ft-lbs to ensure the damper is correctly installed. Then, the new bolt is tightened to 37 ft-lbs and torqued to 140 degrees.

The placement of the steering rack on C5/C6 Corvettes generally requires its removal for the pinning procedure. It is easily unbolted and pulled out of the way, but extreme care must be taken to ensure the steering wheel is pointed straight ahead and held there during the removal process. This can be done by running masking tape (or other low-residue tape) between the top of the steering wheel and dashboard. After the steering rack is unbolted, the individual spindles can be moved, but they must be returned to the original position when the rack is re-installed. A sensor in the steering system detects whether the rack and wheel are aligned; if they are not, drivability may suffer and a trouble code is triggered on the driver information center. The steering wheel should not be touched while the steering rack is unbolted and/or removed.

Replacing the in-tank fuel pump on most LS-powered vehicles requires the removal of the fuel tank, as the access hole is located on the top of the tank. Brass tools should be used when loosening or tightening the lock ring on the fastener, to prevent accidental sparks near the gas fumes.

bolt, it is imperative to prevent the crankshaft from turning. On a manual transmission vehicle, the transmission is placed in fourth gear to prevent movement, while an automatic-equipped vehicle needs a tool to positively hold the flexplate; specialized tools are available for this.

Fuel Pump

The additional air delivered by the blower or turbo must be accompanied by a corresponding increase of fuel in order to make power. And it's not just the quantity of the additional fuel that's important, it's the sustained pressure at which it's delivered.

correctly, the pinned crankshaft and damper are locked together, regardless of the amount of power (or boost) the engine produces.

The pinning procedure is easily accomplished in the vehicle, but depending on the model, it may be necessary to remove the cooling fan assembly and possibly the radiator in order to provide enough room to insert the drill at the proper angle.

On C5 and C6 Corvettes, the process requires the removal of the steering rack for maximum clearance and an unobstructed angle (reinstallation of the rack requires suspension alignment after the project is completed).

It may be very difficult to initially break loose the 24-mm bolt, requiring the added leverage of a breaker bar or something similar. When attempting to remove the

Here is a typical Boost-A-Pump installation. Installation is fairly simple: It is wired into the existing power wire that leads to the fuel pump, with additional wiring leading to the driver-adjustable control knob. On this Corvette, the driver's-side rear wheel well liner was removed to mount the unit. The re-installed liner provides weather protection.

For most LS-powered vehicles using a bolt-on power adder kit and no other internal engine modifications, higher-capacity fuel injectors may suffice; and they should be included with most kits. When larger injectors alone aren't enough, higher-capacity fuel pump(s) and/or a fuel pump amplifier are required.

In most cases, swapping the fuel pump is a simple procedure that involves dropping the fuel tank to remove the stock pump and inserting the new one. While it's true that it's better to have more pump capacity than not enough, it's also possible to have too much. Generally speaking, most supercharged/turbocharged LS engines need a pump rated at a minimum of 190 liters per hour (lph), which is the equivalent of 50 gallons per hour (gph) or 301 pounds per hour (lbs/hr). This suits an engine up to approximately 600 flywheel horsepower.

If the horsepower is expected to be between 600 and about 850, a 255-lph (67-gph/404-lbs/hr) pump should be used. Beyond that, a custom system is likely required that can include an inline "helper" pump. Australia-based turbo kit manufacturer APS offers a dual-fuel pump kit that fits a variety of LS

vehicles and is rated for more than 1,000 hp.

The Kenne Bell Boost-A-Pump

For many LS-powered vehicles (mostly 2003 and later), an alternative to replacing the in-tank fuel pump (or complementing a replacement pump) is the addition of a Kenne Bell Boost-A-Pump. It works essentially like an amplifier for the electric in-tank pump, increasing the voltage by up to 17.5 volts when necessary. It also increases the voltage on demand, such as under boost conditions, and allows normal operation in low-speed, zero-boost conditions.

The principle of the Boost-A-Pump is quite simple: Increase the voltage to the fuel pump to increase fuel flow. But along with increased fuel flow is the necessary requirement

of sustained fuel pressure to ensure a safe air/fuel ratio. Because the electric, in-tank fuel pump is essentially an electric motor, the amount of voltage it receives determines its speed and output. The Boost-A-Pump's increased voltage sustains fuel pressure as long as necessary. Generally, it increases voltage to the pump when boost exceeds 4.5 pounds.

The on-demand operation of the Boost-A-Pump has several advantages, such as not overloading the fuel system during low-speed, no-boost conditions. The manufacturer claims it supports up to 1,000 hp when used in conjunction with the factory, in-tank fuel pump and can actually enhance the life of the stock pump. The system is adjustable, with a control knob that enables between 1- and 50-percent increase in voltage on demand.

If a supercharger or turbocharger kit does not include a Boost-A-Pump, you should consider adding one if fuel pressure fluctuates significantly at WOT.

Fuel Injectors

Fuel injectors should be tailored to the engine's general performance parameters. Like the fuel pump, a slightly larger injector is okay, but injectors too large can lead to

For most supercharger and turbo charger systems, higher-capacity fuel injectors are required. Typically, they're included with bolt-on kits. They must be installed prior to starting the engine with the blower or turbo kit, but the engine should never be started with new injectors until the engine controller is "told" about them through a new tune.

low-speed drivability problems, as well as tuning problems. Injectors are typically "sized" in pounds-per-hour measurements, such as 24 pounds, 36 pounds, etc., based on a general operating fuel-pressure rating of 43.5 psi for the LS-type port-injection system.

Determining the appropriate injector size for a modified engine, with a supercharger or turbocharger system, can be done with the following formula:

Horsepower x brake specific fuel consumption (BSFC) / the number of injectors x the duty cycle

BSFC is the amount of fuel an engine needs to make 1 hp for 1 hour. Generally speaking, that's between .40- and .60-pound per hour, with forced-induction applications at the high end of the range. A .55 BSFC rate is used for the following calculations. The duty cycle is the approximate load on the engine. Most injector calculations use a duty cycle between 80 and 85 percent; a .85 duty cycle is cited in the following calculations.

Therefore, the equation for an estimated 500-hp (at the flywheel) engine with eight fuel injectors would look like this:

$$500 \times .55 / 8 \times .85 = 40.44$$

Rounding up to the nearest standard injector rating is 42 pounds per hour.

Larger injectors work in the application and if additional engine modifications are expected, installing 60-pound injectors or slightly larger injectors would be fine.

Generally speaking, 60-pound injectors are suitable for engines up

to about 700 to 750 hp. After that, 72- to 83-pound injectors work up to about 900 hp. As power approaches 1,000 hp and beyond, even larger capacity injectors are required.

A Word About LS Injectors

From the factory, LS engines have used three injector types:

- LS1 and LS6 engines used tall injectors with a "Minitimer" type of harness connector
- LS2 and some other 6.0-liter engines used tall injectors with the newer-style "USCAR" harness connector
- LS3/LS7/L92 engines used a short injector with the USCAR connector.

The injector types are interchangeable among all engines, but those included with a blower or turbo kit may not match the engine's wiring harness. If that is the case, adapter kits are available from F.A.S.T. They include jumper harnesses with a Minitimer connector on one end and a USCAR connector on the other.

IMPORTANT! Do not attempt to start an engine with upgraded fuel injectors until the engine-control computer has been flashed with new tuning data that includes the new injectors' specifications. Doing so almost immediately fouls the spark plugs and could lead to other problems or engine damage. Start the engine *only* after new injector data has been programmed into the controller.

Spark Plugs

In almost every supercharger or turbocharger installation, the engine's spark plugs should be replaced with

Colder-range spark plugs are a must on supercharged and turbocharged engines. Many engine builders and supercharger/turbocharger kit manufacturers prefer the NGK TR-6 spark plug in boosted LS engines. It has a heat range of 6 and the plug gap is close to spot-on out of the box.

To prevent galling or other problems when installing new spark plugs in aluminum cylinder heads, the plugs' threads should be coated with anti-seize compound.

those of a "colder" range and a tighter electrode gap. In fact, many bolt-on kits include a set of new plugs as part of their standard equipment.

There are two primary reasons for the new plugs: heat range and proper gap. The colder heat range of the plugs helps ward off the pre-ignition and detonation conditions that are crucial to maximum performance and trouble-free drivability. Forced induction generates greater cylinder pressure and therefore more heat, and stock spark plugs that get overheated can glow like the glow plugs of a diesel engine. This promotes pre-ignition since the heat of a glowing plug tip lights off the incoming air/fuel charge before the piston reaches the top of its stroke.

The heat range is a rating of a spark plug's capability of absorbing/removing heat from the combustion chamber. It is determined by design elements such as the plug's center electrode material and insulator design, as well as the length of the ceramic center insulator nose. A longer insulator nose exposes more ceramic to the combustion gases to promote heat retention.

It's important to remember that the heat range has nothing to do with the energy output or voltage transfer of the plug. Heat ranges are indicated on plugs with a numeral, such as 5, 6, or 7; the lower numbers

indicate hotter heat ranges. For example, a plug with a heat range of 5 is hotter than one with a heat range of 6.

Most LS production engines use plugs with a heat range of 5 or lower, as heat retention is desired to warm up the engine more quickly. In turn, that helps the catalytic converter heat up quicker, in order to reduce cold-start emissions.

A heat range of at least 6 should be used on supercharged and turbocharged engines.

As for the importance of a tighter-than-stock electrode gap, it's necessary to ensure a strong, consistent spark that won't get blown out by the increased cylinder pressure that comes with supercharger/turbocharger boost. Think of it as attempting to light a match outdoors when

there's no wind (natural aspiration) versus when there's a stiff breeze (supercharged/turbocharged).

The gap of stock plugs may be sufficient for low-boost, bolt-on kits used with few other modifications, but since it's important to use replacement, colder-range plugs anyway, they should be gapped to suit the supercharger/turbocharger requirements. For most forced-induction applications, a gap of about .030 inch is optimal.

Real-World Project: Camshaft and Valvesprings Swap

Bolt-on supercharger and turbocharger kits can be complemented with a change to a camshaft that's tailored to the airflow and performance potential of the power

A valvespring removal tool (seen here) is required to squeeze the spring's coils to remove the valve keepers and retainers and to also re-insert the keepers and retainers during installation. This spring tool is from Performance Tool (PN W84001) and is available from Northern Tool and Equipment.

The project begins with swapping the valve springs. Access to them is gained by unbolting and removing the ignition coil assembly, followed by the valve covers. When the valve covers are off, the rocker arms are the next to be removed. This is simple, because they're mounted on a fixture that holds all of them. Once it's unbolted, the rocker arms come off as a single assembly. The pushrods should also be removed.

To hold the valves in place when the springs are removed, the cylinder combustion chamber must be pressurized with air (approximately 120 psi). There are specialized air hose fittings for this job, but a compression test gauge also works.

A stock LS2 valve spring (left) is shown with a heavy-duty, higher-rate spring from Comp Cams (right). The stock spring has a single coil and a slight beehive shape. Note the smaller-width top compared to the Comp Cams spring. The replacement spring has a pair of inner and outer coils for exceptional strength. The stronger spring is not only necessary for standing up to the higher valve lift delivered by the new camshaft, but better withstands the cylinder pressure created by the blower or turbo.

With the air line connected at the spark plug hole, the spring tool is lowered onto the top of the spring. A ratchet is used to compress the spring until the retainer and keeper can be removed, freeing the spring. Extreme care must be taken since the spring is under tremendous pressure and could cause an injury or even damage if it breaks loose from the tool.

Prior to the new spring's installation, the new valvestem seal is slipped on. It is a tight fit that generally requires assistance to seat it all the way down onto the cylinder-head surface. In this case, a deep-well socket placed on top of the seal and a few gentle taps from a mallet or hammer does the trick.

New valvestem seals go with the replacement valve springs, so the originals must be removed with the springs. Gentle tugging with pliers is generally all that's needed to pull them off the valve stems.

In the reverse of the process for removal, the compressed valve spring is slipped over the valvestem and seal. Then, the keeper and retainer are installed, and the spring compressor tool is backed off until the spring is held firmly in place.

Replacement of the stock camshaft begins with the removal of the front cover. Like the valve covers, its seals don't require replacement if the removal/installation procedures don't damage them.

Here's one of the cylinder heads with its new set of springs. At this point, it's easier to hold off reinstalling the pushrods, rocker arms, and valve covers until the new camshaft has been installed. If the O-ring-style valve cover seals were not damaged during removal, they do not require replacement.

To remove the camshaft, you must first remove the oil pump and timing-chain set. The oil pump is the first to go, as seen here. Note the large, single bolt on the camshaft timing gear on this LS2 engine. Earlier LS engines were equipped with smaller, three-bolt fastening setups for holding the gear to the camshaft, but later engines were equipped with the large, single-bolt fastener. It is imperative to match the new camshaft and the timing gear, because they are not interchangeable.

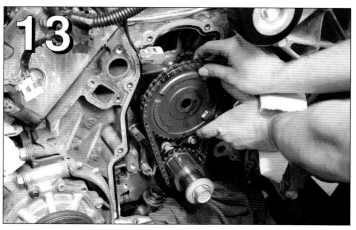

With the timing gear correctly aligned, the cam gear is unbolted and removed. The crankshaft sprocket remains installed on the engine.

The oil pump has fasteners on the bottom edge that are very difficult to reach. Removing them requires a very slim wrench or ratcheting wrench. A rag placed beneath the pump helps prevent the bolts from falling into the engine if they were to slip from the wrench or your grasp.

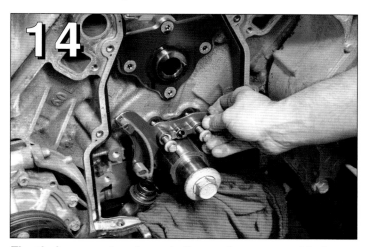

The timing-gear tensioner is the next component to be removed.

Next, the crankshaft is rotated until indicator marks on the cam gear and crankshaft sprocket are aligned. The cam gear's "dot" goes to the bottom, with the crank sprocket's dot at the top. This indicates cylinder number-1 is at top dead center.

After the tensioner is removed, the camshaft retaining plate is unbolted and can be removed, too.

Before the stock camshaft is pulled out of the engine, it must be rotated a few times while still in its bore. Doing so pushes the lifters into a "locked" position that enables the camshaft to be removed without the lifters falling into the engine.

Once the camshaft has been rotated to lock the lifters in place, the camshaft can be removed. Care must be taken when pulling the cam out of the cylinder block to prevent damaging the cam bearings.

Selecting a camshaft with the lift, duration, and lobe-separation-angle specifications tailored to the supercharger or turbocharger kit can enhance the performance and drivability of the new power adder system. (See Chapter 9 for information on choosing the right camshaft.)

adder (see Chapter 9 for camshaft selection details). Because portions of the top and/or front of the engine require removal or disassembly to facilitate the blower/turbo kit installation, swapping the camshaft (and required stiffer, higher-rate valvesprings) is a way of knocking off two birds with the same stone.

The unique details of the LS engine allow the cam and springs to be easily changed without having to remove the cylinder heads. This is because the lifters can be "locked" with a simple full rotation of the camshaft to prevent them from falling into the cylinder block when the cam is removed.

A few unique tools are required for the procedure, mostly to support the valvesprings' removal and installation. They include a compressed-air hose, with a threaded fitting on the end for the spark-plug holes in the cylinder heads, as well as a valvespring compressor/removal tool.

This project was performed at Detroit-area Stenod Performance on a TrailBlazer SS that was also receiving a Magna Charger Roots-type blower system.

Red Loctite thread sealer (or similar) should be applied to the cam gear bolts, as well as to the timing chain guide bolts, prior to installation.

Next, the new camshaft is inserted into the engine. The roller design of the valvetrain, and the fact that the inside of the engine is already well lubricated from regular use, means the application of conventional camshaft lube on the cam lobes isn't necessary.

Finally, the timing-chain guide, timing chain, and cam gear are re-installed. The cam/cam gear must be lined up again with the dot on the crankshaft sprocket to ensure correct ignition timing at startup. If the engine has relatively few miles on it, the original timing chain can be reused. After this step, the remainder of the procedure simply involves re-installation of the oil pump, front cover, and other engine accessories.

Because the replacement camshaft used here features the three-bolt cam gear fastening design of earlier LS engines, the stock single-bolt gear could not be re-used. A three-bolt gear was obtained, along with a replacement timing-gear guide that replaces the more cumbersome stock tensioner.

SUPERCHARGER INSTALLATION PROJECTS

This chapter offers in-depth looks at the two basic types of bolt-on supercharger systems: Roots/screw-type compressors that replace the intake manifold and centrifugal systems that mount to the engine's front accessory-drive system. Both systems are typical in that they are delivered with all of the components and hardware required for installation, including fuel-system upgrades such as fuel injectors. (See Chapter 4 for general information on important details such as fascia removal, fuel-pressure relief, the importance of spark plug selection, and "pinning" the crankshaft).

It's important to note that while this chapter provides a detailed look at the typical procedures involved with the installations, not every step or process is outlined. In other words, it is no substitute for the manufacturer's assembly manual, which should be followed to the letter.

Project 1: Roots/Screw-Type Supercharger Kit

This project involves the installation of a MagnaCharger kit on a 2008

General Tools Required

- Metric wrenches and sockets (standard and deep)
- Metric Allen wrenches/sockets
- Torque wrench
- Phillips-head and flat-head screwdrivers
- Fuel-line disconnection tool (may be included with the kit)
- Drill (possibly requiring angled head)
- Hose cutters and hose clamp pliers
- Trim removal tool

Pontiac G8 GT (LS2 6.0-liter engine). The kit consists of an MP 1900 (1.9-liter displacement) compressor (see Chapter 2) and liquid-to-air intercooling system. It includes almost every piece of hardware required for installation, including a plug-in flash tuner.

Although this project illustrates the installation on the Pontiac G8 GT, the procedures and methods are largely the same for all Magna Charger kits for LS-powered vehicles; and they are very similar to the steps required to install a screw-type

---

blower kit. In the broadest terms, the installation requires the following:

- Replacing the stock intake manifold with the supercharger compressor/manifold assembly
- Swapping the throttle body onto the supercharger system
- Mounting the intercooler's heat exchanger and routing its hoses and hardware
- Replacing the serpentine drive belt in order to accommodate the supercharger drive pulley
- Installing higher-capacity fuel injectors (and any other fuel system enhancements)
- Uploading a revised engine-calibration program to the engine controller

As is the case with most contemporary Roots/screw-type supercharger kits, the Magna Charger system is delivered with the compressor pre-mounted to the intake manifold. This greatly enhances the speed and ease of the installation. It also reveals the only significant downside to the project: additional mass. The lightweight, composite factory intake manifold weighs next to nothing, but bolting on the Magna Charger compressor/manifold assembly adds about 50 pounds over the front axle of the vehicle. Under boost, those extra pounds disappear, but it's not an inconsequential consideration, particularly on finely balanced cars like the Corvette.

Generally speaking, the quality and completeness of the Magna Charger kit is exceptional. It is a bolt-on system in the very best sense of the term, requiring little fabrication and mostly common hand tools. In the case of this G8 project car, no additional fuel system enhancements were required, apart from the supplied, higher-rate injectors; and the self-contained lubrication system eliminates an entire procedure that some other kits may require. In fact, an experienced technician should be able to install the kit within a day—with additional time required for proper tuning and evaluation. The same cannot be said for most bolt-on turbocharger systems, which require considerably longer labor time (see Chapter 6).

The installation outlined here was performed at Dearborn Heights, Michigan-based Livernois Motor-

sports, with tuning completed by Dan Millen, using the company's recently introduced X-Treme Cal Tuning software (see Chapter 7). On Livernois' chassis dyno, the otherwise-stock Pontiac G8 GT recorded 423 hp and 401 ft-lbs of torque at the rear wheels, with a peak of approximately 8 pounds of boost. That represents an increase of more than 35 percent in horsepower versus the stock 312-hp rating and about 20-percent more torque than the baseline 312-ft-lbs rating.

Millen indicated the G8 would have seen a greater response, but the supercharged airflow was hampered at the back end by the stock exhaust system.

"At the very least, a cat-back-style system is needed when you add a supercharger," he said. "Headers and high-flow cats help greatly, too, to uncork the exhaust, because supercharged engines don't need much backpressure to make the most power."

To prove his point, shortly after the installation was completed, Livernois Motorsports performed an identical installation on another G8 GT and Millen uploaded essentially the same tune—but the second car was already equipped with a cat-back

exhaust system. The comparison with the stock-exhaust car was dramatic: 438 hp and 445 ft-lbs of torque at the tires. That's a significant 15 hp and 44 ft-lbs difference. Without a doubt, a less-restrictive exhaust system benefits the greater airflow generated by the supercharger. Such an upgrade should be the standard operating procedure for an enthusiast wishing to maximize the performance benefit from the sizable investment made in the supercharger system.

The photos in this chapter should be referenced as the general steps used for all Roots/screw-type supercharger systems.

Using HP Tuner software, Livernois Motorsports' Dan Millen performed the tuning on the G8, dialing in the new 62-pound/hour injectors and the blower system's other parameters. He was initially disappointed with the comparatively tame horsepower result. Millen attacked his keyboard and came up with 423 hp and 401 ft-lbs of torque at the tires—for more than 35-percent greater horsepower and about 20-percent more torque than the 312 hp/335 ft-lbs baseline figures.

When it comes to attaching a price tag to the supercharger's power increase, the Magna Charger kit typically retails in the $6,500 to $7,000 neighborhood. If you're going to have it professionally installed and tuned, as was done with the project car here, you're probably looking at another $1,000 to $1,500 for labor, miscellaneous service parts, and tuning. Livernois Motorsports' quantity discount for the number of Magna Charger kits it stocked enables it to sell the blower, install it, and tune it for about $6,600. That's a good value in my book.

The Eaton-based Magna Charger supercharger system is delivered ready to bolt on. In fact, the 1.9-liter supercharger was pre-mounted to the intake manifold, as seen here. The satin-black finish looks more "O.E." than the typical bare-metal finish of most blowers. The other primary components of the system include the heat exchanger, electric pump, and coolant reservoir for the charge-cooling system. It is a dedicated system, meaning it is separate from the engine's cooling system and maintains its own circuit of coolant (the same 50/50 mix of water and coolant typically used in engines).

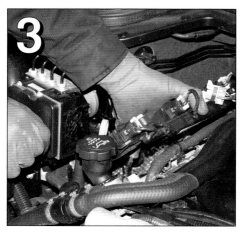

The supercharger kit's charge cooler requires removal of the front fascia. This starts with removal of the front tires to provide access to the myriad of fasteners (most of them plastic pushpin types) on the inside of the wheel well. There are also seemingly endless fasteners on the bottom of the fascia. The car used in this project is wrapped with protective coverings to prevent damage to the body. (See Chapter 4 for more information on fascia removal.)

After the fascia's fasteners are removed, it pulls off as one big component, but still requires some muscle to pull it free from clips holding it to the chassis. It sounds like the clips are breaking when doing this, but when done correctly, no damage occurs. The fascia should be stored safely away from the work area to prevent accidental damage when maneuvering under the hood and/or under the vehicle.

The procedural step with the engine involves the removal of the ignition coils. This is accomplished by disconnecting the plug wires from the spark plugs, disconnecting the coils' individual plug harnesses, unbolting the coil brackets from the valve covers, and lifting them out of the engine compartment. The coils are attached to the bracket, avoiding the need to remove them individually.

After properly relieving the fuel pressure (see Chapter 4), the fuel system is disconnected from the fuel rail in preparation for the intake manifold's removal. Fortunately, the Magna Charger kit comes with a fuel-line disconnection tool, but you should check the kit's contents for it prior to starting the installation. If the supercharger kit does not include the tool, you should obtain the correct one before starting the project.

The intake manifold on most LS-powered vehicles is easily unbolted, although the comparatively restrictive engine compartments of fourth-generation F-cars and the SSR can make access to the rear fasteners more of a challenge. After the disconnection of the fuel system, the air-intake tract and a few miscellaneous hoses are pulled off, and the intake manifold should pull relatively easily off the top of the engine. The lightweight nylon construction of the manifold makes removal easy for one person, but that is not true when it comes to installing the supercharger/intake manifold assembly. You should plan to have another person assist with that portion of the project.

To prevent debris from falling into the engine during the intake manifold's removal and the supercharger's installation, duct tape is laid over the cylinder heads' intake ports. A shop vacuum should also be used on the top of the engine to remove any unseen debris. There's no such thing as too much caution in this area.

With the intake manifold removed, attention turns to the crankshaft balancer and the steps required to add pins between it and the crankshaft hub to prevent unwanted movement of the press-fit balancer on the crankshaft. The Magna Charger kit comes with the pins, as well as a bolt-on template to guide the drill bit into the correct position. (See Chapter 4 for a more complete explanation of this procedure.)

Many of the installation procedures simply prepare the engine to accept the supercharger. Such is the case with this step: adding a new tensioner/pulley to the front of the engine, as the crankshaft-driven supercharger adds a pulley to the accessory drive system. Not seen here is the pulley that bolts to the tensioner bracket after the bracket is secured on the engine.

Next, the front of the engine compartment is readied for the charge-cooling system. That process begins with the temporary removal of the electric cooling-fan assembly from the rear of the radiator. It is secured with a few easily accessed fasteners. The wiring harness must be disconnected, too.

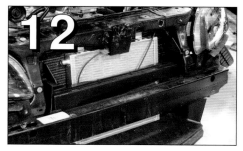

Although the installation procedure varies among vehicles, the charge-cooler heat exchanger always mounts in front of the radiator. In the case of this project G8 GT, installation requires disconnecting the radiator (including the removal of the radiator hoses and draining of the coolant) in order to push it back a few inches to slip the heat exchanger in front of it.

The heat exchanger for the G8 has brackets that hook on to the top of the radiator to hold it in place. In fact, adhesive-backed rubber pads are used for a tight fit at the top of the radiator and no bolts or other fasteners are used. This isn't the same for all LS vehicles, but holds true for many of them.

Here is the heat exchanger nestled in front of the radiator. Because it is essentially a radiator of its own, air freely passes through it and into the engine radiator, so the vehicle needs no further cooling-system upgrades. Some vehicles with compromising radiator positions and/or tight engine compartments (such as the fourth-generation F-cars and C5/C6 Corvettes) may benefit from a larger-capacity radiator to ensure cooler overall engine operation, as the supercharger generates more heat to dissipate.

The next step in the installation procedure involves extending the length of the throttle-body wiring harness for vehicles equipped with an electronically controlled (fly-by-wire) throttle. It starts with exposing the individual wires of the harness by pulling them out of the protective cover.

After the individual wires for the throttle-body harness are exposed, they are cut and extension wires are inserted. The Magna Charger kit comes with extension wires matched to the colors of the original harness, making the task simpler. To prevent the joints of the extensions from bundling together in a bulky pack, the original wires were cut at different points for different lengths. This spaces out the joints for a cleaner, more finished product that fits within the protective loom cover.

Here's the extended harness assembly, with the wires tucked back inside a longer cover. When done correctly, the modification looks factory, with the cleanly spaced extension joints fitting easily within the cover. The extension is required to accommodate the modified mounting position of the throttle body when it is installed on the supercharger, as well the additional reach required for it around the supercharger system's components.

This application (along with most similar Roots/screw-type systems) requires a different cylinder-head-coolant crossover vent tube to accommodate the supercharger and new intake manifold. It is easily swapped with the help of a 10-mm socket, because the original intake manifold is out of the way. There are O-ring seals on both ends of the vent tube that must be transferred to the new tube.

Another accommodation for the supercharger on the G8 GT, as well as some other vehicles, is providing adequate clearance around the cowl/firewall area. In the case of the G8 and the Magna Charger system, it includes trimming a small piece from the leading edge of the plastic cowl trim. An air-powered cutoff wheel slices easily through the material, leaving a cleaner-looking cut. The edges of the modified sections should be finished or filed slightly to remove excess "flash" material from the plastic.

With most of the engine and engine-compartment preparations for the supercharger system completed, work turns to prepping the super-charger itself. Here, the new fuel injectors and fuel rails are added to the intake manifold. Be clear about whether the kit includes the injectors or you must obtain them separately. Most supercharger manufacturers offer lower-cost "tuner" kits that do not include items like injectors, spark plugs, and other parts. Those kits are designed for installation by profes-sional shops that likely stock such parts. Complete kits should include the injectors, plugs, etc.

While preparing the supercharger, the installer at Livernois Motorsports noticed the rearmost manifold bolt on the passenger side would be a tight fit during installation, as it was sandwiched directly under the super-charger drive belt. Pre-checking for installation issues such as this prevents larger headaches from developing once the assembly is on the engine and in the vehicle. It was determined that hand-threading the bolt would be required until there was sufficient room to get a box-end or open-end wrench on the bolt head. As the mounting position and super-charger design are largely the same for all LS engines, this is a common challenge with a Magna Charger installation.

The last step before installing the supercharger/manifold assembly on the engine is installing gaskets on the intake manifold itself. The Magna Charger kit uses convenient, snap-on gaskets that are held in place perfectly until the manifold is fastened to the cylinder heads. Correspondingly, the ports on the cylinder head should be slightly lubricated with a mild soap-and-water solution to ensure a more precise, leak-free fit.

At last, the supercharger/manifold assembly is carefully lowered onto the engine. Because of the weight and awkward size of the assembly, it is a two-person task. On some vehicles, a replacement valley cover (including the transfer of the oil-pressure sensor) is required and included with the kit, but that was not the case with this G8 application. Also, some vehicles may require the removal or relocation of a factory engine-installation bracket or, on vehicles with an automatic transmission, the relocation of the automatic transmission fill tube. Again, this was not the case with the G8. Once the assembly is in place, the manifold bolts are tightened to the manufacturer's recommended torque specification.

With the supercharger assembly bolted in place, the fuel injector harnesses are connected to the injectors. It is important to make sure the injectors used with the supercharger are compatible with the harness connectors, as there are primarily two types used with LS engines. Jumper harnesses are available to accommodate non-matching harnesses and injectors, but you should check the harness/injector compatibility prior to reaching this stage in the installation.

Next, the ignition-coil brackets are re-installed. There should be no clearance problems, as none of the supercharger system's hardware affects the location or placement of the brackets, coils, or plug wire routing.

After the ignition coils come the spark plugs. Colder-range, NGK TR-6 plugs with a tighter gap are used on this project and recommended for most forced-induction systems. (See Chapter 4 for more information on the importance of selecting the right spark plug.)

Next, the new serpentine belt is installed on the engine, including its routing on the supercharger pulley. One of the appreciated features of the Magna Charger kit is the integration of the supercharger pulley into the accessory drive system. Some systems may require separate belts and/or greater modification of the accessory drive components.

All of the small details become increasingly important as the "button-up" stage of the installation is underway, and that means following the manufacturer's assembly manual closely. Here is the comparatively minor (yet very important) step of installing the O-ring seal for the throttle body.

This photo shows the throttle body installed on the supercharger, as well as its lengthened wiring harness plugged into it. It also shows the myriad of other hoses, connectors, and fasteners re-attached to the engine and/or supercharger/manifold assembly. Despite their common LS engine architecture, different vehicles have different connections, sensors, and other hardware. Again, the manufacturer's assembly manual should be followed closely to ensure all of the connections have been made. A few items to check include the Idle Air Temperature (IAT) sensor, EVAP lines (which may require modification or replacement on some vehicles), purge solenoid, vacuum hoses, and MAP sensor/wiring harness.

Another important re-connection step is the installation of the fuel-feed line. Because of the "push-lock" design of the connector, it simply pushes into place and a positive "click" sound indicates it is correctly installed. Unlike the removal process, a special tool isn't required.

Among the plumbing changes brought on by the supercharger system (at least on the G8 GT depicted here) is the need for longer heater hoses. Typically, they're included with the inclusive kits and may not be included with "tuner" kits.

A new brake-booster check valve should be included with all supercharger systems to optimize the boost/vacuum pressure created with the supercharged engine.

The brake-booster connection finishes off the connections related to the engine, so the final step is the installation of the charge-cooling system components. On the independently circulated liquid-to-air system with the Magna Charger system, installation begins with mounting the system's electrically driven water pump (arrow).

32 The charge-cooling system also includes a coolant reservoir. Mounting positions vary from vehicle to vehicle, but they are typically mounted higher in the engine compartment, while providing easy access to the fill cap.

33 There is also add-on wiring associated with the electric water pump. It simply splices into the factory, underhood fuse box.

34 With all of the charge-cooling system's hoses securely connected, the reservoir is filled with a 50/50 mix of coolant and water, just as in the engine. Depending on the system, it takes 1 to 2 gallons of mixed coolant. Activating the pump without the engine on helps circulate the coolant to quickly fill the system. This is also the appropriate time to refill the engine radiator with the coolant that was drained previously

35 Next, the coolant hoses are routed to and from the heat exchanger between it, the water pump, and the reservoir tank. Again, routing and placement of the hoses varies among vehicles; and it typically requires the modification or removal of components located behind the vehicle's front fascia. In the case of this G8, it requires creating a passage-way through a plastic "wall" located beneath the bumper.

Here's the finished installation. It looks as neat as a pin and, with that black blower case, nearly factory. At this point, refer to the assembly manual to double check that all required connections are made. This car also has an aftermarket cold-air induction system that is not part of the Magna Charger kit.

With the supercharger and charge-cooling systems installed, the final stage of the project involves uploading the new programming tune to the engine-control module. For most vehicles (whether using the kit's supplied programmer or a custom tune), a connection must be made with the OBD port located beneath the dashboard. On other vehicles, add-on and/or supplemental control modules must be spliced into the factory control module. On the G8 GT project vehicle, the tune was simply uploaded through the OBD port.

Project 2: Centrifugal Supercharger Kit

This project concerns the basic installation of a centrifugal supercharger. Unlike the Roots/Lysholm-type blower that essentially replaces the intake manifold, a bolt-on centrifugal kit typically retains the stock intake manifold, but adds the supercharger to the front of the engine, much like other engine-driven accessories like the air-conditioning compressor or power-steering pump.

Generally speaking, the installation of a centrifugal supercharger is more complex than a Roots/screw-type system, but not significantly so. I followed the installation procedures of both the Magna Charger system and the centrifugal system and found the Magna Charger system was easier to install and took less time to do so. That said, the centrifugal system wasn't necessarily dif-

The Magna Charger kit comes with its own tuning software and programmer, but Livernois Motorsports' Dan Millen uses his company's X-Treme Cal Tuning software. Here, he feeds the G8's controller his tune. It is vitally important to never start an engine with non-original fuel injectors until the tune is uploaded, as engine damage will occur almost immediately! Once the engine is started for the first time, it should be turned off after a few seconds to check for any fuel, oil, or coolant leaks; serpentine belt alignment; and a general underhood examination. Also, make sure the fuel tank is filled with premium gasoline, as the tuning is typically dependent on at least 91 octane.

On Livernois Motorsports' dyno, the newly blown G8 put down 423 hp and 401 ft-lbs at the tires. It was a good result, but would have been even better with a less-restrictive cat-back exhaust system. Nevertheless, the car made more than 35-percent-greater power than when it entered the shop a few days earlier. Throttle response and overall drivability is excellent, too, with the blower's presence only heard and felt on demand.

ficult to install, but required more steps and greater finesse.

The centrifugal blower system outlined here involves an A&A Corvette kit for a C6 Corvette with an automatic transmission. It uses a Vortech V-2 Si compressor and a custom intercooling system. The blower is fitted with a 3.8-inch-drive pulley that enables approximately 12 pounds of boost. The kit includes a bypass valve, 60-pound fuel injectors and a Kenne Bell Boost-A-Pump.

The installation was performed by Troy, Michigan-based Stenod Performance. It took roughly a day and a half to complete the installation, while the Magna Charger kit was installed in a single business day. Both installations were handled by

professional shops using vehicle lifts and, where necessary, air tools. The accompanying photos should not

General Tools Required
• Metric wrenches and sockets (standard and deep)
• Metric Allen wrenches/sockets
• Torque wrench
• Phillips-head and flat-head screwdrivers
• Fuel line disconnection tool (may be included with the kit)
• Drill (possibly requiring angled head)
• Hose cutters and hose clamp pliers
• Trim-removal tool

be considered a how-to guide for installing a blower on a Corvette, but a reference of the basic steps for all centrifugal supercharger systems.

Because the processes for pinning the crankshaft, mounting the intercooler heat exchanger, routing the intercooler coolant tubes, and other details are similar to the Roots-type installation, this project focuses on the aspects of the installation that make it different. That includes mounting the supercharger bracket and compressor. It should be noted that the kit shown here required an oil-feed line tapped into the oil pan. That is not the case with all centrifugal kits (see Chapter 4 for more details on that procedure).

Prior to receiving the supercharger, the Corvette used in this project was enhanced with L92 cylinder heads and intake manifold, as well as a blower-spec camshaft (see Chapter 9). These modifications increased the airflow capability of the engine to better exploit the capability of the supercharger. The work paid big dividends, too, as the Corvette put down 508 hp and 439 ft-lbs of torque to the rear wheels on Stenod Performance's Mustang Dynamometer chassis dyno.

Here are the basic components of a centrifugal system, minus the intercooler hardware. The mounting brackets hang the supercharger on the front of the engine. This kit (from A&A Corvette) includes a large blow-off valve (at bottom of photo), which is a necessary accessory for preventing excess boost from being forced into the engine when the throttle is closed.

As with the Roots blower kit, preparation for installation includes the removal of the front fascia to enable mounting of the intercooler system's heat exchanger and related hoses and hardware. The cooling system is also drained and the radiator removed. Although not necessarily required for every vehicle installation, removing the radiator is quick and easy, and it opens up tremendous working space under the hood while preventing inadvertent damage to the cooling fins.

After pinning the crankshaft, an oil-feed line was routed from the engine in preparation for the supercharger. Some centrifugal superchargers (Vortech blowers, mostly) require this external lubrication. The oiling circuit also includes an oil return line that must be tapped into the oil pan. (See Chapter 4.)

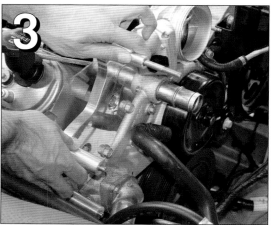

The next step involves mounting the rear portion of the supercharger support bracket. In most cases, it replaces the factory tensioner or idler pulley, although the location and placement varies among vehicles. The passenger-side location on this Corvette is typical.

The front part of the bracket is then mounted to the super-charger compres-sor. The bracket contains a tensioner that replaces the factory unit, which was removed to make room for the supercharger.

Because of the tight fit and/or awkward routing, it may be easier to pre-install the serpen-tine belt on the super-charger bracket prior to installing the supercharger on the engine. This makes it easier to accurately route the belt on the rest of the engine's accessories.

The supercharger and front mounting bracket are installed together and loosely threaded onto the rear mounting bracket. None of the fasteners are torqued until the general fitment and clearances around the brackets, blower, and belt are double checked.

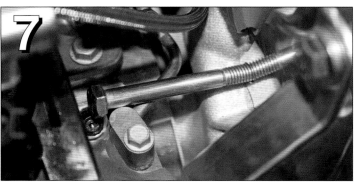

It's vitally important to follow the assembly manual closely. Here, the installer made an assumption about the blower mounting bracket's hardware, but didn't take into account the interference of the cylinder heads' coolant crossover tube, which prevented one of the bracket's bolts from sliding into its mounting hole. Rectifying the problem required backtracking, which added unnecessary time to the project.

With the supercharger and its mounting-bracket components securely tightened, the oil-feed line from the engine is connected to the compressor.

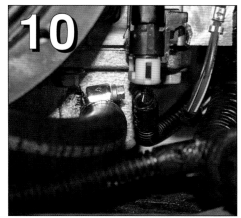

Complementing the oil-feed line is an oil-return line routed from the compres-sor (left) to the fitting that was added to the oil pan (right).

Next, the intercooler heat exchanger is mounted in front of the radiator. The procedure for the coolant circuit and hose routing for it is similar to the procedures outlined in the Magna Charger installation projecton page 60.

Like the Magna Charger installation, routing the intercooler's plumbing required modifying some of the vehicle's plastic underbody components to enable pass-through room for the hoses. Note the circular template for the hole, which is easily cut into the soft plastic material of the part.

After routing the intercooler plumbing, attention turns to the fuel system. The kit's higher-capacity, 60-pound/hour injectors were swapped onto the stock fuel rail. Then, the fuel rail was simply pushed back into place on the intake manifold.

Here's the finished installation. There was more fabrication required than the Roots-type supercharger installation outlined on pages 62-67, but some of it is due to the tighter confines of the Corvette engine compartment. Nevertheless, the installation is relatively easy and straightforward for a professional shop or an individual who has the necessary experience and tools.

Depending on the engine and vehicle, greater fuel pressure and/or a higher-capacity fuel pump may be required. In the case of this LS3-powered C6 Corvette, the kit included a Kenne Bell Boost-A-Pump to amplify the power of the stock fuel pump. Using it eliminates the costly and time-consuming need for removing the fuel tank to swap fuel pumps.

Because of the additional modifications, including cylinder heads and a camshaft, the manufacturer's tuning software wasn't sufficient for this project. A custom tune was created at Stenod Performance and the Corvette delivered 508 hp and 439 ft-lbs of torque at the rear wheels through an automatic transmission. This was on a Mustang dyno that typically isn't as optimistic as comparable chassis dynos from other manufacturers. That's a significant 170 hp/110 ft-lbs jump over the baseline 338 hp/329-ft-lbs numbers.

TURBOCHARGER INSTALLATION PROJECTS

Unlike most bolt-on supercharger systems, which can easily adapt to a variety of vehicles, turbo kits present unique challenges. There is more to contend with in the routing of inlet and outlet tubing between the exhaust manifolds, turbocharger(s), and engine intake. At the minimum, major changes are required of the exhaust system. Of course, all that plumbing changes for different vehicles, whereas adapting a Roots blower, for example, requires comparatively minor revisions to suit mostly the accessory drive and intercooler mounting for different vehicles.

So, while complete turbo kits aren't as plentiful as the range of supercharger systems, they can be created by essentially running enough tubing between the basic elements: turbocharger, wastegate, blow-off valve, and intercooler.

Real-World Project: Lingenfelter System

This project is the installation of the Lingenfelter Performance Engineering's twin-turbo system on a Corvette Z06 (re-bodied by Specter Werkes/Sports). Although it is a system Lingenfelter has installed a number of vehicles, it's not exactly an off-the-shelf kit. Because of the natural variances between production vehicles, Lingenfelter custom-fits elements like the water and oil lines after the turbochargers are installed. It's a very precise, well-engineered system, but again underscores the difficulties in developing a true bolt-on turbo kit. With that in mind, this installation should be seen as representing the common components, connections, vehicle modifications, and other details that are common to all turbo systems. The caveat is that the system is specific to Lingenfelter Performance Engineering and the Corvette Z06. In other words, it should be viewed as a general overview of the parts and procedures involved, but by no means a definitive blueprint for all LS-powered vehicles. It should also be noted that this installation does not show every procedure, but highlights primary procedures and details.

The Lingenfelter system is designed for use in cars driven primarily on the street, so it works around existing vehicle systems and components. There was no sacrificing of air conditioning, power amenities, or anything like that. In a nutshell, it uses a pair of medium-size Garrett water-cooled, oil-lubricated ball-bearing turbos and an air-to-air intercooler. Here are the basics:

- A single blow-off valve
- Custom air-to-air charge cooler
- High-capacity fuel injectors
- Kenne Bell Boost-A-Pump
- Upgraded oil cooler
- Custom Corsa/Specter Werkes low-restriction exhaust system
- Custom tuning

Although boost is always tunable, the base system delivers about 10 to 12 pounds of boost to help the 7.0-liter engine produce 800 hp. More importantly, Lingenfelter's package for the twin-turbo system includes rebuilding the high-compression LS7 engine with stronger internal components, lower-compression (9.0:1) pistons, and a number of other related details. The turbo system isn't installed until the engine is removed, rebuilt, and reinstalled (all the work is performed at Lingenfelter's Decatur, Indiana, shop). One of the benefits of the system for many customers is improved fuel economy in "normal" driving conditions. That's mostly due to the engine's lower compression ratio and the lack of parasitic drag; the turbochargers don't affect drivability or fuel economy until they start generating boost.

An advantage to having the work performed at Lingenfelter's shop (or any reputable shop that does custom turbo systems) is experienced fabricators. The minor, yet important, vehicle-to-vehicle variances between otherwise-identical vehicle models typically requires fabrication work that is not easily accomplished in a home garage.

Whether it's a true bolt-on system or a blend of bolt-on and custom-fabricated, such as the Lingenfelter system, installation takes time—perhaps two or three times as long as a bolt-on supercharger system. Keep that in mind (and its implication on labor costs at the installation shop) as you consider such a modification.

The turbo system is designed to mount the turbochargers directly to custom, heavy-duty exhaust manifolds. In the low-slung Corvette chassis, that still puts them at the bottom of the engine compartment, which helps keep heat farther away from the engine and air-intake system.

Lingenfelter's basic system uses a pair of mid-size Garrett GT30-series water-cooled, oil-fed ball bearing turbochargers and Forge wastegates. The medium-size bodies of the turbos make them ideal for easier fitment and quick spool-up. The A/R ratio, as noted on the casting seen here, is .50:1.

This turbo installation project takes place on a Specter Werkes/Sports GTR built around a Corvette Z06. All of the mechanical work was performed at Lingenfelter Performance Engineering's Indiana facility.

Prior to installing the turbo system, Lingenfelter removes the Z06's LS7 engine and rebuilds it to suit the demands of turbocharging. That involves rebuilding the short-block with a new, forged-steel crankshaft, forged-steel connecting rods, and lower-compression, 9.0:1 pistons. The heads also receive high-temperature-resistant Inconel exhaust valves.

The first evidence of custom fabrication on the kit is the welded-on elbow added to each turbocharger's air outlet, which is necessary to orient the outlet toward the front of the vehicle.

A thick, 3/4-inch flange is attached to the exhaust manifold, where the turbocharger mounts. This is necessary to prevent warping under the extreme temperatures generated when the system is producing maximum boost. Also note the heat shield attached to the manifold.

Turbo systems invariably require custom or modified exhaust systems, so before installation began, the original system was removed and set aside.

One of the other pre-installation procedures involves prepping the engine for the oiling requirements of the turbos. That involves swapping the stock oil cooler for an aftermarket model, fitting a scavenge pump to pull returned oil from the low-mounted turbos and adding a feed line (seen here) to the oil pan that sends the circulated oil back into the pan.

The system's installation started with bolting on the exhaust manifolds. With the hood removed and considerable chassis clearance on the Corvette, it was easy to do from the top of the engine compartment. Other vehicles require careful installation of the manifolds from the bottom of the engine compartment.

The all-important oxygen sensors are threaded into the exhaust manifolds next, as doing so later would be more difficult with more of the turbo system's components in place. Wideband sensors are installed for more precise part-throttle tuning.

With the exhaust manifolds and their oxygen sensors in place, the first turbocharger is hoisted into position, sliding onto the mounting studs protruding from the exhaust manifold's mounting flange. In this photo, the passenger-side turbo is being installed.

Lingenfelter uses many hard lines in the system, including the oil-feed and oil-return lines at the turbo, which require custom fitting to account for the slight variances among vehicles. After the first turbocharger was installed, for example, this line was measured at cut to fit the oil-feed line to it.

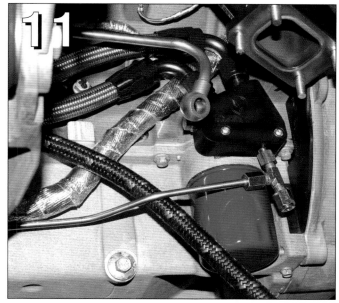

The hard oil-feed line wraps under the oil pan and up to a T-junction in an aftermarket oil cooler. The bottom fitting is reserved for the driver's-side turbo's oil-feed line.

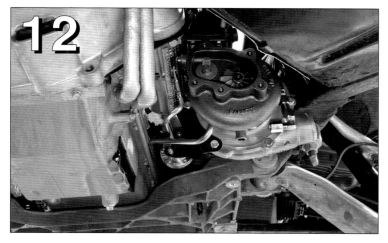

The installed oil-feed line is seen routing away from the turbo and along the oil pan rail. Installing the line at this point in the project is necessary, because access to it would be almost impossible after the down tube and other sections of the system are installed.

With the passenger-side turbo and its oil-feed line in place, the driver's-side turbo is installed and its oil-feed line attached.

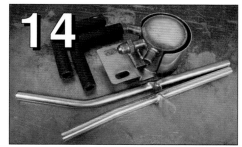

At the other end of the turbos' oiling system is a scavenge system that draws oil cycled through the turbochargers back into the engine's oiling system. Because the turbos are mounted low on the engine, gravity is not sufficient for draining to the oil pan, so Lingenfelter designed a small oil tank that collects the return oil from the turbos and, with the help of an electric pump, draws it out and back into the oil pan.

The turbochargers are also water cooled, which requires tapping into the vehicle's cooling system for feed and return. Inserting a junction in the heater hoses does the trick. As seen here, it's double-clamped on both ends to ensure a leak- and blow-proof seal.

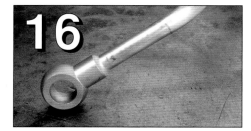

To make installation easier in the tight confines on the bottom side of the engine compartment, banjo-type fittings are used to connect the coolant system to the turbochargers.

Although a metal gasket was used between the turbochargers and exhaust manifolds, the down pipes are mated to the turbos with Permatex Ultra Copper high-temperature silicone gasket maker. It is spread liberally on the mounting flange.

The custom oil-scavenge tank also mounts to the bell housing. The hard lines feeding the tank carry gravity-fed oil from the turbochargers, while the large flexible hose draws out the oil with vacuum pressure from a pump mounted at the front of the engine. The oil is then reintroduced to the engine oil circuit.

Like the oil lines, the water lines to and from the turbos are hard lines. They're also routed around the oil pan. This configuration is more time-intensive to fabricate and install, but if the lines were simply run directly under the pan, they'd be susceptible to damage if the vehicle were to scrape the ground.

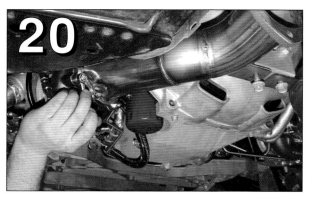

tubes. Look closely and note the careful routing of the hard lines for the oil and water systems, as well as the unique oil-scavenge tank. From here, the installation focuses on the intake tubes, intercooler, and reinstallation of numerous engine/exhaust system components.

Next, the down tubes (the pipes that connect the exhaust outlet of the turbos to the vehicle's exhaust system) are installed, but not before they're test-fitted to ensure there are no interference issues with any of the other turbo system or chassis components.

With the copper gasket maker on the flange, one of the down tubes is cinched down against the turbocharger. Note how both down tubes are further supported by mounting tabs that attach to the transmission bell housing.

From under the Corvette you can see the basic installation and orientation of the twin-turbo setup, prior to the fitting of the air-intake and air-discharge

The silicone hoses are carefully routed from the turbochargers along the chassis rails, with numerous checks and inspections to ensure they don't bind or interfere with the suspension and steering systems.

Filter-capped intakes are mounted in the front corners of the front fascia. The air-discharge tubes from the turbos feed the intercooling system's heat exchanger that is to be located in front of the radiator.

When the intake tubes are routed and securely attached, the project moves into the final stages, with buttoning up a myriad of details, including installing the mass air sensor (seen here), reconnecting the fuel system, and performing a number of wiring duties.

The intercooler's heat exchanger slides down in front of the stock radiator, necessitating the relocation of the oil cooler's heat exchanger. A Y-pipe connects both outlets of the exchanger and feeds the air charge straight into the throttle body. Like other aspects of the installation, the Y-pipe is custom-fitted to each vehicle. After that, the heat exchanger and intake tube are painted black.

The final major task in the installation involves re-installing the exhaust system. As is the case with most turbo installations, a modified exhaust system is required. In the case of this Z06-based project, it also required re-imaging the converter system, because the close-coupled, high-mounted catalytic converters on the stock exhaust system were eliminated. Lingenfelter's solution involves using a pair of aftermarket converters and a lightly modified Corsa C6 Corvette flow tube to fit within the vehicle's underbody tunnel. The rest of the exhaust system was modified in order to keep the mufflers in the stock location.

Fuel-system upgrades are necessary for an engine producing about 300 more horsepower than stock. To that end, Lingenfelter installs a set of 60-lbs/hr injectors and supports them with a Kenne Bell Boost-A-Pump fuel-pump voltage amplifier.

An interesting detail on this system is the re-use of the vacuum port that used to actuate the factory's two-stage exhaust system. It now is used to actuate a fuel-pressure regulator mounted at the rear of the vehicle, near the fuel tank.

Lingenfelter uses flexible silicone hoses for the air-intake tubes and the discharge tubes that feed the boosted air charge to the intercooler. They're custom made a little longer than necessary to enable precise fitment with a little trimming.

Custom Turbo System Fabrication

Rather than a system designed for racing, the vehicle's owner, DiabloSport chief Mike Wesley, wanted an integrated system for the street. That meant the system had to work around existing vehicle systems and components. There was no sacrificing of air conditioning, power amenities, or anything like that. Wesley turned to Stenod Performance to design, fabricate, and install a custom system. It uses a pair of Garrett ball-bearing turbos and an air-to-air intercooler. Initially, because the turbochargers were blowing into a stock LS2 engine, boost was kept to a detonation-avoiding 5 pounds. That was enough to deliver tread-melting performance from all four of the all-wheel-drive TrailBlazer's tires.

Soon, Wesley returned to the Stenod shop for a power boost. The engine was removed and rebuilt with the requisite forged internals and lower-compression pistons, as the wick would be turned up on the turbos to deliver approximately 10 to 12 pounds of boost. The original Garrett turbochargers were retained, but the wastegate actuators were swapped to allow the greater boost (a boost controller was not used).

Basics of the system and supporting hardware include:

- Two Garrett GT28R ball-bearing turbochargers with integral wastegates
- One TiAL 50-mm blow-off valve
- Custom air-to-air charge cooler
- 60-lb/hour fuel injectors
- Walbro 355-lph in-tank fuel pump
- Stock radiator with fourth-generation F-car cooling fans

Adding a turbo system to the TrailBlazer SS presents the same problem for many LS-powered vehicles: There isn't a bolt-on kit available in the aftermarket (at least not as this book was published). A custom turbo system was designed, built, and installed by Stenod Performance. Fortunately, there was enough room under the hood and around the chassis to facilitate the installation with minimal impact on the surrounding factory components. As is the case with almost all intercooled forced-induction systems, the project began with the removal of the front fascia, grille, and headlamp components to enable mounting of the intercooler heat exchanger and related plumbing.

- and C6 Corvette fan-control unit
- SLP Performance low-restriction exhaust system
- Retention of the stock mass air metering system, but with a 3-bar MAP sensor
- Re-programmed factory controller with HP Tuner

On a completely custom build, every inlet, discharge, and intake tube requires fabrication. If you are seeking to have a custom turbo system made for your car should do so only through a shop with similar experience. Inspecting other customers' cars and interviewing them about their experience are musts before entrusting your car and money to any shop. The design and fabrication of the TrailBlazer's system required turbocharger mounting brackets, air intake flow tubes, discharge flow tubes, intercooler tubing, and exhaust tubing. Additionally, a number of oil and coolant hoses were routed into and away from the turbochargers, requiring modification of the engine's coolant lines to merge the turbochargers' cooling lines with the engine's water system.

One of the more advantageous aspects of the system's design is the mounting of the turbos out of the engine compartment. They are located down and away from the engine, effectively straddling the

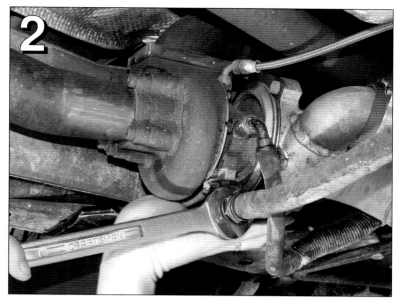

The turbo system includes a pair of Garrett GT28R water-cooled, ball-bearing turbochargers. Seen here is one of the turbochargers mounted to an exhaust extension that bridges between the turbo and exhaust manifold. Because of this arrangement, the turbocharger is located at the bottom of the engine compartment, in the approximate area of the original catalytic converter. The lower mounting position not only reduces underhood heat, but the thermal barrier for the converter also provides heat shielding.

Here is the passenger-side turbocharger/exhaust extension assembly attached to the exhaust manifold. Note the Y-fitting with large-diameter hoses at the center of the photo. It is part of the scavenge system that draws oil away from the turbochargers and back into the engine-oil circuit. Like the turbos described in the Lingenfelter installation earlier, the turbochargers on this system are water-cooled and externally lubricated. Because of the heat generated by the turbos, very durable, heavy-duty hoses, including braided lines, are used with AN-type fittings.

transmission. This placement takes the turbos away from the exhaust manifolds, saving the time and money of fabricating custom manifolds, while also reducing underhood heat. In fact, factory shielding on the underside of the vehicle, where original exhaust components were located, provides an excellent thermal barrier for the turbochargers.

Upon completion of the upgraded turbo system, the Trail-Blazer was tested on an AWD-capable chassis dyno, where it produced more than 600 hp and 550 ft-lbs of torque to all four wheels. It was stunning performance for a vehicle that is driven daily, but performance that is well within the capability of a carefully designed, installed, and tuned turbo system.

The other major component of the turbo system is the intercooler, which includes a custom heat exchanger built by Stenod Performance. It's an air-to-air intercooling system, meaning the pressurized air from the turbo system simply flows through the exchanger and is cooled by air entering through the grille or from the electric cooling fans. There is no liquid coolant circulating in the heat exchanger, as would be the case with a liquid-to-air intercooler. Stenod started with a Bell core and built the inlet/outlet caps to fit the Trail-Blazer. It mounts to a removable header that's part of the TrailBlazer's radiator core support, making installation and removal very simple.

When it came to the coolant lines for the turbochargers, the inlet and outlet hoses were routed from the aluminum hard-line sections of the heater hoses. That required drilling holes and welding fittings to the factory lines. There are other ways to tie into the factory cooling system to provide the same effect, but with one of the hard lines dedicated to inlet and the other a dedicated outlet, this method is foolproof, even if it required careful, labor-intensive aluminum welding.

With most of the coolant and oil lines routed and connected, the turbos' air intake and discharge tubes are mounted. The relatively large chassis and generous ground clearance of the TrailBlazer SS allowed Stenod Performance to route them easily under the engine K-member, where they feed into the bottom of the intercooler heat exchanger.

The air intake filters are mounted as far away from the heat of the turbo system as possible; in this case, at the far corners of the front bumper cover. Note the vacuum hose attached to the intake tube. It's part of a crankcase breather system.

The fabricated portions of the exhaust system also included provisions for oxygen sensors: one on each side, after the turbochargers. This system also incorporates oxygen sensors *before* each turbocharger, to satisfy the parameters for wideband tuning.

At the top of the engine, the intake tube is sandwiched between the throttle body and intercooler. It is a large, 4-inch-diameter tube to feed as much air as possible to the engine. The convoluted shape of the tube again demonstrates the careful, custom fitment required of each tube to fit with other factory-installed components. For vehicles that aren't matched with an aftermarket turbo kit, such custom fabrication is the only option. Stenod Performance incorporated a TiAL 50-mm blow-off valve into the intake tube. A blow-off valve should be located in the intake section between the discharge port of the intercooler's heat exchanger and the throttle body, which is right where this one is located.

The supporting elements of the turbo system are focused mostly on fuel requirements. They include a higher-capacity, 355-lph tank-mounted fuel pump that required the removal of the fuel tank for installation. At the other end of the fuel system, a set of 60-lbs/hr injectors was installed in the intake manifold.

The stock radiator was retained, but the cooling fan assembly was swapped with the twin-fan setup from an LS1-powered fourth-generation F-car. The fans are driven with the controller from a 2005-later Corvette, because it offers almost infinite adjustability when tuning the engine, including varying the fan speed to suit different demands. Most other electric fans, such as the fourth-generation F-car fan, are not adjustable—when they're on, they're on full-blast.

The STS Option

As described in Chapter 3, Squires Turbo Systems (STS) offers a non-conventional method of adding a turbo system to a vehicle. Rather than mounting the turbocharger(s) on the exhaust manifold(s), it is moved far back on the underside of the vehicle, typically near the rear axle. The reasons for this include reduced underhood temperature, lower air-charge temperature, lower cost (an STS kit eliminates the need for expensive, purpose-built headers or exhaust manifolds) and, perhaps most importantly, comparatively easy installation.

Because the turbo and its plumbing are mounted beneath the car, there is far less need for fabrication and relocation of underhood components. In most cases, installing an STS kit is comparable to a centrifugal supercharger—and perhaps slightly easier and less time consuming.

When STS turbo kits first hit the market, skeptics wondered whether a turbo hanging near the rear axle was the best place for it, citing concerns over its exposure to the elements, rogue road debris, and water ingestion. Generally speaking, those fears have proven to be unfounded. In fact, the systems have proven to deliver on their promise of lower temperatures, both at the throttle body, overall, and under the hood. It seems the long tubing of the system, running front-to-rear on the vehicle, delivers a passive intercooling effect. Many of STS's kits include conventional intercooling systems, because the high compression ratio of stock LS engines demand it. Of course, like any turbo system, an STS system is adjustable, allowing you to adjust boost pressure to make more power.

The following basic installation procedures of an STS kit are performed on an LS1-powered Pontiac GTO (similar to the Holden Monaro). Of course, different vehicles and different engines require different installation procedures, but the steps outlined here provide an excellent look at the basic mounting of the turbo and routing of its inlet and outlet plumbing.

This underhood shot of the STS-equipped GTO reveals no clues that there is a turbocharger installled, apart from clearly non-original air intake that snakes down and under the engine compartment. The uncluttered appearance is a hallmark of the STS kit, as it doesn't require tricky fabrication to squeeze the system beneath the hood.

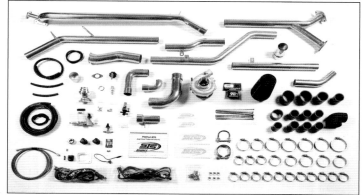

Here's an STS kit all laid out. Basically, the kit is comprised of tubing, clamps, and the hardware required to install the turbo and its supporting components. Not seen here is a separate intercooling system that is partnered with many of the kits. Additional components are also required, including higher-capacity fuel injectors and a fuel-pump booster. (Photo courtesy Squires Turbo Systems)

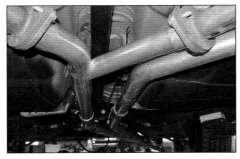

At the top of this photo, the Y-pipe illustrates the merge of the left- and right-hand exhaust outlets and its flow rearward to the turbocharger. The separate tube at the right is the flow tube carrying the boosted air charge to the intercooler and, after that, to the engine. The length of the tubes and their distance from the exhaust manifolds provide a passive intercooling effect.

Looking up at the chassis, with the left-rear tire on the right side of the photo, you can see STS' mounting location for the turbocharger. It's the location of the original muffler, which is eliminated with this system (although that is not true for all STS kits). A benefit of this mounting position is the factory heat shield that was originally designed for the muffler.

There's no down pipe or other exhaust system with STS's GTO kit. An exhaust outlet pipe simply mounts where the exhaust or down pipe would attach on a conventional system. The exhaust note with this design is acceptable and, the close-coupled catalytic converters that are mounted right off the exhaust manifolds are retained.

This view looking up at the front of the car shows the inlet pipe from the turbo coming in from the right, with the outlet to the engine intake on the left. What's missing in between is the heat exchanger for the intercooler.

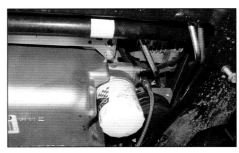

An oil-feed line for the turbo is added at the oil filter mounting pad, tapping into an existing, but unused port. A return line is also required and routes back through the oil-fill hole in the valve cover. An electric pump scavenges the oil from the turbo, forcing it back into the engine.

The unconventionally mounted turbo system requires conventional upgrades to the fuel system and ignition system. The LS1-powered GTO sufficed with a set of 42-pound injectors and a Kenne Bell Boost-A-Pump. Also, NGK TR6 spark plugs replaced the originals.

Here's a look at the finished installation. The blow-off valve is visible, but the system doesn't hang much lower than a regular exhaust system. A vehicle with a solid rear axle would benefit from better, over-the-axle tube routing, but the independent rear suspension of GTOs/Monaros, G8s/Commodores, and fifth-generation Camaro demands tubing that runs under the axle.

One of the unique aspects of the system is an electric pump that circulates oil between the turbo and engine. This isn't always necessary with a conventional turbo system, but definitely required on the STS kit, as there's no way gravity would return oil to the engine.

For the record, the project car produced 480 rwhp, with a Garrett G-67 turbo producing about 8 pounds of boost. The LS1 engine was internally stock, but was equipped with an LS6 camshaft and valvesprings.

Building a Race Car around a Turbo System

The custom turbo kit on the TrailBlazer SS and the STS turbo kit mentioned earlier represent a system designed to fit within the confines of essentially stock vehicles. For vehicles intended more for the drag strip than the street, accommodating the turbo system is the priority, with the vehicle's bodywork and chassis modified to support it.

For the popular "street car" and pro-modified-style classes, the engine system typically includes one or two very large turbochargers, a custom intake system, and a large-capacity, liquid-to-air intercooling system (often using an interior-mounted reservoir of ice water). Simply put, these race cars are built around the turbo system, with priority given to the desired location of the turbo(s).

"We start with where the turbochargers are going to be mounted, and go from there," says Stenod's Joe Borschke. "The customer tells us, for example, that the rules for his class allow a 106-mm turbo. That's a big turbo and it's going to take up a lot of room, as is the tubing routed in and out of it."

Although there's not a necessarily perfect location to mount a turbocharger, Borschke typically mounts them at the very front of the bodywork, exposing the air inlet side to the atmosphere.

"For a race car, you want as much exposure to fresh air as possible, as any restriction will affect the maximum boost," he says. "It's for this very reason that you wouldn't duplicate such a system on a street car; you need adequate air filtering on the street."

Another important aspect in race car turbo design is optimal wastegate location, with tubing that avoids sharp bends.

"The wastegates have to be priority-fed," says Borschke. "Air must go through the wastegates first [before the turbochargers] to maintain proper boost control."

As for those large intercooler tanks typically seen in the interiors of race cars, there are several reasons for locating them in the cabin. First of all, they are just plain large and don't fit easily in the engine compartment. Also, when filled with ice water, they're quite heavy, so mounting them in the interior helps distribute weight more evenly on the chassis.

Another race car under construction shows a smaller, front-mounted intercooler and more conventional mounting of the turbochargers. But while this setup seems tame when compared with the twin-turbo setup outlined in the previous photo, it nonetheless involves removing the bumper beam and other underhood accessories to support the system's components. Again, this is not a system for the street.

Here is a typical turbocharged race car under construction. The turbochargers were mounted up front on a fabricated brace, replacing the original bumper beam. Note how the turbos are fed by reversed, marine-style headers, with the wastegates located before the turbochargers. The air outlets from the turbos merge into a single, large-diameter tube that is routed on the outside of the engine compartment (underneath the passenger-side front fender) to the passenger compartment, where it is cooled by a large, liquid-to-air intercooler. The cooled air charge is then fed through a hole in the firewall to a reverse-facing inlet atop the intake manifold. This is not designed for street use, as all of the typical accessories found on a street car are eliminated to make room for the turbo system's tubing.

Aaron Schoen's 500-rwhp Silverado

Homebuilt Turbo System on a Budget

Disproving the conventional wisdom that turbo systems are complicated and expensive, Ohio resident Aaron Schoen built one essentially by himself with used parts from a variety of sources. Its 5.3-liter engine generates 503 hp and 535 ft-lbs of torque to the wheels; and it has sent the heavy Chevy down the drag strip in 12.9 seconds at 114 mph.

In a nutshell, Schoen scratch-built an intercooled turbo system, using a single turbo and air-to-air charge cooler, along with a methanol injection system. There are a couple of other things you should know, too: It was built out of his single-stall, apartment-complex garage, and he spent less than $1,500 on the parts. Here are the highlights of his recipe:

- $300   Stock 5.3-liter short block
- $300   6.0-liter (LQ4) cylinder heads
- Free   LS1 camshaft (a gift from an uncle who'd swapped the cam in his 2002 Trans Am)
- $25   LS6 valve-springs (take-off parts from a 2005 GTO)
- $200   Garrett T61 turbocharger (60-mm inducer/85-mm exducer)
- Free   39-pounds/hour fuel injectors (traded some stuff for them)
- $350   Miscellaneous tubing and hoses
- $90   TrailBlazer torque converter
- Free   Corvette servos from a 700R-4-equipped TrailBlazer 4x4
- $30   Electric fan (a Chevy Corsica part from a salvage yard)

Schoen says he was inspired by the unique turbo kits of Utah-based STS. The turbo system flows into and out of the Garrett T61 turbocharger. Because he didn't have the tools to fabricate the necessary tubing, Schoen took his truck and turbocharger to a local exhaust shop. Schoen showed where he wanted the turbo located—on the passenger side of the chassis, under the cab—and had the shop bend the necessary

Aaron Schoen built an intercooled turbo system for his 2004 Chevy Silverado using almost all used parts, but all the basic elements are there and work very well together, including a single turbo, wastegate, blow-off valve, and air-to-air intercooler. There's also a methanol injection system.

3-inch tubing to accommodate the design.

Of course, the elements of the turbo system include the flow pipes from the engine's exhaust manifolds, which merge and feed the turbocharger's turbine. From there, more tubing runs to the front of the engine compartment, where the boosted air charge (tuned right now for a maximum of about 11 pounds) flows into an air-to-air heat exchanger that came off a 1989 Toyota Supra. Then, the air is sent into the 5.3-liter, iron-block engine's stock throttle body. An electric pump is required to re-circulate oil from the turbo back to the engine; it returns to the crankcase by means of a fitting drilled into the oil fill cap on the valve cover.

One of the additional benefits of this system design is it retains the stock exhaust manifolds, which saves a big chunk of change, as more conventional systems typically require thick, expensive cast-iron manifolds to support the high-heat turbo.

In fact, the entire engine is essentially production-based, although not entirely stock for a 5.3-liter engine. The cast crankshaft, rods, and pistons are used, with Speed Pro rings fitted to the 8.4:1 pistons. Even the intake manifold is stock, although equipped with

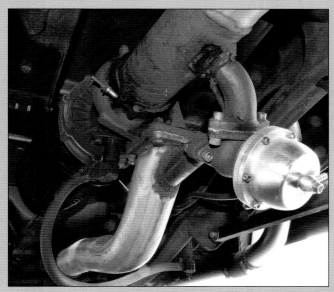

The turbo is mounted under the cab, on the passenger side. It is a Garrett T61, with a 60-mm inducer and 85-mm exducer. The turbo inlet tube from the engine exhaust is clearly visible at the lower-center of the photo. At the far right is the outlet from the turbo, sending the boosted air charge to the engine. It runs along the perimeter of the frame.

The outlet tubing from the turbo runs up and into an air-to-air charge cooler from a 1989 Toyota Supra. Note the mounting of the blow-off valve on the outlet tubing of the charge cooler. It is the connection between the charge cooler and throttle body. The valve bleeds off the air charge when the throttle closes.

This photo of the entire engine compartment shows the tubing from the intercooler routed to the engine. Also of note is the homemade methanol injection system, which includes a pump and reservoir located in the upper corner of the passenger side of the engine compartment. The reservoir is a take-off piece from a salvage-yard car.

Aaron Schoen's 500-rwhp Silverado *(continued)*

39-pound fuel injectors. The low-compression pistons help stave off detonation, but so does the methanol injection system that Schoen rigged up, using a junkyard windshield-washer container and an auto-parts-store electric pump. Methanol injection enables the use of higher-octane fuel and more aggressive tuning to maximize horsepower.

Backing the turbocharged 5.3 engine is a Hydra-Matic 4L60-E electronically controlled automatic transmission that's been beefed up to support the added torque that comes from the turbo system. The torque converter for it is yet another take-off part, coming from a stock TrailBlazer. Additional drivetrain components include a 4.10:1-geared rear axle fitted with an Eaton TrueTrac limited-slip differential.

When it came to tuning his combination, Schoen used tried-and-true HP Tuner software. He went with a speed density air-metering system, too.

"There were a lot of reasons I went with speed density," he says. "One of the most important was the fact that, with a 2-bar speed density system, I had more tuning range beyond 6 pounds of boost. The stock, 1-bar mass airflow system is only good to about 10 pounds of boost." (See Chapter 7 for more information about 1-bar and 2-bar MAP considerations.)

Pure and simple, Schoen's combination works. It starts, runs, and drives excellent, with no flat spots in the tuning. Turbo lag is minimal and the boost comes on smoothly and progressively. In short, it is a project that proves how excellent forced-induction performance need not break the bank.

To enable higher-boost tuning with the 5.3-liter engine's standard, 1-bar MAP sensor, Schoen converted the engine from mass airflow air metering to a 2-bar speed density system. He uses HP Tuner and a laptop to make adjustments.

Tuned for a maximum of 11 pounds of boost and running on 93-octane pump gas (with 8.4:1 compression), Schoen's truck produces more than 500 hp and 535 ft-lbs of torque to the rear wheels. Turbo lag is minimal and the entire system was hand-built for comparatively little money.

TUNING FOR SUPERCHARGED AND TURBOCHARGED ENGINES

In the most basic terms, electronically controlled engines must be carefully calibrated to take advantage of engine modifications that affect airflow and fuel delivery requirements. That is more imperative for forced-induction engines, which process significantly more air than a comparable, naturally aspirated engine—and do it under positive manifold pressure.

The various calibrations, whether adjusting fuel and spark delivery or "telling" the controller about new injectors or sensors, fall under the broad heading of tuning. The importance of accurate, pinpointed tuning changes all boils down to a central goal: optimizing fuel and spark throughout the RPM range and under all load conditions.

All of the other changes and adjustments to the engine controller's programming circles back to maintaining a safe air/fuel ratio. Too little fuel leads to a lean condition that can lead to detonation, burned pistons, and worse.

Experienced tuners "sneak up" on a supercharged/turbocharged engine's programming, keeping the fuel mixture rich and spark timing conservative at first. After establishing a safe zone of performance, the air/fuel mixture is refined to maximize horsepower. It can be a painstaking process with many adjustments. Novices are advised not to experiment with their newly force-fed car, as incorrect tuning can quickly lead to expensive problems with an engine under boost.

There is far more to engine tuning and computer programming than found in this single chapter, which covers the basics of what's involved in the procedures and requirements for forced-induction combinations. For a more in-depth look at tuning, I recommend Greg Banish's detailed books *Engine Management: Advanced Tuning* and *Designing and Tuning High-Performance Fuel Injection Systems* as excellent guides (go to www.cartechbooks.com for more information).

Custom tuning for a forced-induction system (beyond uploading the pre-programmed tune included with a kit) requires experience and isn't advised for the novice. It is best to seek a knowledgeable tuner who uses an engine chassis dynamometer facility for accurate, safe tuning. WARNING: Do *not* start or drive a newly supercharged or turbocharged engine with higher-capacity fuel injectors if the controller is not programmed for them.

Air + Fuel = Horsepower

Of course, the entire reason for adding a supercharger or turbocharger is increasing the airflow through the engine. And with more air, more fuel is required it to maintain an optimal air/fuel ratio across the RPM band. If sufficient fuel isn't added as RPM and boost increase, the engine runs lean, possibly leading to detonation or worse—burned pistons or catastrophic engine failure.

The factory engine-control systems of LS-powered vehicles ensure optimal combustion, based on a programmed set of engine parameters, including displacement, the size of the throttle body, the capacity of the fuel injectors, and even the specifications of the camshaft. Anything done to the engine that significantly alters the engine's parameters, from a simple cam change to 10 pounds of boost, requires updated programming. Otherwise, the controller "fights" the changes, as it tries to deliver fuel based on its program.

Without question, a supercharger or turbocharger system radically alters the parameters of the engine's airflow and manifold pressure, so the controller's programming must be altered to directly feed the engine more fuel. In a nutshell, that's the goal of tuning. However, a few clicks of the keyboard are not the only way to produce great horsepower in a safe manner—the fuel system must support it. That means the fuel pump and injectors must be matched to deliver fuel at a rate matched with the engine's airflow.

To put it simply, without sufficient fuel to match the boosted air charge from the blower or turbocharger, all the tuning tricks in the world won't produce safe, sustainable performance.

Mass Airflow vs. Speed Density

To ensure the engine receives the precise amount of fuel it needs to match the incoming air, the engine controller relies on an air-metering system. There are two basic types: mass airflow and speed density. From the factory, LS-powered vehicles come with a mass airflow system.

In the simplest explanation, mass air systems directly measure air, while speed density systems estimate it from a variety of inputs. Mass airflow systems use a sensor to provide a direct reading on airflow through the intake tube, ahead of the throttle body. Basically, the sensor tells the controller how much air is entering the engine and the controller

The boosted air charge of a force-inducted engine requires not only a matching increase in fuel, but the engine controller must be programmed with the specifications of the new parts in order to control the fuel delivery. Inaccurate programming prevents the engine from performing to its full potential or, even worse, allows an unchecked lean condition that could damage the engine.

responds by matching that airflow with the appropriate amount of fuel. With a speed density system, there isn't a direct reading of airflow, but it is calculated based on a variety of inputs, including manifold pressure, RPM level, and air temperature.

One of the benefits of a mass airflow system is its ability to roll with certain airflow changes without major tuning alterations. If the increased airflow is within the air meter's sensor range, it simply signals the airflow reading to the controller, prompting increased fuel delivery (assuming the fuel system is up to the task). That's not the case with a speed density system, which requires tuning updates for all airflow changes. Also, mass airflow systems compensate for engine wear over time.

Generally speaking, the factory mass airflow systems work with low-boost forced-induction systems and has helped make LS-powered vehicles among the easiest to tune for great

power increases. Factory mass airflow systems provide excellent performance and optimal air/fuel for up to approximately 15 pounds of boost. In fact, the pre-programmed, uploadable tuning software that comes with most bolt-on blower and turbo kits is designed to work with the factory mass airflow system and provide good drivability and performance.

After 15 pounds of boost, tuning becomes difficult with factory mass airflow systems because the manifold absolute pressure (MAP) sensor cannot provide accurate readings to the controller. Swapping the stock, 1-bar MAP sensor with a 2-bar or 3-bar sensor alleviates that problem.

Some builders prefer speed density systems with higher-boost combinations, because they aren't limited by the range of the mass airflow sensor. They also enable higher boost with 1-bar MAP sensors. However, speed density systems have "fixed" programs, meaning that the

The factory mass airflow meter/ sensor assembly is used without modification on most Roots- and screw-type supercharger kits. Larger-diameter meters allow more air, but slightly diminish maximum boost. Changes to the meter's diameter or the sensor must be addressed in the controller's programming

The custom intake systems of most centrifugal supercharger and turbocharger systems require swapping the stock mass airflow sensor into the intake tract. For the most accurate airflow readings, the sensor should be placed in a section of the intake that allows a straight flow path across the sensor element.

The bypass valve (lower left) for a centrifugal supercharger system mounted on a C6 Corvette is shown with the front fascia removed. When installed on a vehicle with a factory-style mass airflow system, the bypass valve must be mounted between the intercooler outlet (flowing toward the engine) and before the mass airflow sensor. The intercooled air charge must only pass the mass airflow sensor once, or accurate air metering is impossible. That means bypass air shouldn't be introduced back into the intake stream ahead of the air meter; and bypass air released to the atmosphere shouldn't be vented after the air meter.

Most modern Eaton superchargers and twin-screw compressors have an integrated bypass valve, negating the need to insert a separate bypass valve in the intake system.

Speed density air metering is the way to go with racing engines, because, generally speaking, it can be programmed to handle more power than a mass air-metered engine. It is also necessary on setups like this twin-turbo engine, where air enters the intake plenum in two places and uses multiple throttle bodies.

Map Sensors

controller is programmed to suit the exact parameters of the engine to ensure the air/fuel ratio. Anything done to the engine that changes the airflow characteristics, or volumetric efficiency, requires a new program for the controller—and that goes for engine wear over time and, sometimes, extreme temperature swings. Also, drivability can suffer somewhat, when compared with a properly tuned mass air system. Generally, however,

speed density systems are used more with very-high-boost/racing combinations, where stoplight-to-stoplight smoothness isn't a great concern.

Bottom line: For most street and street/strip combination of low to moderate boost, the factory-style mass air system is preferred.

Whether used with a bolt-on kit on an internally stock engine or on a custom-built engine, a MAP sensor that's capable of "reading" higher levels of boost must be used. Forced-induction engines making approximately 8 to 10 pounds of boost usually work fine with the 1-bar MAP sensors that are equipped on most naturally aspirated LS production engines.

When the boost level is expected to exceed 10 pounds, at least a 2-bar MAP sensor should be used. The 6.2-liter LS3 engine uses a 2-bar pressure sensor, while the LSA and LS9 use a trio of sensors—one on the inlet side before the supercharger, and two on the outlet side, after the supercharger and intercooler. The LS3 sensor, along with the inlet sensors for the LSA and LS9, are the same GM PN: 12591290. The outlet sensor on the factory supercharged engines is a 2.5-bar MAP, PN 12592525.

The 2-bar sensors are interchangeable with 1-bar sensors, but the engine-control module must be modified to reflect the change. For experienced tuners, it is a quick and easy adjustment. The recommended sensor is the more common PN 12591290 part. The only factory LS-engine MAP sensor that doesn't directly swap out with the others is found on the naturally aspirated LS7. Its sensor has a different-size pin end.

There are aftermarket 2-, 3-, and 4-bar MAP sensors, but for most higher-boost combinations, the GM 2-bar sensor is adequate.

GM Controllers

Generally speaking, all of GM's production LS engine controllers can be tuned to work with supercharged and turbocharged engine combinations. Commercial tuning is available for all of them and each works well with low- and moderate-boost systems.

The later E38 and E67 controllers are the most flexible, offering greater parameter ranges, but the E67 is the most flexible of them all. For high-boost, custom-engine combinations, it is the best option—to a certain point (see page 94, "Standalone Control Systems"). It is available from GM Performance Parts under PN 19166569.

Here's a quick look at the most common factory controllers used with LS engines.

The MAP sensors for LS engines are mostly interchangeable, except for the LS7 sensor. Here's the factory 2-bar sensor for LS9/LSA engine. Adding a higher-pressure sensor must be accounted for when programming the controller.

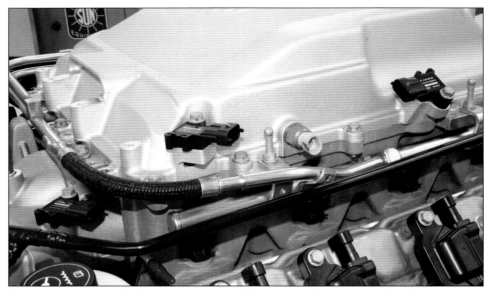

The three factory MAP sensors are visible on this LSA engine. For the most part, aftermarket supercharger systems use only the single MAP sensor from the stock, naturally aspirated engine. If the system is tuned to produce more than 10 pounds of boost, the factory 1-bar sensor should be swapped with at least a 2-bar MAP sensor, and the flash memory for the controller must be updated to accommodate it.

GM's E38 and E67 controllers are the most flexible for tuning of those matched with factory LS powertrain systems, with the E67 being the best for forced induction. For higher-boost engine combinations that also incorporate other significant engine modifications, it is the best choice for tuning up to approximately 1,000 hp. It is available through GM Performance Parts, under PN 19166569.

LS1A: Used on early LS1 engines equipped with a cable throttle and 24X reluctor wheel. Also features integrated transmission control and a wiring harness with LS1 fuel injector connectors.

LS1B: Used on later LS1 engines and compatible with electronic throttle control with separate throttle actuator control (TAC) module, and a 24X reluctor wheel. It features integrated transmission control and uses LS1-style injector connectors.

E40: Not as common as the LS1 controllers or the later E38 and E67 controllers, the E40 works with a 24X wheel and electronic throttle control, but the harness uses LS2-style fuel-injector connectors; no integrated transmission control.

E38: Works with a 58X wheel and electronic throttle control; uses LS2-style injector harness and compatible with integrated, automatic 6-speed transmission control.

E67: Same basic capability as the E38: 58X, electronic throttle, LS2 connectors and integrated 6-speed automatic transmission control—but with a greater range of parameters and increased tuning flexibility. It is the controller used with the factory LSA and LS9 engines, along with several other naturally aspirated LS engines.

It's important to note that the later controllers, including the E38 and E67, were incorporated based on vehicle and system requirements, so different LS-powered vehicles built in the same model year were equipped with different controllers. The 2010 Camaro SS, for example, was equipped with the E38 controller, while the same-year Cadillac CTS-V received an E67. In other words, the next-generation controller didn't necessarily supersede

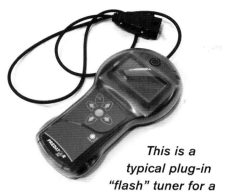

This is a typical plug-in "flash" tuner for a supercharger kit. There's no need for a laptop computer, because if the directions are followed correctly, re-programming the factory controller is as easy as pushing a few buttons. What it doesn't allow is tuning for additional engine modifications.

the previous generation in production vehicles—different vehicles received different controllers based on their control-system and vehicle electrical architecture.

Pre-Packaged Programming

The vast majority of supercharger and turbocharger kits include some type of uploadable, pre-programmed tuning system, usually a hand-held device that plugs into the vehicle's OBD (on-board diagnostics) port beneath the dashboard. When the instructions are followed correctly, the engine controller has all the information it needs to operate the engine safely. For do-it-yourself enthusiasts and those without convenient access to independent tuning shops, it's the only real option for tuning the car.

Because a measure of safety is built into those pre-programmed systems—ensuring adequate fuel delivery and spark control for a number of variables including fuel type, engine load, altitude, and more—it is

Flash tuners upload their programming to the engine-control module or powertrain-control module via the OBD-2 port located inside the vehicle, under the dashboard.

possible to achieve greater horsepower results with custom tuning. More importantly, the pre-packaged tuning *cannot* be used if other major engine modifications have been made, including a camshaft swap, stroker crankshaft, higher-flow cylinder heads, or even fuel injectors of a different capacity than what was included with the kit. To put it simply: Anything beyond the blower kit is not accounted for with a kit's included programming.

Some manufacturers have technical hotlines that allow custom tuning, but the modifications beyond the stock configuration must be conveyed before the kit is shipped. (See page 93, "Livernois Motorsports' X-Treme Cal Tuning System," for an alternative.)

Aftermarket Flash Software

One of the reasons LS-powered vehicles are so popular among high-performance enthusiasts is the comparative ease with which their controllers can be reprogrammed to accommodate the air/fuel changes that come with engine modifications. Aftermarket software packages enable professional and knowledgeable private tuners to edit and/or alter the operational parameters of the engine-controller program and upload the changes through a flash procedure.

The ability to alter the flash memory of engine controllers is a big change from earlier computer-controlled systems that used control-module "chips" that required separate ones to be "burned" for basically every modification. All LS-powered production vehicles use the modern flash-style memory systems that are easily accessed via the OBD-2 (onboard diagnostics, second generation) port under the dashboard.

The primary sources for LS-engine flash memory tuner software utilities are HP Tuners EFILive and Carputing LLC, a company whose products are collectively known by the name LS1 Edit. Like software for a home or business computer, the utilities offered by these companies are licensed either on a singular basis for a specific vehicle or for tuning shops that use the software for multiple vehicles. They are priced accordingly, too, with single-vehicle systems costing several hundred dollars and multiple-vehicle licenses costing several thousand dollars.

Boiled down to their most basic functions for tuning, these products enable the user to read the engine-controller flash memory and save it to a file that can be altered/modified to suit new performance and engine-component parameters. HP Tuners' VCM Editor utility, for example, enables manipulation of not only fuel and spark parameters, but RPM limit, cooling-fan operation, transmission shift points, and more. It also incorporates an automatic recovery feature that protects against re-flashing problems.

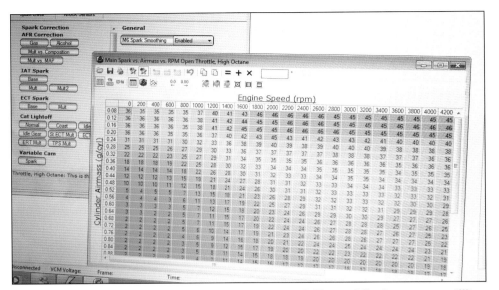

Here's an example of an editable screen from HP Tuners' flash memory utility. When the tables are adjusted, the settings are saved and uploaded to the engine controller. It then directs the engine and/or transmission as programmed. Knowing which values to change and what to change them to is the trick of tuning. An understanding of how the values affect the engine and transmission is necessary before modifying them.

This is an HP Tuners interface module that connects between a computer and the OBD-2 port inside the vehicle. It is what enables modifications in the flash memory to be made, saved, and uploaded. Whether using HP Tuners' system or the LS1 Edit system from Carputing LLC, software is included to facilitate modifications.

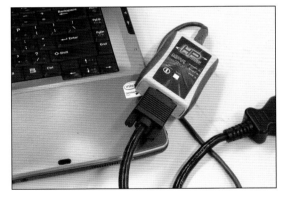

Lidio Iacobelli, from Alternative Auto Performance, performs a common test-and-tune procedure, whereby a test drive of a modified vehicle determines the need for further tuning adjustments. With a laptop connected to the HP Tuners interface and plugged into the OBD-2 port, Iacobelli inputs the value changes and saves them to the controller's flash memory. Then, it's out for another test drive to find out whether the changes delivered the desired results.

Currently, HP Tuners' latest tuning utility is VCM Suite 2.22, which incorporates updated Editor features along with the company's VCM Scanner. System highlights include:

- Windows Vista compatibility
- "Tunerlock" support for GM's E38 controller (preventing access by unauthorized tuners)
- More than 450 updated parameters for GM's 6L80 automatic transmission (along with Alison transmission and Duramax Diesel engine support)

As with HP Tuners, the editing utilities from Carputing LLC (LS1 Edit and LS2 Edit) enable manipulation of the controller's flash memory. The LS2 Edit utility, which covers most later-model LS-powered vehicles, regardless of whether they actually have an LS2 engine, accommodates those vehicles' split powertrain controller system that operates on a controller area network (CAN). That means the engine and transmission controllers perform mostly independently, but are linked via the CAN.

Regardless of the utility, you must have a working knowledge of the base fuel, spark, and air/fuel ratio requirements of the engine, recognizing them in the myriad of tables the flash tuner software is equipped with and the proper approximate values for tuning the system to accommodate new performance parts.

This is where a book like Greg Banish's *Engine Management: Advanced Tuning* becomes essential. Both HP Tuners and Carputing, LLC, offer online assistance for basic tuning issues and troubleshooting. Many popular online enthusiast forums, as well as HP Tuners' Web site, devote space to flash-memory tuning. If you are contemplating custom tuning for the first time familiarize yourself with the basics, because even a relatively small mistake at the keyboard could result in serious engine damage.

Livernois Motorsports' X-Treme Cal Tuning System

Enthusiasts who perform installations at home or don't have convenient access to a good, reputable tuning shop are challenged when it comes to proper tuning on a combination that exceeds the parameters of a manufacturer's pre-packaged programming, such as a cam-and-heads swap in addition to a bolt-on blower kit. As noted earlier, the flash memory upgrade included with most bolt-on systems does not account for additional engine modifications.

Livernois Motorsports' solution is an interface system that allows an easily uploadable, customized flash-memory upgrade based on an individual's specific requirements. It's called X-Treme Cal Tuning Interface and it essentially works like this: The customer receives the interface kit from Livernois Motorsports, which includes a pre-programmed tune based on that customer's specific vehicle equipment—a 2009 Pontiac G8 GT with a Magna Charger blower kit, LS3 cylinder heads and a hotter camshaft, for example. Based on the experience of similar combinations, Livernois Motorsports creates an appropriate tune and loads it on the interface module. After receiving it, the customer uploads the new tune to the controller, just as he or she would with the pre-packaged tune from the supercharger kit.

"It allows us to achieve results equivalent to dyno tuning for simple bolt-ons or more elaborate power adders that normally would require custom tuning at our dyno facility,"

Livernois Motorsports' X-Treme Cal Tuning Interface includes a software disc, interface module, and cables required to connect between a laptop computer and the OBD-2 port.

Among the benefits of the X-Treme Cal Tuning Interface system is how Livernois Motorsports stores each customer's tuning files. This allows them to quickly modify and forward a revised tune if further changes are planned for the particular engine combination.

says Livernois Motorsports' Dan Millen. "The X-Treme Cal Tuning Interface is a single VIN unit with the ability to data log, so it is the customer's to keep. We can send updates to the customer with our tuning files as they become available, or the customer can update his own tune—within reason—to accommodate further modifications."

According to Millen, the X-Treme Cal Tuning Interface reads the factory controller program, which can be saved, to return the vehicle to stock specifications. The system includes software, a USB-to-laptop computer cord, and an OBD-2 interface cord.

Standalone Control Systems

Although very adaptable to tuning, the factory controllers on GM vehicles have their limits. In general terms, it's about 1,000 hp. After that, the requirements to fuel the engine demand things the factory controller isn't designed for. Mostly it's injector-driver control, because the high-output, aftermarket-performance injectors are known as the "peak and hold" type and GM's controllers aren't designed to operate them.

Joe Alameddine, of ACCEL/DFI provides a more thorough explanation: "Most of the injectors found in the market today that flow significant amounts of fuel for high-horsepower applications are typically low-impedance injectors [less than 12 ohms]. The injector drivers in the stock computer do not support the current levels necessary to drive them properly. Also, the few, specialty high-impedance injectors that are available have a very slow opening rate that causes poor stability at idle and high RPM. The effect is magnified further if

The ACCEL/DFI Gen 8 engine-control module is one of the most advanced engine controllers on the market and is capable of driving a variety of high-performance fuel injectors. It can fire up to eight ignition coils simultaneously. It features three integrated micro-processors capable of supporting engines spinning to 15,000 rpm and producing more than 3,000 hp. Additional highlights include: the capability to drive low-impedance fuel injectors common on racing engines; programmable inputs to support cooling fan control; 64 channel internal data logging, and more. Real-time programming software helps dial in combinations very quickly. There are several PNs of the Gen 8 for different applications; the one compatible with LS engines carries PN 75807.

the user increases fuel pressure. With an aftermarket computer, such as ACCEL/DFI Gen 8, these issues are not a problem, as each injector driver can handle up to 8 amps. This equates to very finite control at just about any engine speed and compatibility with an injector carrying an impedance rating of 1.5 ohms."

Alameddine further suggests a computer swap in a force-inducted setup with a high-performance camshaft.

"The stock racing-oriented computer cannot compensate for a high level of valve overlap, causing cold-startup issues and general poor-idle quality—and mass airflow sensors typically have a glass ceiling for measurement of airflow, limiting potential power levels," he says. "While there are many flash programs available to compensate at some level, usually the end user fights some degree of performance to dial in the whole package."

Another popular standalone engine controller is F.A.S.T.'s XFI system. Like the ACCEL/DFI Gen 8 controller, it handles high-performance, low-impedance injectors and enables the use of up to 16 injectors (a trait factory controllers don't have). Another benefit is the XFI system's ability to store four separate engine mapping programs (tune ups), allowing the user to switch fuels (pump gas to racing gas or E85, for example) without having to re-flash the memory. The different tunes can be accessed with the simple flip of a switch.

A chassis dynamometer is a wonderful tool for gauging before-and-after results of a supercharger or turbocharger, as well as ensuring the air/fuel ratio is adequate at WOT. Generally speaking, automatic transmission-equipped vehicles lose more of the engine's power before reaching the drive wheels. Testing automatic-transmission-equipped vehicles can be difficult on a chassis dyno, because their factory lockup-style converters don't always lock up. That means full engine power isn't being transmitted to the drive axle. However, a knowledgeable dyno operator can get the converter to lock and take an accurate measurement. All-wheel-drive vehicles (like the TrailBlazer SS) also pose a unique challenge. They require a dyno with both front and rear rolling drums, which can be difficult to find, even in metropolitan areas with numerous tuning shops.

After a "pull" on the chassis dyno, the technician notes the recorded horsepower and torque measurements at the rear wheels and compares them with the baseline numbers that were recorded prior to the installation of the supercharger or turbo system. The graphs generated by the dyno pull not only point out the peak power numbers, but graph them in RPM increments, showing where in the rev range the power increases are most effective. If the vehicle is equipped with wideband oxygen sensors, air/fuel ratio measurements are also compared.

Along with the products from ACCEL/DFI, standalone control systems are also available in the forms of F.A.S.T.'s XFI electronic fuel-injection system and Big Stuff 3's GEN3 Pro SEFI control system.

Chassis Dyno Tuning

Whether a modified vehicle uses a pre-programmed software program or a custom tune, it is highly recommended that the vehicle be tested and fine tuned with the assistance of a chassis dynamometer. It more closely replicates the real-world performance of the engine by putting a load on the drivetrain. Of course, it also indicates the horsepower and torque levels of the engine. Those numbers are generally referred to as "at the wheels" power numbers, because they're measured at the drive wheels on the dynamometer's inertia drums (the large rollers on which the vehicle is loaded).

Depending on the type of dyno used, the at-the-wheels power numbers can be corrected by a factor of about 15 to 20 percent to indicate the true horsepower and torque output of the engine. The difference between the engine and drive wheels is the result of parasitic losses from the engine turning the transmission, driveshaft, rear axle, etc., before the horsepower and torque get to the pavement.

Most tuning shops use chassis dynos from either Mustang Dynamometer or Dynojet. Generally, the same car tested under the same conditions reveals slightly more at-the-wheels power on a Dynojet dynamometer than a Mustang dyno, although many tuners suggest the Mustang unit imposes a more real-world load on the vehicle that produces a result closer

A wideband oxygen sensor simply replaces the standard narrowband sensor in the exhaust system. One should be used in each position originally occupied by a narrowband sensor; most range in price from $50 to $100 each. If you plan to tune the engine yourself, it is a worthy investment. If you use a professional shop for tuning, the shop can usually swap out the standard sensors for wideband sensors during tuning sessions.

Part-throttle performance is more accurately tested on the road, with air/fuel ratio measurements recorded through a wideband oxygen sensor. Wideband sensors are also used on the chassis dyno during WOT tests, but they are acutely effective at helping fine-tune low-speed drivability and ensuring adequate fuel is available at all RPM and throttle levels.

to what the vehicle will deliver on the street.

Confirmation of a newly modified vehicle's power output is certainly important, but ensuring adequate fuel delivery under load is the most important aspect of dyno tuning. It is imperative to know that the engine is free from detonation at WOT and under full boost. For vehicles undergoing a custom tune, such testing helps determine the precise fuel requirements throughout the RPM range.

Frankly, some tuners are better than others—and a professional shop that's adept at installing parts and fabricating custom systems may not have a staff member who is experienced at the finer points of tuning electronically controlled engines. It is incumbent on the vehicle owner to seek the most qualified tuner to ensure a costly investment in a blower or turbo kit isn't going to end prematurely with burned pistons. The Internet makes it relatively easy to probe whether a tuning shop has a good reputation, while old-fashioned asking around at the drag strip or a car show may also help find a knowledgeable local tuner.

Wideband Tuning

As helpful as chassis dyno tuning is, the measurements on the dyno are generated with the engine at WOT. Ensuring a safe air/fuel ratio and adequate fuel delivery at full throttle is, of course, vitally important, but part-throttle driving makes up the vast majority of conditions for street-driven vehicles. Tuning for those conditions ensures not only the appropriate air/fuel ratio across the RPM band, but optimizes idle quality, overall drivability, and even fuel economy.

The most accurate way to account for "real world" driving conditions is through what is known as wideband tuning, which requires a wideband oxygen sensor and sup-

porting components. By replacing the original narrowband oxygen sensor with the wideband one, a greater range of air/fuel ratio detection is enabled. The value of the variation from the ideal, stoichiometric 14.7:1 ratio (when using gasoline) is expressed with the Greek letter Lambda (λ).

With the factory-style narrowband oxygen sensor, its capability is basically limited to determining whether the post-combustion air/fuel ratio is at the optimal 14.7:1. If not, it triggers the "Check Engine" light and registers a code in the computer. A diagnostic check reveals if the difference was because of a rich condition (more fuel than air) or a potentially engine-damaging lean condition (more air than fuel).

Unfortunately for tuners of modified vehicles—especially those with supercharged or turbocharged engines—the narrowband sensor signals rich or lean, but cannot indicate

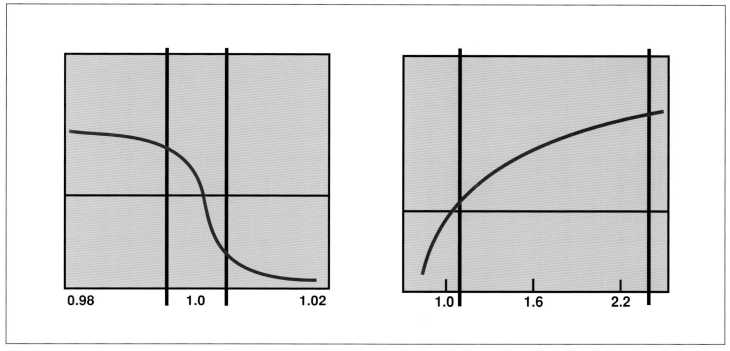

These graphs illustrate the difference in air/fuel measurements recorded by narrowband (left) and wideband (right) sensors. In the narrowband graph, the measurement within the 1.0 value section depicts the limited sensing range of the sensor, whereas the wider sensing range with the wideband sensor is clear. More importantly for tuners, the wideband sensor tells how lean or rich the mixture is, while the narrowband sensor merely indicates a rich or lean condition.

the precise air/fuel ratio that triggered the code. A wideband system has the capability of precise measurements. Typically, a wideband oxygen sensor identifies air/fuel ratios between 9.65:1 and 20:1.

Because incorrectly tuned forced-induction systems can quickly lean out the air/fuel ratio, wideband tuning should be considered a must. In fact, for engine safety's sake, many tuners build in a slightly rich ratio to ensure adequate fuel for any operating or engine-load condition. Typically, such tuning scrubs off a few horsepower, but the tradeoff is often welcomed because it brings with it peace of mind. Without wideband tuning, it would be difficult to accurately measure the air/fuel ratio and optimize it to ensure a safe tune that doesn't drastically affect the engine's output.

Electronic Throttle

Some builders have discovered a problem with the electronically controlled throttle body of some LS engines, particularly LS2 engines found in TrailBlazer SS and SSR models. The issue involves the throttle blade being pushed open unintentionally by the supercharger/turbocharger boost pressure.

The condition is usually detected through uneven performance, bucking, and even an illuminated "Check Engine" warning. It is believed the culprit is a comparatively weak spring within the throttle body and the cure is the installation of another production throttle body with a stronger spring mechanism. Builders who've dealt with this issue report the 2005–2007 Corvette LS2 engine's throttle body has sufficient spring

strength to stand up to considerable boost pressure. Another possible culprit may be an insufficiently strong bypass valve.

Another throttle-related issue seems to affect the TrailBlazer SS, Hummer H3, and other all-wheel-drive vehicles. The comparatively violent acceleration caused by a full-throttle blast with a force-inducted engine can upset the factory stability-control system called StabiliTrak. When this occurs, a warning message may flash on the dashboard and temporarily disable the stability system. It may also cause the stability system to perform in a manner where it believes it is intervening in a potentially hazardous driving situation. If that happens, the spark may be retarded and the throttle position reduced—even under boost—because that's what the stability system is programmed to do.

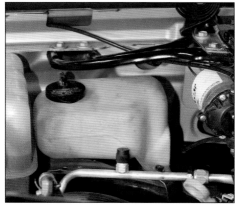

Most Gen IV LS engines use electronically controlled throttles, but they're not all manufactured with the same internal components. A strong throttle spring is necessary to prevent boost creep that affects tuning and could possibly harm the engine. Higher-boost supercharged and turbocharged engines must all have adequate bypass valves and/or blow-off valves or waste gates.

A homemade methanol injection system is relatively easy to build. A salvage-yard windshield-washer reservoir makes a perfect storage tank for the methanol solution. Filling up with windshield-washer solution is cheaper and easier than tuning the engine to run on high-octane racing gas, too.

Also required for a methanol injection system is a pump to deliver the solution to the intake system. Unfortunately, the pump for the windshield-washer system that pairs with the reservoir isn't strong enough to generate the pressure necessary to provide a finely atomized spray of the alcohol solution in the intake tract. This example is from methanol injection specialist Snow Performance.

Lingenfelter Performance Engineering has a simple module that "tricks" the stability system with a more appropriate torque signal and it works for most—but not all—LS-powered all-wheel-drive vehicles. It's called the Delivered Torque Output Limiter (DTOL) and its PN is L460021105.

Methanol Injection

Pushing the edge of the envelope with boosted performance has inherent risks in engine combinations using stock rotating assemblies, not the least of which is detonation.

Even with the necessary air-to-air or air-to-liquid intercooling systems, the boundaries of sustainable, pump-gas performance can be easily reached with only moderate boost levels. One of the ways some tuners expand the pump-gas safe range is with a methanol injection system.

In a nutshell, an alcohol-based solution—usually a 50/50 mix of methanol and water or even blue windshield-washer solution—is injected with the regular fuel supply and delivers a pair of significant advantages: lower inlet temperatures and a greater effective octane rating. Essentially, methanol injection acts

as a secondary intercooler. Injection of the solution is done in the intake stream, ahead of the throttle body, much like the nozzle does for a dry nitrous system.

Of course, a methanol-injection system must be accounted for in the tuning, but the lower inlet temperature and higher octane rating enable more aggressive programming. Snow Performance is the aftermarket industry authority on methanol-injection systems. It offers installation kits, as well as a pre-mixed methanol solution.

The user must closely gauge the range of the alcohol solution to ensure it matches the gas tank. In other words, if the methanol tank runs dry before the gas tank, a larger methanol tank is needed. In very general terms, a gallon of methanol/water solution should last roughly the range of an average fuel tank. Of course, larger vehicles, such as the G8/Commodore and trucks have larger gas tanks.

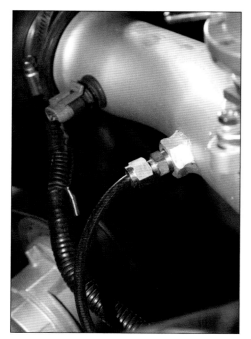

The impressive Martin SS 427 Camaro, with 727 hp and 700 ft-lbs of torque, gets its ample power from a 7.0-liter engine based on the car's original 6.2-liter LS3.

The intake tract is drilled to accept a nozzle for the methanol injection system, just as it would be for a bolt-on nitrous system. Fortunately, no fuel-system modifications are required for methanol injection, but tuning is necessary to optimize its advantages.

The Martin SS 427 Package

It delivers more than 725 supercharged horsepower from 427 ci and does so with the docile driving manners of a family sedan. That's the Martin SS 427—a package for the fifth-generation Camaro from longtime Pro Mod drag racer and racing-shop proprietor Harold Martin.

More than a bolt-on blower kit, the SS 427 package is based on a larger-displacement version of the standard LS3 engine, which grows from 376 to 427 ci through greater bore-and-stroke dimensions. Along with that is a set of modified LS3 cylinder heads and a ProCharger D-1SC centrifugal supercharger and intercooler system that generates

A ProCharger D-1SC blower and intercooler are used on the Martin SS 427, generating about 11 pounds of boost at the throttle body. A smaller pulley is used on the blower to generate more boost for the larger-displacement engine. The factory E38 controller is used with this engine combination and enables excellent drivability.

around 11 pounds of boost. Martin's claimed rating for the engine is 727 hp and 700 ft-lbs of torque.

Importantly, the completely modified engine uses the stock E38 controller that was carefully tuned for the combination. The engine starts, idles, and pulls through the rev range without stalling, hiccupping, stumbling, or any other tuning issues. It's a daily-drivable, 727-hp street car.

BUILDING AN *LS* ENGINE: CYLINDER BLOCK AND ROTATING ASSEMBLY

Builders seeking performance beyond the realm of bolt-on supercharger and turbocharger kits—exceeding about 10 pounds of boost, or so—likely need to consider the construction of a custom engine assembly designed specifically for forced induction. In the simplest terms, that means replacing the factory cast rotating parts with premium, forged components; ensuring greater head-clamping power and optimizing the compression ratio.

Even vehicles with bolt-on forced-induction systems benefit from a purpose-built engine that supports the power adder, as the engine will likely offer greater durability, resistance to detonation, and more overall power. Although any engine buildup is not regarded as inexpensive by most builders or enthusiasts, there are methods to simplify the process and keep the overall cost to a minimum.

The seemingly easiest and least-expensive option is simply upgrading the vehicle's existing engine with a forged rotating assembly and boost-compatible, lower-compression pistons. Of course, choosing this option or a more extensive engine buildup

requires the removal and disassembly of the original engine. In other words, with the heavy lifting required to remove the engine, making the investment in the engine is better justified in the long run.

It's important to keep in mind that while GM's LS engines are commendably robust, durable, and reliable, only the recent LS9 and LSA versions were designed explicitly for supercharging—and all of the engines were tested and validated to perform within carefully engineered parameters. That means, for example, the rods and pistons of the LS7 engine are designed to deliver the 505 rated horsepower within the stated RPM range with a small percentage buffer, but strong as that engine may be, its components were not validated for forced induction.

Building in strength and durability is paramount in the engine's overall success and longevity. The tremendous power gain delivered by the supercharger or turbocharger lessens the effective differences that lower-mass (lighter) components offer on a naturally aspirated engine. That means the instinct to use, for

example, lighter-weight pistons to maximize performance isn't necessarily the correct one, as a heavier forged-alloy piston may slightly increase friction, but ultimately prove stronger under maximum boost. And at, say, 20 pounds of boost, the marginal weight difference won't be noticed. In other words, using the strongest rotating parts in addition to a strong cylinder block and premium fasteners is worth the few RPM they may sacrifice in the long run in order to ensure optimal cylinder pressure.

Cylinder Block

Unless you are planning to use the original engine from your vehicle as the starting point, there is almost an unlimited number of options when it comes to selecting an appropriate cylinder block to use as the new engine's foundation.

Production automotive (and some truck) LS engine blocks are aluminum and reasonably robust for moderate boost pressure. If your plans for the engine exceed the roughly 800-hp range, a high-performance cylinder

The GM Performance Parts LSX cylinder block was designed with forced induction in mind. Its cast-iron construction is not only strong, but makes it very economical; less than $2,000 from most retailers. It is offered in two deck heights: standard (PN 19166454) and tall-deck (PN 19166097). Tall-deck versions (delivered with a 9.700-inch semi-finished deck) require spacers for intake manifolds, because the heads are moved farther apart than with the standard, 9.240-inch deck height.

Most significantly, the LSX block includes two additional head-bolt locations per cylinder (for a total of six) that greatly enhance clamping strength to prevent head-gasket blowouts under high boost. Street/strip engines with up to about 15 to 19 pounds of boost will likely survive with conventional, four-bolt blocks, but if the engine is projected to use 20 pounds (or more) of boost, a six-bolt block is highly recommended. A second-generation LSX block was introduced in 2009 that offered several design and machining improvements, but retains the original PN. A first-generation block is shown here.

block is recommended. Although the strength of the block is crucial, the more important factor is the capacity for greater cylinder head clamping through the use of six head bolts per cylinder. Production blocks (including the supercharged LS9) use only four bolts per cylinder; although the LS9 uses larger, 11-mm head bolts versus other LS engines' 10-mm head bolts.

There are high-performance LS blocks on the market, including the following.

GM Performance Parts LSX Block

Introduced in 2007, the LSX block is designed to support extreme high-performance combinations, especially high-boost engines. GM Performance Parts claims the block can support turbocharged engines mak-

ing more than 2,000 hp and more than 20 pounds of boost. This is due largely to the provision for six bolts per cylinder.

The LSX block has a siamese-bore design, with 3.99-inch bores that must be finished to 4.00 inches—with a 4.25-inch recommended maximum bore. The maximum stroke can reach 4.25 inches, but rotating-assembly interference on the cylinder must be taken into account for strokes greater than 4.125 inches. It is offered in a production-style standard deck height (delivered .020-inch taller for machining purposes); and a tall-deck version with a 9.70-inch height.

In the LSX block's favor is its sturdy design, machining flexibility, six-bolt head-clamping strength, the availability of high-flow heads, and a very low retail price. Working against

Another advantage of the LSX block's iron makeup is its capacity for machining. Its thick, siamese-type cylinders can be bored to 4.250 inches while retaining a minimum of .200-inch wall thickness. And, with machining, the standard-deck version can accept a 4.250-inch stroke, while the tall-deck version can take a 4.500-inch stroke. Proper machining, including the use of a deck plate as seen here, delivers a more accurate finished product that ensures greater cylinder sealing.

the LSX is the extra weight of an iron casting versus a production aluminum block.

GM Performance Parts C5R Race Block

When the only other choices for engine builders were production blocks, many turned to the unique C5R racing block that GM developed for its factory-backed Corvette racing team. It afforded a 427-ci displacement, and the block was considerably stronger than production blocks.

Although it makes a great foundation for moderately powered engines, it's not optimal for higher-boost combinations. That's because the C5R block was designed to support 500 to 600 naturally aspirated horsepower. Most notably, it does not offer six-bolts-per-cylinder clamping. It is also expensive, although prices have come down in recent years.

The C5R is a wonderful piece of engine exotica, but the other cylinder blocks described in this section are better suited to supercharged and turbocharged applications.

Racing Head Service LS Race Block

New in 2009, the LS Race Block from Racing Head Service (RHS) is targeted at maximum-performance combinations, including forced induction. Like the LSX block, it features six-bolt head clamping, including a thick .750-inch deck. In fact, the head-bolt pattern is the same as on the GM Performance Parts LSX block, allowing great interchangeability with cylinder heads. Anything that fits the GM block fits the RHS Race Block. However, the LS Race Block is a lightweight, all-aluminum casting.

The block features a siamesebore design, but with pressed-in,

The GM Performance Parts C5R cylinder block (PN 12480030) is very stiff and its specially machined, 356-T6M-alloy aluminum casting is X-rayed and "hipped,"which is a reference to the hot isostatic pressure process that pressurizes, heats, and cools the casting to virtually eliminate any chance for porosity. It is a time-consuming procedure that contributes to the block's nearly $6,000 list price. But for all its strength, the C5R was designed for about 750 to 900 naturally aspirated horsepower and, thus, does not include six-bolt head clamping as does the LSX block.

The C5R block was introduced prior to the LS7 engine, making it the only alternative for a larger-displacement, aluminum-block LS engine. But, availability of the LS7 block (PN 19213580) makes it a more economical choice for a lower-boost engine that doesn't necessarily require six-bolt head clamping. It is typically offered at less than half the price of the C5R block.

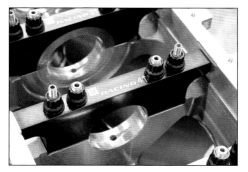

Although the relatively economical LS7 cylinder block is robust enough for low- and mild-boost engines, there are definite product advantages to the more expensive C5R. The main bearing caps are a great example. On the left is the C5R and its racing-bred billet steel main caps and premium ARP studs and fasteners. On the right is the production-based LS7 block's main caps and fasteners; they're still strong pieces, but there's a definite edge with the more expensive C5R.

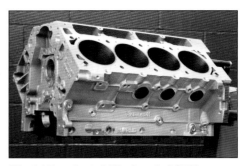

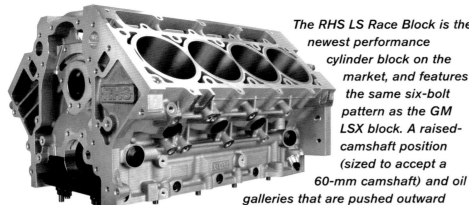

The RHS LS Race Block is the newest performance cylinder block on the market, and features the same six-bolt pattern as the GM LSX block. A raised-camshaft position (sized to accept a 60-mm camshaft) and oil galleries that are pushed outward enable a generous 4.600-inch stroke without rod-to-block interference. Various bore sizes are available, with the largest being 4.165 inch. Coupled with the maximum stroke, this aluminum, six-bolt block can offer more than 500 ci.

World Products' Warhawk LS7X cylinder block is offered in four-bolt and six-bolt configurations, with the six-bolt versions (standard-deck 9.240 inches and tall-deck 9.800 inches) being the logical choice for forced induction. GM cylinder heads bolt right up to the standard four-bolt locations, but the six-bolt configuration is exclusive to World Products. This means using the World's own six-bolt LS cylinder heads, which use 7/16-inch studs in all positions. The iron cylinder liners can be machined to 4.155 inches that, with the tall-deck block's 4.500-inch stroke capability, enables a 488-ci (8.0-liter) displacement. On the bottom side are billet-steel main caps that used ARP 200,000-psi main studs.

spun-cast-iron cylinder liners. It is available with a minimum 4.125-inch-bore diameter and up to 4.165-inch bores. Both production- and tall-deck 9.750-inch versions are available. RHS also touts the LS Race Block as "long-arm friendly," with a raised camshaft centerline and outboard priority main oiling that enables greater rod clearance. A maximum stroke of 4.600 inches is achievable, delivering more than 500 ci with 4.165-inch bores.

Big displacement capability, interchangeability with GM LSX heads, and aluminum construction are the LS Race Block's highlights. A comparatively high price is the only real negative.

World Products Warhawk LS7X Block

Long Island, New York–based World Products was the first to market with a high-performance, six-bolt, aftermarket LS cylinder block—beating even GM Performance Parts' LSX block.

As with RHS' Race Block, World's Warhawk LS7X block is a lightweight aluminum casting. It offers six-bolt head clamping and is available in standard- and tall-deck (9.800-inch) versions. Billet steel main caps are standard and it weighs only about 135 pounds with the main caps installed. Additional details include:

- Range of cylinder bore diameters, from 3.990 inches to 4.115 inches
- Tall-deck version accommodates up to 4.500-inch stroke; standard deck takes up to 4.00-inch stroke, for a maximum displacement of more than 454 ci
- Priority main oiling; the oil circulates to the crankshaft first and the top of the engine is at the end of the oil circuit
- Cast-in provisions for standard small-block Chevy engine mounts, meaning a Warhawk-based engine is more easily installed in an older GM car
- Provisions for an external oil gallery that enables greater displacement capability
- O-ring seals on the cylinder liners that prevent hot oil from squeezing between the block and liners, and heating the cylinders

This is what the World Products Warhawk block looks like with the deck sliced off for an inside inspection. Note the cylinders and head-bolt holes are completely surrounded by a very generous water jacket, yet there is very thick material surrounding the cylinders. The extra-thick material adds strength to the cylinder areas, while also serving as a better insulator as the block warms and cools.

The biggest detractor of the Warhawk block is that its six-bolt head pattern is unique. It is not the same as on the GM LSX or the RHS LS Race Block, meaning the only six-bolt cylinder head options come from World Products. That's not necessarily a bad thing, as World's heads offer tremendous flow attributes, but they're the only six-bolt choices for the block.

Katech Re-Sleeved LS2 Cylinder Block

Katech Performance offers a modified version of the GM LS2 (6.0-liter) aluminum cylinder block. The company removes the stock, 4.000-inch iron cylinder liners and replaces them with larger, 4.125-inch-diameter bores that are also machined at the bottom to accept a 4.000-inch-stroke crankshaft. This enables a final displacement of just about 428 ci, or 7.0 liters. The bores can be honed out to 4.130 inches, too, for a 429-ci maximum displacement.

Katech offers the enlarged cylinder block with standard or billet steel main bearing caps. And while the larger displacement of the lightweight aluminum block is desirable, it retains the four-bolts-per-cylinder head-clamping pattern. That means an engine built with this block should be aimed at 1,000 hp or less and/or limited to less than 20 pounds of boost (assuming an all-forged rotating assembly).

If building a larger-displacement engine isn't a main priority for your project, all of GM's production-based, four-bolt LS cylinder blocks provide adequate strength for low- and moderate-boost engines.

This is GM's standard 6.0-liter LS2 cylinder block, which is adequate for low-and moderate-boost engines that see primarily street and limited strip duty. Using a production-based, four-bolt block means keeping boost below 20 pounds. Production blocks are very affordable over the counter from GM dealers, and used cores are becoming less expensive as more show up at salvage yards. An even cheaper alternative (if you don't mind the weight penalty) is an iron LS block from a truck, such as the Silverado or Suburban.

Rotating Assembly

A forged crankshaft, forged rods, and forged pistons should be the ingredients that comprise the rotating assembly, but there are other factors to consider.

Crankshaft

Assuming a new engine build uses a forged-steel crankshaft, it's important to understand that not all forged crankshafts are created equally. From the factory, only the LS7, LSA, and LS9 engines include a forged crankshaft; all other LS production crankshafts are cast iron.

It is possible to use the LS9 forged crankshaft in other LS engines and brand-new assemblies, but it has a considerably longer snout to support the dry-sump oiling system's larger, gerotor-type oil pump, as well as a unique flywheel bolt pattern. It is possible to modify the crankshaft to work with other oil pumps and front-engine accessory drive systems, but it is easier and less expensive to spec a forged crankshaft from one of the well-known performance crankshaft manufacturers, such as Callies or Eagle.

But even under the banner of "forged steel," there are different levels of forgings, based on the materials incorporated with the steel to enhance hardness and durability. The most common forgings used in performance engines are 4130 and 4340. Here's what those numbers mean:

- The "4" refers to a steel alloy that is mixed with molybdenum for greater overall strength—the more "moly," the tougher the crankshaft.
- The "1" and "3" numbers refer to other materials mixed in the

alloy; the "1" indicates a steel alloy with chromium added, while the "3" in 4340 indicates nickel and chromium are part of the steel alloy, for even greater strength.

- The "30" and "40" numbers refer to the percentage of carbon added to enhance hardness; "30" refers to approximately 30-percent content and "40" indicates an approximate 40-percent content.

While both 4130 and 4340 forged-steel crankshafts are superior to standard cast-iron crankshafts, the 4340 forging is stronger than the 4130 because of its nickel content and higher percentage of carbon. Of course, that greater strength comes with a higher purchase price, but for racing applications it's worth the investment. A street/strip engine does just fine with a properly prepared 4130 crankshaft.

Proper heat-treating can significantly strengthen the crankshaft, while crankshafts used in engines designed primarily for racing should also be shot-peened for maximum strength. Some builders also have the stress risers on the rod throws removed to improve performance and longevity.

To optimize lubrication, the engine may benefit from slots machined in the crankshaft journals that direct oil at higher RPM. Some racing-engine builders also use full-groove bearings to ensure maximum oiling for the rods. Avoid cross-drilling the crankshaft, however. While it was a common procedure years ago, most professional builders no longer believe it is effective. In fact, it may do more harm than good in the long run.

A forged-steel crankshaft is a must for forced-induction engines in order to build strength into the engine assembly. They're capable of supporting tremendous power levels of up to 1,500 hp or more. Billet-steel crankshafts are also available at a greater cost, but there is conflicting opinions on whether they deliver greater strength than a forged-steel crank made of the same material. As the name implies, billet-steel cranks are cut from a single piece of stock, while a forged crank is "pounded" into shape.

A 4340-alloy steel forging is the strongest available for crankshafts, while traditional heat-treating methods such as nitriding and induction hardening can enhance strength. With nitriding, the crankshaft is placed in an oven and ionized nitrogen is vacuum deposited on its surfaces; a process that can double the surface hardness. Induction hardening, where the sections of the crankshaft are subjected to a magnetic field for intense heating and cooling, can produce a harder surface, but only where the process was applied. Nitriding treats the entire crankshaft at once. Another common "trick" is knife-edging the crank's counterweights to reduce windage, but that has generally proven to be counter-effective to performance. The most efficient design is a rounded edge, as seen on the crankshaft being installed in this LSX block.

The crankshafts of production LS engines have a press-fit damper, and the only one with a crankshaft keyway to prevent slippage is the forged crank of the LS9. When building an engine for supercharged or turbocharged performance, a keyway is a must and you should spend the time and few extra dollars to have one machined into the nose of the crankshaft. Shown here is a "budget" supercharged engine build using a LS3's cast crankshaft with a keyway cut into it.

When it comes to installing the crankshaft and main bearing caps, the cap fasteners should be the best you can afford. Rather than using the production-style combination of studs and bolts, all of the main caps should be secured with studs and nuts for more accurate fastening and repeatable removal and installation on an engine that will see moderate to frequent teardowns. ARP's 200,000-psi studs and 12-point bolts (seen here) are the best on the market and should be highly considered.

This is Thomson Automotive's LS main bearing removal tool, and it's pretty cool. The tight tolerance of the main bearing caps fitted to the long-skirt LS-style cylinder block makes their removal difficult and time consuming. Thomson Automotive has come up with a simple, yet ingenious solution: a tool that hooks beneath the caps and uses the leverage of a pair of aluminum handles to yank the caps quickly and smoothly out of the block. Anyone who has struggled with removing LS main caps will appreciate this simple, but very useful tool.

Most of the fasteners on the LS engine feature torque-to-yield specifications. This means rather than a conventional foot-pound or inch-pound torque rating, the fasteners are final-tightened to a specific torque angle, such as 40 degrees or 60 degrees. So, a standard torque wrench is not enough and you will need to complement it with a torque angle wrench or a modern combination torque wrench (seen here) that includes pound readouts (and Newton meters) as well as angle degrees.

Reluctor Wheel

The crank-triggered ignition system of the LS engine requires a "reluctor" wheel (also known as a "tone" wheel) mounted on the crankshaft. It's a toothed wheel that helps determine crankshaft position to ensure spark-timing accuracy. Early LS production engines came with a 24X (24 tooth), while later engines—including all those equipped with electronic throttle control—used a 58X (58-tooth) wheel.

Generally speaking, either wheel can be used on a custom engine build, but selection depends primarily on the engine controller to be used. The more common, later-style GM E38 and E67 controllers support the 58X wheel and electronic throttle control, while earlier LS1A and LS1B controllers support the 24X wheel. The 58X wheel can be used with earlier LS engines and later controllers, but revisions to the camshaft-position sensor requires an LS2/LS3 front cover on LS1/LS6 and some truck engines.

For example, a 24X wheel should be used if you plan to retain the original engine controller on an engine built for a 2002 Trans Am that was originally equipped with the LS1 engine. If, however, you plan to install an LS7 engine and supercharger, the LS7's 58X wheel must be changed to a 24X wheel if the stock LS1 controller is to be used. Additionally, Lingenfelter Performance Engineering offers a conversion module that allows the 58X wheel to be used with earlier controllers, without the need for sensor or other wiring changes.

Aftermarket, standalone control systems, such as those from F.A.S.T. and ACCEL-DFI, are compatible with either the 24X or 58X wheel.

Pistons

The two most important factors for pistons in a forced-induction engine are cylinder pressure and strength. Simply stated, the cast-aluminum pistons of most production LS engines (only the supercharged LS9 comes with forged pistons) are adequate for low-boost, bolt-on power adders, but builders seeking higher power need stronger, forged-aluminum pistons that deliver a lower static compression ratio.

At a glance, here's how to tell the different GM reluctor wheels apart. The 24X wheel (left) is found on LS1, LS6, and other engines through about 2007, while the 58X wheel (right) is used on later engines, although there is some model-year overlap between the reluctor wheel types on LS2 engines. The 2005 Corvette and most 2005 Pontiac GTOs use the LS2 with a 24X wheel. Generally speaking, the 58X wheel is used with Gen IV LS engines that moved the camshaft position sensor from the top rear of the engine block to the front of the engine, near the timing gear. In a custom project that will use a standalone control system, there's not a significant reason to use one type of wheel over the other, but when building an engine for a primarily street-driven vehicle that was originally equipped with an LS engine and retains the original controller, it is best to use the original reluctor wheel design to ensure controller compatibility.

Although commendably light-weight and durable in naturally aspirated applications, the factory cast pistons' high silicon content makes it rather brittle when compared with a forged-aluminum piston. That brittleness doesn't stand up well to the excessive pressure generated by the blower or turbo; and it is especially susceptible to damage if detonation occurs.

Forged pistons are manufactured through a process that forms the part by essentially pounding it into shape rather than the poured metal of a cast piston. They are still comprised of alloys, but the manufacturing process brings greater material density and eliminates the chance for porosity, which greatly enhances strength. They're also more ductile—the opposite of a casting's brittleness—and they typically resist heat better than cast pistons. The best forged-aluminum pistons suitable for boost have less than 1-percent silicon con-

tent. (Production pistons are referred to as hypereutectic because of silicon content greater than 12 percent.)

Generally, there are two grades of high-performance forged-aluminum pistons: 4032 and 2618. The 4032 forgings (which contain a small amount of silicon) are less expensive, but not as strong as silicon-free 2618-forged pistons. If there's a trade-off with forged pistons, particularly 2618 forgings, it is increased cold-start engine noise due to thermal expansion. The silicon in hypereutectic pistons minimizes the piston's expansion when the engine warms up, allowing for a much tighter piston-to-cylinder-wall tolerance, but the low silicon content of forged pistons means they "grow" more in the cylinder bore. Consequently, forged pistons need greater piston-to-wall clearance, with 2618 pistons needing the most.

In general, a 4032-forged piston needs approximately .0025- to .0035-

Lingenfelter's TRG-001 conversion module is designed to enable later LS engines with the 58X reluctor wheel be used in vehicles with the earlier, 24X-based control systems without sensor or wiring changes. It plugs into the wiring harness and original sensors, although some early Gen IV engines may need a jumper harness to extend the camshaft position sensor wiring.

inch piston-to-wall clearance, while 2618 pistons need about .0035- to .0045-inch clearance. That extra clearance means forged pistons typically generate an unsettling knocking noise known as piston slap when the engine is cold. The noise goes away as the cylinders and pistons heat up, causing the pistons to grow and fill up the space. (If the noise doesn't abate after the engine warms up, it may indicate an incorrect engine assembly or other, more serious engine problems.)

Other attributes that contribute to a stronger "blower piston" include reinforced pin bosses (the areas on either side of the piston skirt where the pin slides in) and a thick piston crown. That's the area between the top ring and the top of the piston. A thicker crown better withstands the punishment of detonation, as well as the generally hotter temperature and cylinder pressure that come with a highly boosted engine.

Besides selecting a forged-aluminum design, the pistons for a supercharged or turbocharged engine should be targeted to deliver a compression ratio between 8.5:1 and 9.5:1. This typically means using a D-shaped head with a dish (also known as an inverted dome) or strictly a dished piston and matching it carefully with the projected combustion chamber volume. Most LS production engines came from the factory with relatively high compression ratios, including greater than 10.25:1 (the LS7 engine has 11.0:1 compression). That's too much compression for a forced-induction engine, making it difficult to prevent detonation.

One more thing: Along with strong, forged pistons, you should also employ heavy-duty piston wrist pins, even at the expense of adding weight to the assembly. As mentioned earlier, the overall weight of a forced-induction engine or its rotating assembly should be secondary to ensuring it is robust enough to withstand the pressure generated by the turbocharger or supercharger. To that end, heavier-yet-stronger wrist pins

Here is a common, forged-aluminum piston design for LS engines. The flat-top design, however, is not conducive to optimal forced-induction performance, as it would likely deliver too high of a compression ratio. Excessive compression can lead to engine-damaging detonation under boost.

Here's a look at the production, forged-aluminum LS9 piston. Note that it is dished to minimize compression ratio, but that there is also a slight dome within the dish. It helps reflect the incoming air/fuel charge back toward the spark plug for greater combustion efficiency. It also has a unique ring pack that uses relatively thick top and secondary rings and a very thin, minimal bottom oil-control ring. The specialized machining process of the block enables tighter tolerances that, in turn, allows for the thinner, lower-friction oil-control ring. Also note the friction-reducing Teflon coating on the skirt. In short, the LS9 piston is all about low friction and high rpm. It would make a good choice for low- to moderate-boost engines projected to make about 750 to 800 hp. (Photo courtesy General Motors)

A better piston selection for a supercharged or turbocharged street/strip LS engine is seen here in the "D"-shaped dish that provides a large, relatively efficient quench area. Quench is described as the squishing effect on the air charge as the piston reaches top dead center. The shape of the piston's dish helps squeeze air through the combustion chamber in a manner that generally helps even out the temperature throughout the chamber and reduces the chance for detonation. The depth of the dish affects the compression ratio.

The side profile of a piston shows the crown height (defined as the space between the top ring land and the top of the piston). The minimum crown height for a forced-induction LS engine should be .200 inch; .300 inch is optimal. Production LS pistons don't have such a thick crown, which (in addition to their cast construction) is why they're not great in high-boost supercharged or turbocharged applications.

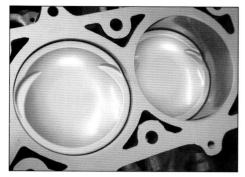

Ceramic-coated pistons can minimize both heat absorption and friction, but the builder must be extremely careful to ensure the coating is applied by a knowledgeable, experienced vendor or by the manufacturer itself. Poorly applied coating material or an incorrectly prepped piston can result in the very hard coating flaking or peeling off in the cylinder. This can cause catastrophic damage, as the coating will typically score, scratch, or gouge the cylinder walls—effectively ruining the cylinder block. This risk is typically not worth it on street/strip engines producing less than 1,000 hp and/or less than 15 or so pounds of boost. Use coated pistons on high-power racing engines where engine temperature will be greater.

Coated-steel piston rings or nitrided-steel wire rings are the strongest and most resistant to the heat that comes with forced induction (with temperatures that can exceed 600 degrees F). Because blow-by is a greater concern with turbo-charging and supercharging, a tight ring end gap is necessary, but like other engine components, piston rings grow as the engine heats. That means the end gap is wider when the engine is cold and becomes narrower as the engine warms. Too tight of an end gap when the engine is cold can force the ring ends together with excessive pressure when the boosted engine generates greater heat, leading to failure. A general rule of thumb for forced-induction engines is a top ring gap of .006 inch for every inch of bore diameter. That means a 4.125-inch bore should have a top ring end gap of .025 inch. Consult the ring manufacturer in order to select the best parts, specifying the engine's intended duty, operating range, and approximate power and boost levels.

that are either larger in diameter, or have a thicker wall than those typically used in a naturally aspirated engine, should be considered.

Piston manufacturers such as JE Pistons and Diamond offer a variety of forged applications for LS engines and have excellent technical advisors to guide the builder into selecting the most appropriate parts.

Ceramic-Coated Pistons

On engines designed for higher boost and higher power levels, the use of ceramic-coated pistons is an effective way to combat excessive cylinder and combustion heat, while also reducing friction. Most piston manufacturers and companies with bearings for high-performance and racing engines offer parts with ceramic coatings. The coatings are generally based on Swain Tech products.

On a piston, a coating on top reduces the heat absorbed by the piston, helping prevent burning or other damage under high-boost and leaner-fuel conditions. A coating on the skirts of the piston reduces heat-building friction and the same goes for coated main bearings. These coated parts come at a premium cost over non-coated components, but the hedge against the damage caused by excessive heat makes them wise investments.

Some builders use coated main bearings, too, but this is more of a preventative measure against the possibility of oil starvation, rather than a performance enhancement.

Piston Ring and Ring Pack

Piston rings service the vital job of sealing the cylinders to prevent combustion gases from entering the crankcase, while also controlling oil on the cylinder walls and stabilizing the pistons within the bores. Under the high pressure of supercharger or turbocharger boost, those jobs are all the more important, as maintaining cylinder pressure is essential to performance.

Piston manufacturers that offer "blower" pistons for forced-induction engines generally optimize the ring-pack location to provide a generous crown for greater overall strength. But LS pistons nevertheless have a ring pack that is located closer to the crown than, say, old-school small-block engines. The rings are typically thinner than previous-generation engines, but bring increased stability with reduced friction.

With the higher ring pack and pressure from forced induction, LS piston rings are subjected to significant heat. For the most part, that means using the strongest, most heat resistant rings you can afford. That typically means the top ring is moly-coated or similar. Ductile iron has long been the mainstay of rings, but steel is used increasingly for its strength and durability.

Generally speaking, when it comes to ring end gaps, the tighter the gap, the better, as this generally maintains cylinder pressure and resists blow-by longer. Total Seal offers unique, two-piece gapless top and second rings that offer greater resistance to blow-by by preventing a conventional gap from opening between the ring ends.

While production engines' ring sizes vary, most aftermarket LS pistons are manufactured to support 1.5-/1.5-/3.0-mm rings. Thinner rings can be used to reduce friction, but they are made from specialized material that makes them very expensive. They should only be used in a racing engine that will see repeated disassembly, as thinner rings wear out sooner and require more frequent replacement. Stick with thicker rings for street and street/strip combinations.

One more thing about piston rings: You should make sure they're available for your desired bore size before ordering the pistons or having the cylinder block machined. Assembly plans go right off the tracks when the pistons arrive and there are no rings to fit them.

Gas Porting

The trick to gas porting involves drilling holes strategically in the piston to force the compression ring against the cylinder wall. The idea behind it is that this pressurized ring seal prevents the ring from fluttering at higher RPM, while extending the power curve.

Two types of gas porting are typically used: vertical and horizontal. Vertical gas ports are drilled from the piston deck into the top ring groove and behind the ring. This method is employed more by drag racers. Horizontal gas porting involves drilling holes through the bottom side of the top ring land, extending to the back wall of the ring groove. It is used more in circle track/road racing.

Generally, gas porting is best left to dedicated racing applications, where sustained performance at high RPM delivers the greatest benefit. Also, carbon builds up in the ports, so an engine that does primarily street duty (and does not get regular, between-race teardowns) quickly loses the advantage of gas porting when the ports clog. The pressure on the rings also significantly reduces the ring's lifespan—another reason to avoid gas porting for street engines.

Connecting Rods

The higher the expected horsepower, the stronger and beefier the connecting rods need to be. Rod failures typically arise from high RPM strain and/or exhaust-stroke pressure. In general, greater horsepower increases the compressive force on the rods, while greater RPM increases tensile strain. These attributes are amplified considerably with forced induction.

Most LS production engines use powdered-metal rods that, like their corresponding cast-aluminum pistons, are surprisingly robust in an unmodified engine. As mentioned earlier, factory engine components are designed to operate in a performance window within a few percent of the advertised horsepower and torque ratings. Consistently pushing beyond that range puts a strain on the internal components they weren't designed for.

To withstand the strain under boost, high-performance connecting rods need to deliver greater compression strength and tensile strength. The typical upgrade is to a forged-steel material, such as 4340 steel or 300M. Beyond the greater strength that comes with the denser material, these performance rods are typically thicker in key areas to enhance strength, too.

In most cases, builders choose between I-beam-style and H-beam-style connecting rods. Each is known for delivering strength, but each delivers it slightly differently. The I-beam looks more like a conventional connecting rod, but is very thick through the middle, allowing it

Here's an example of a gas-ported piston intended for drag racing, you can tell it by the the holes drilled through the piston head. Because those tiny holes can get clogged with carbon over even a relatively short period of operating time, gas porting is not an effective idea for street engines. The pressure created on the cylinder rings also wears them out much faster, requiring frequent replacement.

Typical example of I-beam (left) and H-beam (right) are shown here. In terms of strength, they are comparable when made of the same material, offering similar compression strength. The differences, then, are more subtle, and selecting one design over the other comes down to other engine assembly factors. Typically, an H-beam rod is lighter than an I-beam, but its big end is generally larger, too, which can mean a greater chance for cylinder block interference on a long-stroke combination. If block interference is not a concern, the extra rev capability enabled by lighter H-beam rods is preferred to offset the other higher-mass, heavy-duty rotating parts. Also, most professional builders insist on using a solid bushing on the small end, rather than the more common and cheaper split bushing.

to handle great compressive loads. H-beam rods have a thin center section, but wide, flat outer sides that provide tremendous stiffness and resistance to bending.

Assuming all other attributes are equal, the I-beam and H-beam offer comparable compressive strength, but the thinner center portion of the H-beam typically makes it lower in mass than an I-beam. The lighter H-beam design can make more of a difference with primarily street-driven vehicles, where more low-end power is desired.

Problems with performance rods can arise, however, with internal clearance within the cylinder block. Thick, racing-type I-beam rods on larger-stroke combinations (generally, engines greater than 427 ci) can interfere with the bottoms of the cylinders and other walls inside the block. Extreme care must be taken to gently rotate the rod/piston assembly to check for clearance problems. Notching the bottoms of the cylinders, making clearance for other areas within the block, and even

machining the small and/or big ends of the rods may be required.

Performance connecting rods and rods used with stroker crankshafts may also cause interference issues with the windage tray. After the rotating assembly moves freely within the block, the windage tray should be installed and the engine carefully and slowly rotated to check for clearance problems. If any of the rods hit the windage tray, washers can be used as shims on the bolt studs. Two or three washers per stud are generally all that's required to ensure adequate clearance.

4340 vs. 300M and Forged vs. Billet—and Aluminum

The common steel connecting rod forging is made from 4340 steel, which contains up to 2-percent nickel, along with smaller percentages of chromium, silicon, molybdenum, and manganese. It is an extremely durable material for connecting rods, but 300M alloy is gaining favor with many builders. It

contains more silicon (approximately 1.5 percent) along with more moly and carbon.

Rods made from 300M can be more expensive, but they are generally stronger than a comparably sized 4340 rod, which enables the manufacturer to downsize the center section by up to 20 percent and still offer the strength of 4340 steel. In a supercharged/turbocharged engine that is already using a number of higher-mass components to reinforce overall strength, the investment in 300M rods can offset a significant source of rotating mass.

Another choice is to choose billet-steel over forged-steel connecting rods. As the name implies, billet rods are cut from a single piece of steel on a CNC machine. This is generally used for custom applications where a manufacturer may only make a few sets of a particular design that wouldn't be cost effective to set up in a conventional forging operation.

A billet-steel rod *can* be stronger than a forged-steel rod, but only if the steel used is of higher quality than the 4340 or 300M recipes. Because the material does not have to be as malleable as the steel used in forging, it enables the manufacturer to use very strong steel.

As for forged-aluminum connecting rods, they offer very good strength and the obvious benefit of low mass—an attribute that helps offset the weight of heavy-duty piston and wrist pins. But aluminum rods have only about half the tensile strength of a steel rod and are much more susceptible to stretching and fatigue, so they are typically quite "chunky" in size in order to maintain their shape longer. This can cause cylinder-bore interference problems, requiring machining that could ultimately reduce overall strength. Aluminum rods are also considerably more expensive than forged-steel rods.

Aluminum rods are not recommended for street and street/strip engines. They are suitable for racing engines that will see frequent inspections and teardowns.

LS7/LS9 Titanium Connecting Rods

The titanium connecting rods of the LS7 and LS9 engines are strong and lightweight, enabling very quick RPM buildup, but not necessarily the best option when building a boost-ready engine. That's because the rods are designed for the operating parameters of their respective factory engines.

Because the rods are validated to the strength requirements for their respective engines, higher boost and higher horsepower strain their compression-strength resistance. That's not to say these rods are weak by any measure, but they're simply not designed for use

This is a typical forged-aluminum connecting rod and at a glance it's easy to see it is physically larger than a comparable forged-steel rod. Aluminum rods tend to stretch the most during the cold-start period and during the compressive loads of varied RPM, which makes them particularly unsuitable for sustained use in a street vehicle. By some estimates, the lifespan of an aluminum rod is only 1/10 that of a forged-steel rod. They work best in a drag-racing engine where the engine is quickly brought up to high RPM and more or less left there during the run. There is an unquestionable impact on RPM capability with aluminum rods, but their fatigue rate makes them best left to racing-only combinations.

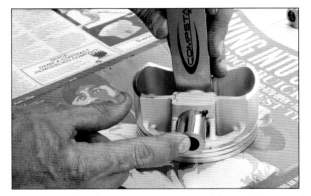

Note the extra-thick wrist pin being inserted into this piston/rod combination. In high-performance, forced-induction engines, the wrist pin absorbs tremendous bending and radial pressure, so to shore up rotating assembly it should be large, robust, and made of a strong material, such as a 4130 forging for a street engine. For racing engines, perhaps the ultimate wrist pin is offered by Bill Miller Engineering in the form of its 9310 VAR (vacuum-arc-re-melt) steel pins.

A common issue with long-stroke engines and/or those using aluminum or even some forged H-beam-style rods is cylinder-block interference. The rotating assembly should be slowly and carefully turned after installation to check for potential interference, as seen here. This LSX-based engine will require additional machining to clear bulky forged-aluminum rods.

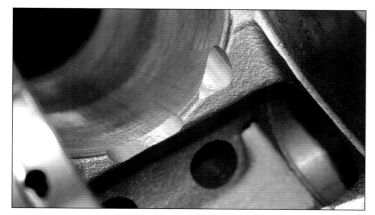

Looking upward at the bottom of the cylinder, here's the machined block, showing the notched areas required for connecting-rod clearance. Although time consuming, as it must be accomplished on all of the cylinders, it is a relatively easy procedure to perform on an iron cylinder block. More care is required when dealing with the iron liners in an aluminum block. In fact, the machining requirements simply may not be possible on some aluminum blocks, forcing the use of different, lower-profile rods, a shorter-stroke length, or both.

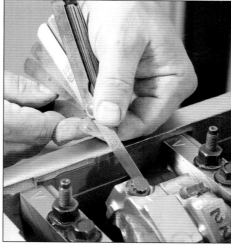

Beefier connecting rods can squeeze the tolerance of the rod ends on the crankshaft journal. The rod side clearance should be between .00433 and .0200 inch.

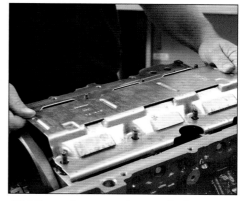

All LS engines employ a windage tray. During assembly, it should be checked for interference with the crankshaft and rods. The process includes bolting down the tray after the rotating assembly has been installed and all the fasteners torqued to specification.

Machining material off aluminum rods is another method of making them fit the tight confines of a big-stroke combination, but doing so can adversely affect strength and lower the lifespan of an already-stretch-prone component that doesn't have the tensile strength of steel.

With the tray in place, slowly rotate the crankshaft and check for rod or crankshaft interference. Even if the assembly turns without hitting the tray, check for a too-close relationship that could lead to interference during engine operation.

in, say, a 700-, 800-, or 1,000-hp forced-induction engine.

Sacrificing low-speed RPM capability for the assurance and longevity of a forged-steel rod is a worthy tradeoff.

Pre-Assembled Short-Block or "Crate Engine" Assembly

Several engine builders offer short-block and crate engine assemblies that are targeted at supercharged applications. Starting an engine with one of these can be a cost-effective and time-saving option, as you receive a pre-assembled portion of the engine with a correctly engineered engine base.

Generally speaking, a short-block assembly includes a cylinder block fitted with a crankshaft, rods, and pistons. Typically, there is no oil pump, oil pan, camshaft, or other components. An assembled long-block or crate engine generally adds cylinder heads, camshaft, oil pump, and perhaps oil pan, with other accessories and the induction system left up to you. More complete crate engines generally include an intake manifold and other accessories, such as a water pump.

A good example of ready-to-go short-block assemblies are Katech Performance's Value 402 (6.6-liter) and Value 427 (7.0-liter) kits. Each is built with a re-sleeved LS2 6.0-liter aluminum cylinder block, a premium 4340-forged-steel crankshaft,

This is an example of GM's factory titanium connecting rods from the LS7 engine. The primary advantage to titanium rods comes in their lower mass (about 20-percent lighter) not superior strength over forged-steel rods. Titanium is very hard, but comparatively brittle when compared with steel, so the part must be designed for the RPM capability of the engine. Also, GM's titanium rods use a split-style small-end bushing that some builders don't like. Some companies, such as Katech Performance, offers the rods with replacement, solid bushings. (Photo courtesy General Motors)

If a windage-tray interference issue is discovered, stacking washers on the main cap studs that also secure the windage tray is the easiest method of curing the problem. Start with a single washer on each stud and re-check the clearance, adding washers until a satisfactory clearance is achieved.

Katech Performance's Value 402 short-block kit is typical of blower-friendly assemblies. It uses all forged rotating parts, along with D-shaped, dished low-compression pistons. The balancing and blueprinting steps performed during assembly make it a very good starting point for a home builder who wants to finish the engine with his heads and induction system. Similar short-blocks are available from World Products, using their Warhawk block, as well as other LS engine builders.

forged-aluminum pistons and forged H-beam connecting rods. The components are also balanced and blueprinted during assembly.

The rough cost of the Katech short-blocks is between $6,000 and $7,000, and while that may seem expensive compared to the budget small-block engines many enthusiasts grew up with, the aluminum block and other high-performance parts for the LS engine simply come at a higher price. Nonetheless, one of these short-block assemblies—or a similar assembly from another engine builder—makes a smart starting point for an engine combination.

GM Performance Parts' Boost-Capable LSX376 Crate Engine

In 2009, GM Performance Parts announced the LSX376 crate engine (PN 19171049). It is designed as a boost-friendly, lower-compression assembly that mixes production and specialty performance parts for a comparatively affordable foundation for a supercharged or turbocharged engine. Indeed, it would be difficult to assemble a comparable long-block for the same money when selecting brand-new parts.

The LSX376 is more of a traditional long-block assembly, as it is delivered without an intake system, oil pan, or other components. The "376" designation in its name refers to the cubic-inch displacement, or 6.2 liters. At its core, the LSX376 uses components designed to withstand greater boost pressure. The cylinder block is the economical and sturdy iron LSX block and it's fitted with forged-aluminum pistons. The crank is cast and the rods are powdered metal. The engine assembly also includes a set of L92-style aluminum cylinder heads and the same roller camshaft used in the LS3 Corvette engine.

The heads use 2.16-inch/1.59-inch valves and feature 68-cc combustion chambers; the valvetrain includes roller-tip rocker arms with a 1.7:1 ratio. The camshaft specifications include .551-inch lift on the intake side and .522-inch lift on the exhaust, with 204/211-degrees duration (intake/exhaust) and a 116-degree lobe-separation angle.

The compression ratio is approximately 9.0:1 (using forged pistons) and the engine includes a 58X crankshaft reluctor wheel.

GM Performance Parts' LSX376 crate engine is more of a long-block assembly, as it does not come with an intake manifold, oil pan, or other accessories. What it offers, however, is a pre-assembled engine with a forged crank, 9.0:1 forged pistons, and high-flow LS3 cylinder heads. Its four-bolt head clamping (on the six-bolt-capable LSX block) and powdered-metal rods aren't ideal for high-boost/high-RPM combinations, but for low- to moderate-boost street/strip engines, it's more than adequate—and a comparative value.

BUILDING AN *LS* ENGINE: HEADS, CAM AND INDUCTION

With a stout short-block filled with an all-forged rotating assembly, the remainder of a boost-ready engine assembly includes the cylinder heads and crucially important camshaft. All LS engines benefit from excellent cylinder-head airflow—some more than others—but it is the camshaft that is the key not only to optimal power but drivability characteristics.

Cylinder Heads

There isn't sufficient room in this chapter to describe all of the cylinder-head choices available to the LS engine builder—and more seem to arrive every month. The use of heads with six bolts per cylinder isn't an absolute requirement on an engine making less than 1,000 hp or less than about 15 pounds of boost, but they should be strongly considered for racing applications generating high boost and high horsepower.

The other crucial detail only applies to the installation of supercharger systems that mount the compressor in place of the intake manifold. For these applications, the

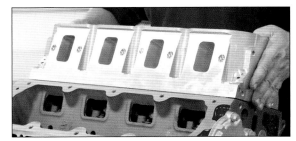

There is an almost endless list of possibilities when it comes to boost-friendly cylinder heads for LS engines. The excellent port design and large-capacity runners allow for easy and efficient cylinder filling. Ensuring intake manifold compatibility with the heads' intake ports is the only major caveat when selecting them for a supercharged or turbocharged combination.

cylinder-head intake ports must be compatible with the intake ports of the supercharger manifold's ports. Mostly, that means the difference between LS1/LS6/LS2-style cathedral-port heads and later-style rectangular-port heads. In fact, even the later heads don't all have matching port shapes—the LS7 head ports have a more square design, while the LS3/L92-style ports are taller and narrower.

Also, because of the comparatively small bores of LS1 and LS6 engines (3.89 inches), when compared with the later 6.0-liter and larger engines, they can only use LS1, LS6, and LS2 heads. Using the heads of 6.2-liter and larger engines causes valve-to-block interference. However, the larger 4.00-inch bore of

the LS2 enables it to use LS1/LS6 heads, as well as L92-style heads (including LS3, LS9, and LSA engines). The 6.2-liter engines (LS3, L92, etc.) can use any head except the LS7 and C5R, while the 7.0-liter LS7 and C5R blocks can use any LS-series head. The C5R head is not recommended, as it is an expensive part with a unique intake port design that requires a custom intake manifold, as well as a small combustion chamber that promotes a high-compression ratio that's incompatible with forced induction. The LS2, LS3/L92, and LS7 heads use production intakes, offer greater port volume and larger combustion chambers that are desirable with forced induction.

In general terms, higher-flow cylinder heads make the same horsepower with lower-boost pressure than a comparable engine combination with lower-flowing heads. Put another way, the boost of the supercharger or turbocharger overcomes the relative inadequacies of "smaller" heads, as the boost pressure fills the ports, and then some. That's not to say the cylinder head isn't important, but for most street/strip applications, the already high-flow characteristics of factory LS heads perform more than adequately with forced induction.

Later-style rectangular-port heads (whether LS7- or LS3/L92-style) are larger and have greater airflow attributes than cathedral-port heads. They are well suited to forced induction, but the ultimate selection may be influenced by bolt-on Roots/Lysholm-type supercharger systems, because not all supercharger intakes are currently compatible with all cylinder-head port designs.

When it comes to combustion-chamber design, the factory configuration is adequate, and conventional porting/blending provides a modest benefit. More crucial, however, is chamber volume, as it contributes to the engine compression ratio. A larger chamber volume lowers the compression ratio, while a smaller volume raises it. A good rule of thumb is somewhere in the 64- to 68-cc range.

Another consideration for engines projected to generate more than 15 pounds of boost is the use of cylinder heads with six head bolts per cylinder, rather than the factory-style four bolts per cylinder. When used with the appropriate cylinder block (see Chapter 8), the additional clamping power—at least 50 percent greater—of the six-bolt heads does much to

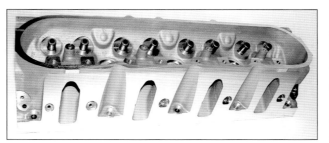

The LS1/LS6/LS2-style cathedral-port cylinder head (seen here) doesn't offer the maximum flow characteristics of later heads that are based on the rectangular port design of the LS7 engine, but they are adept at generating excellent torque. With minor adaptations, later heads can be swapped on LS1/LS6 engines to maximize the airflow offered by the power adder. Also, 6.0-liter engines can use 6.2-liter L92/LS3-style heads to great effect, but again, they must be matched with the correct intake manifold. A 6.0-liter intake, for example, doesn't fit LS3 heads; and the LS7 intake fits only LS7 heads.

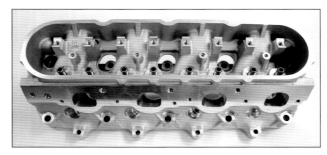

GM Performance Parts offers a range of LSX six-bolt cylinder heads with LS3/L92- and LS7-style rectangular ports, as well as an LSX-DR (drag race) head that offers raised runners, an 11-degree valve angle, and a design the requires shaft-mounted rocker arms. Taking advantage of the six-bolt clamping power, however, requires they be used with LSX or RHS six-bolt cylinder blocks. The standard LSX heads use standard LS intake manifolds, while the LSX-DR requires a unique, carburetor-style manifold (PN 19166954) that can be adapted for use with racing-oriented turbo and centrifugal supercharger systems.

prevent head-gasket failure. GM Performance Parts and Trick Flow offer six-bolt heads that fit the LSX cylinder block, although the Trick Flow heads are only available in LS1/LS6/LS2-style cathedral-port styles. World Products also offers a six-bolt head, but it doesn't match the bolt pattern of the LSX block, meaning it must be used with the company's complementing six-bolt-capable Warhawk cylinder block.

When it comes to other aftermarket cylinder heads, they are of the standard, four-bolt style. There are numerous choices, although most are based on the cathedral-port LS1/LS6/LS2-type head. They make

great, higher-flowing choices for the 5.7- and 6.0-liter engines, but GM's production and performance heads from GM Performance Parts are currently the best options for the larger-displacement engines that use rectangular-port heads.

Here are some of the available aftermarket heads:

- AFR (Air Flow Research) offers "Mongoose" CNC-ported cathedral-port heads in 205-cc (66- or 76-cc chambers) and 225-cc (62-, 65-, or 72-cc chambers) intake runner sizes.
- Edelbrock's cathedral-port heads are CNC-ported by

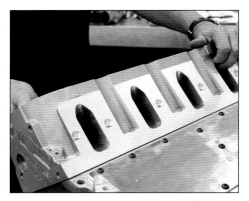

An aftermarket alternative to GM heads is World Products' Warhawk cylinder heads, offered in LS1X and LS7X styles. Each has a six-bolt design that corresponds with World's Warhawk cylinder block, but can be bolted to a GM block using the standard four-bolt pattern. The LS1X features cathedral ports, a 15-degree valve angle, 235-cc intake runners, 2.080/1.600-inch valves, and is available with 64- or 72-cc combustion chambers. The LS7X head has rectangular ports, a 12-degree valve angle, 285-cc runners, 2.250/1.625-inch valves, and 64- or 72-cc chambers. On either head, selecting the smaller chamber volume will promote a higher compression ratio, so it must be matched with an appropriate dished piston design to keep the compression around 9.0:1 and 9.5:1 (or lower).

Perhaps the ultimate in strength and durability for a forced-induction engine is the factory head for the supercharged LS9 engine. Based on the 6.2-liter LS3/L92 head's port and chamber design, it is made of a premium alloy and manufactured with a unique "roto-cast" process that spins the mold as the molten aluminum is poured to provide a more even, denser casting that all but eliminates porosity. They are available over the counter under PN 12621774. The LS9 heads, however, do not have a six-bolt design, but use larger 12-mm head bolts to increase clamping strength (other LS engines use a mix of 11- and 8-mm bolts). Adapting them to other LS engines requires resizing the head-bolt holes in the block to accommodate them. (Photo courtesy General Motors)

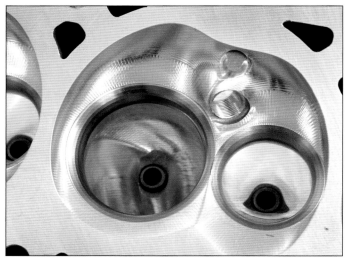

The telltale CNC porting finish on this head reveals a comparatively expensive machining job that won't necessarily pay off with substantially greater performance. The general design of LS heads is very well suited to forced induction, with large intake runners and well-designed combustion chambers. It is true that porting and other machine work can achieve flow characteristics that typically can't be matched with an as-cast head, but the effect of that work is marginalized because the supercharger or turbocharger is cramming as much air into the chambers as they can take. My recommendation? Unless the heads are offered in a CNC-ported design out of the box, leave porting for naturally aspirated engines.

Lingenfelter Performance Engineering and feature 202-cc intake runners and 65-cc combustion chambers.

- Pro-Filer cathedral-port heads are offered in 215- and 235-cc intake runner sizes, with 62-cc combustion chambers..
- Trick Flow offers a number of cathedral-port heads, including some with a six-bolt configuration that fit GM Performance Parts' LSX cylinder block.

Additionally, a large number of companies offer modified versions of production GM heads that typically include CNC port work. These ported heads offer notable flow increases that are helpful on cathedral-port heads, but their relative expense doesn't provide as much of a return on investment on the high-flowing rectangular-port heads. As-cast rectangular-port heads flow very well for supercharged and turbocharged engines.

GM Cylinder Head Comparison Chart (Production and GM Performance Parts)					
Cylinder Head	Port Shape	Port Size (cc)	Chamber Colume (cc)	Valve Sizes (intake/exhaust in inches)	Notes
LS1	Cathedral	200	67	2.00/1.55	Introduced basic 15-degree valve angle and bolt-down rocker configuration. Use only on 5.7L engines.
LS6 (production)	Cathedral	210	64.5	2.00/1.55	Originally equipped with hollow-stem/sodium-filled valves. Use only on 5.7L engines.
LS6 CNC-ported (GM Performance Parts)	Cathedral	250	61.9 or 65	2.00/1.55	Offered in two PNs: 88958622 (small chamber) and 88958665 (low compression); use lower compression for forced induction.
LS2 (production)	Cathedral	210	64.5	2.00/1.55	Can be used on 5.7L (LS1/LS6); originally equipped with solid-stem valves.
LS2 CNC-ported (GM Performance Parts)	Cathedral	250	64.5	2.00/1.55	Comparable to CNC-ported LS6, but less expensive; recommended upgrade to LS6 hollow/sodium valves.
L92 (production)	Rectangular	260	70	2.165/1.59	Can be used on 6.0-liter and larger engines with 4.00-inch bores; originally equipped with solid-stem valves.
L92 CNC-ported (GM Performance Parts)	Rectangular	279	68	2.165/1.59	Similar to production L92, but with approximately 8-percent greater intake port volume.
LS3 (production)	Rectangular	260	70	2.165/1.59	Can be used on 6.0-liter and larger engines with 4.00-inch bores; originally equipped with solid-stem valves.
LS7	Rectangular (varied from LS3/L92)	270	70	2.20/1.61	Requires LS7-specific intake manifold; titanium intake valves and sodium-filled exhaust valves; requires minimum of 4.100-inch bores.
LS9	Rectangular	260	70	2.165/1.59	Special roto-cast manufacturing method and unique alloy material; titanium and sodium valves.
LSX-LS3 (GM Performance Parts)	Rectangular	260	70	2.160/1.59	Six-bolt head clamping design.
LSX-L92 small-bore	Rectangular	260	70	2.00/1.55	Six-bolt configuration; designed for smaller-bore engines, including LS1 and LS6, but with production-style L92 port design. Uses LS3/L92-style intake manifolds.
LSX-LS7	Rectangular (varied from LS3/L92)	270	70	2.20/1.61	Six-bolt configuration; production-style titanium and sodium valves.
LSX-LS9	Rectangular	260	70	2.165/1.59	Six-bolt configuration; production-style titanium and sodium valves. Not manufactured with production roto-cast method.
LSX-DR	Rectangular	313	50	2.25/1.60	Unique design requires specific intake manifold; small combustion chamber promotes high compression—may not be suitable for forced induction without modifications.

Stainless-steel intake valves are hard to beat when it comes to strength and heat resistance. High-boost super-charged and turbocharged engines should employ thermally active exhaust valves, such as sodium-filled or inconel material, to withstand severe heat. The largest valves used in production LS engines are the LS7's 2.20-inch intake and 1.61-inch exhaust valves.

Valves

Superchargers and turbochargers, especially turbochargers, generate more heat than a normally aspirated combination. Valves with the strength to withstand that heat are critical to the engine assembly. The factory-supercharged LS9 engine of the Corvette ZR1, for example, uses titanium intake valves and sodium-filled exhaust valves.

The titanium valves are extremely durable and low in mass, but comparable performance and heat resistance can be found with stainless-steel intake valves, although they don't have the weight advantage of titanium. As for the exhaust side, the use of sodium-filled valves have long been an effective way to combat exhaust heat, but like titanium intake valves, inconel-material exhaust valves offer a less-expensive, yet heavier alternative. Also, some builders shy away from sodium valves because of their multi-piece

Surprisingly, no production LS engines use roller-tip rocker arms; they're all stamped-steel, flat-tip rockers. Later, rectangular-port heads use offset intake-side rocker arms (as seen here) that accommodate the valve position for both the large valve heads and the large ports within the head. Beehive-style tapered valve-springs are LS-standard, too, but don't stand up well to the increased pressure from a higher-lift cam or the cylinder pressure of high boost.

construction and resulting damage that could occur if the pieces separate at high RPM, but contemporary products have proven very durable.

Valvetrain Components

Stronger, higher-rate valvesprings typically go hand in hand with higher-lift camshafts, but even if the camshaft profile remains relatively close to the stock cam, the boost pressure of a forced-induction engine generally demands stronger springs. That's because the increased pressure in the cylinders wants to push the valves open or, at the very least, make it more difficult for them to close—and the greater the boost, the stronger the springs need to be.

Lifter type plays a role here, too, as a roller-type lifter can withstand

Shaft-mount rocker arms, such as the Jesel Pro J2K 1.8:1-ratio rockers (seen here), offer exceptional stability and virtually eliminate problems with valve lash as the engine quickly revs to the upper-RPM band. However, valve cover clearance is an issue when using shaft-mounted rockers, requiring machining of the valve cover rails on the heads and/or a valve cover spacer to prevent interference. Some aftermarket heads, such as World Products' Warhawk heads and GM Performance Parts' LSX heads, are cast with taller rails to accommodate taller rocker-arm assemblies.

about twice the valvespring pressure of a flat-tappet type. High spring pressure and high boost can affect the longevity of the camshaft, however, as greater pressure is transferred to it. So, a roller lifter is strongly recommended.

Production LS engines use non-roller rocker arms with, generally, a 1.5 or 1.6:1 ratio. Using roller-tip rocker arms reduces friction and a higher-ratio arm (typically 1.7 or 1.8:1) delivers the effect of a mild increase in cam lift. But because of the intake-side pushrod position on LS7/LS3/L76/L92 heads, the rocker arms are offset. There are few choices currently for roller-tip rockers for these offset-style arms, but SLP Performance has a set that fits LS3, L76, and L92 engines (PN 50189). The rockers have a 1.85:1 ratio.

Although there are several choices for roller-tip rocker arms for the conventional rocker arms of LS cathedral-port heads, there are only a couple options when it comes to upgrading rectangular-port heads with offset rockers. T&D Machine Products offers these 1.7:1-ratio, shaft-mount roller-tip rockers for rectangular-port heads.

A premium, multi-layer steel head gasket is an absolute must when building a force-inducted LS engine, particularly on higher-boost engines that don't have the benefit of six-bolt head clamping. Fel-Pro and Cometic Gasket manufacture what have become the preferred gaskets for professional builders.

The factory LS9 cylinder head gasket is comprised of a whopping seven layers of specially treated steel. It fits other 6.2-liter engines (PN 12622033), but its added thickness when compared with standard four-layer gaskets slightly reduces the compression ratio. That's perfectly acceptable on a supercharged or turbocharged engine. (Photo courtesy General Motors)

Higher-rate valvesprings are a must on a purpose-built forced-induction LS engine, especially if the combination includes a camshaft that exceeds about .510-inch lift. Shown here are the components of Comp Cams' 1.30-inch dual-coil valvespring, which withstands up to .600-inch lift without binding. The dual-coil design is heavier than the production-style beehive design, but offers exceptional strength and resistance to boost pressure. Using titanium retainers with the springs helps offset their additional weight over the stock springs.

Stronger-than-stock valvesprings are recommended with increased-ratio rockers.

Cylinder-Head Gaskets

Because cylinder head sealing is crucial for forced-induction LS engines, the head gasket is a vital component in building a durable engine that stands up to great pressure. The factory-style gasket is a multi-layer steel (MLS) design that has proven very strong and reliable in naturally aspirated conditions and lower-boost engines of up to about 700 to 750 hp. However, the pressure of a supercharger or turbocharger, particularly when used with production-style four-bolt cylinder heads, often makes the head gasket one of the primary failure points on otherwise-stock engines.

The MLS head gaskets from Ohio-based Cometic Gasket have proven to be very strong and durable in forced-induction engines—and most importantly, they're available in a variety of bore sizes for the six-bolt pattern of the GM LSX block and the RHS LS Race Block. They are constructed of two embossed, Viton-coated stainless-steel outer layers sandwiched around a variable stainless inner layer.

Also, Fel-Pro's four-layer gaskets have proven to be very durable at higher horsepower. Copper gaskets or O-ring-style gaskets are suggested for racing engines producing more than 2,000 hp.

Camshaft

The camshaft needs for forced-induction engines are different than those for naturally aspirated engines. And while supercharged and turbocharged engines both feed pressurized air to the combustion chambers, there are differences that can affect the optimal camshaft profile, particularly the exhaust duration.

Before getting into the specifics of camshaft selection, here's a quick primer on common cam terms.

Lift: The distance the valve head is raised off its seat when the camshaft lobe is at its highest position (and in combination with the rocker arm). Lift is measured in fractions of an inch or millimeters. In theory, greater lift enhances performance by creating a wider opening to the combustion chamber and allowing a larger air/fuel charge to be packed in it.

Duration: The amount of time a valve is held open, measured for both the intake and exhaust valves in degrees of crankshaft rotation; i.e., 250 degrees on the intake valve and 255 degrees on the exhaust side. In general terms, longer duration enhances performance at higher RPM or helps extend the RPM range of the engine.

Lobe/Lobe Ramp: The part of the camshaft that interfaces with the lifter, with the ramp section being the part that initiates the lifting and descending of the lifter. The profile of the lobe determines the speed or rate at which the valve opens and closes.

Symmetrical/Asymmetrical Lobe Ramps: A camshaft with symmetrical lobes has matching opening and closing ramps on both the intake and exhaust. An asymmetrical cam has different opening and closing ramp profiles on each lobe.

Base Circle: The lowest point of the camshaft lobe and the place in the camshaft's rotation when the valve is completely closed.

Lobe Separation Angle: The distance in camshaft degrees between the maximum lift points of both the intake and exhaust valves. It affects performance by affecting valve overlap to impact the overall performance range of the engine. In a nutshell, a narrow angle promotes a steep, immediate power curve and a wider angle spreads the power out across the RPM band.

Valve Overlap: Measured in degrees of crankshaft rotation, it's the amount of time both the intake and exhaust valves are opened in a combustion chamber. It takes place as the exhaust stroke ends and the intake stroke begins. In general terms, greater overlap builds power at higher RPM by helping pull the fresh air/fuel charge into the chamber. Great lift and duration increases overlap, as does reducing the lobe-separation angle.

Intake Centerline: The point of greatest lift on an intake lobe, measured in crankshaft degrees after top dead center. In an assembled engine, it is measured by the crankshaft degrees between top dead center and the point of maximum valve lift.

Hydraulic Flat Tappet vs. Hydraulic Roller: All production LS engines feature hydraulic lifters, but not hydraulic roller lifters, which are the friction-reducing rollers that interface with the cam's lobe ramps.

Camshaft selection is very important when it comes to maximizing the performance of a force-inducted engine. In general terms, both super-charged and turbocharged engines respond best with a camshaft that has a lobe-separation angle of around 114 degrees, but the nature of how boost is produced and processed (including the role of overlap) requires markedly different approaches to the duration specifications.

A solution to the longtime debate between high-power street/strip and racing-oriented engines is the use of a hydraulic-roller camshaft versus a solid-roller cam. As with normally aspirated engines, a hydraulic roller cam is suitable for high-power street and street/strip engines. It's not until the engine is expected to turn extremely high RPM and the cam's lift specs reach the .750-inch range (and higher) that the more positive valve-train actuation offered by a solid roller is required.

In general, a camshaft for a super-charged or turbocharged engine should have a wider lobe-separation angle (LSA) than a naturally aspirated engine in order to spread the power across the RPM band and deal with the increased cylinder heat that comes with forced induction. The rule of thumb for the LSA is 112 to about 114 degrees, although several LS engines' stock cams feature a 112-degree LSA—and the LS2 cam's LSA spec is a wide 116 degrees, for example, while the factory supercharged LS9's lobe-separation angle is an extra-wide 122.5 degrees.

The optimal LSA must be matched with the appropriate exhaust duration to better handle exhaust pressure. Again, in general terms, a supercharged engine needs more exhaust duration than a naturally aspirated engine, while a turbocharged engine needs less duration.

Turbocharger Camshaft

Generally speaking, a turbocharged engine benefits from a milder cam (one with lower duration) in order to make the most of the exhaust-gas pressure that drives the turbocharger's turbine. In a nutshell, the camshaft should be used to keep heat out of the cylinders. (For a good example of the camshaft needs of a turbocharged engine, refer to Chapter 1, page 17, "Real World Project: Steve Gilliland's 1,000-hp Twin-Turbo Corvette Z06.")

Ideally, the boost pressure of a turbo engine should be greater than the exhaust pressure at the low end of the power band, as the engine nears its peak torque. The boost pressure and exhaust-gas pressure are nearly equal when the engine approaches its peak horsepower. However, at peak horsepower there is typically greater exhaust back pressure than boost.

For optimal efficiency and maximum effectiveness of the turbo system, the boost should exceed (or at least be equal to) the exhaust back pressure over the RPM range. When this doesn't occur, a too-small turbocharger can be the culprit.

The original LS7 engine's cam had .591/.591-inch lift, 211/230 degrees duration and 121-degree lobe separation angle specs. Katech Performance used a camshaft with greater lift (.615/.613-inch) to maximize airflow; slightly more intake valve duration (220 degrees) and *less* exhaust valve duration (229 degrees). The cam's lobe separation angle was also dialed back to a more appropriate 116 degrees.

The reason a turbo engine needs less duration than the supercharger cam is because the turbocharger itself is an exhaust restriction that increases exhaust gas pressure—and it's the exhaust-gas pressure that spins the turbo. Therefore, a milder cam with lower duration helps exploit boost-enhancing exhaust-gas pressure.

A supercharged engine's boost is generated at the front of the engine's air stream, so a cam with greater duration than what would be used with a turbo engine helps expel exhaust gases more completely, clearing the chamber and promoting

LS Engine Factory Camshaft Specifications			
Camshaft	**Lift Intake/Exhaust (inches)**	**Duration (at .050 degrees)**	**Lobe-Separation Angle**
LS1 (1998-2000)	.497/.498	202/210	116
LS1 (2001-2002)	.467/.479	197/208	116
LS6 (2001)	.525/.525	207/218	116
LS6 (2002-04)	.551/.547	207/217	117
LS2	.525/.525	207/217	116
LS3	.551/.522	204/211	116
LS7	.591/.591	211/230	121
LS9	.562/.558	211/230	122.5
LSA	.480/.480	198/216	122.5
LQ9 (truck engine)	.479/.467	207/196	116
L92 (truck engine)	.500/.492	195/201	116
LS Hot Cam (GM Performance Parts)	.525/.525	219/228	112

The LSX iron cylinder block can be machined for a Jesel belt-drive timing-belt system.

unrestricted airflow. But as Comp Cams' Billy Godbold pointed out, the camshaft for any forced-induction engine should have less overlap to prevent boost from escaping through the exhaust port.

Cam Talk

Notes on LS Camshaft Selection with Comp Cams' Bill Godbold

I spoke with Comp Cams' Billy Godbold about selecting the right camshaft for a supercharged or turbocharged LS engine. And while he points out that every combination is unique, there are guidelines to help get you started in the right direction. Here's what he had to say:

How should a builder approach camshaft selection for a forced-induction LS engine?

The more complete a picture the builder has of the project and its intended use, the better the component selection will be. That includes details such as the true RPM range the engine will perform. Is it primarily a street car or a race car? for example. Answering that question is why good cam guys ask so many questions about gear ratios, transmission type, tire size, vehicle weight and converters.

Many people have a hard time setting out a good plan. They want the 10,000-rpm Pro Stock cam, but want to cruise coast-to-coast down the interstate at 1,800 rpm. You generally can't have it both ways. The engine needs to be built around a given RPM range and application; that's what separates the really great combinations from the merely good and not-so-good engines.

The second part is as simple as the first: Go to people you trust and take their advice. I'll pick a camshaft for myself, but not the ignition, transmission, converter, induction system, pistons, rods, rings, or radiator. I go to the experts in those fields for advice. Even the best builders in the world rely on others for parts selection, but often it's the novice or inexperienced builder who fails to seek advice. Don't worry about sounding like you don't know everything about building an engine. Few people do. That's why we—and other companies—have a staff of professionals to help.

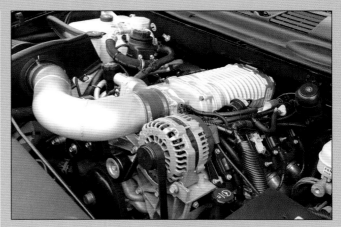

A carefully selected camshaft complements the airflow attributes of the supercharger or turbocharger system to maximize efficiency and build more power. The camshaft, however, shouldn't be selected blindly. It should be discussed with a specialist who understands the engine displacement, cylinder head selection, and power-adder capacity, as well as the primary use of the engine.

Generally speaking, how do LS engines respond with superchargers and turbochargers?

A typical LS1 combination will run well to about 6,000 to 6,500 rpm with very similar intake and exhaust duration. With a blower, you'll typically want to add 4 to 12 degrees of duration to the exhaust. With the rectangular-port heads (even with normal aspiration), the LS3 and L92 engines want more than 8 degrees added to the exhaust. Both the cathedral [LS1/LS6-style] and rectangular heads will respond very well to camshaft changes, but they should be "cammed" carefully to match the airflow characteristics of the cylinder heads.

Does a camshaft swap make a meaningful difference on an otherwise-stock engine that has a bolt-on supercharger or turbo kit?

Yes. LS heads flow great when compared with older overhead-valve V-8 heads. Including a modern camshaft design tailored to the application's intended use makes the combination that much better. A great cam selection will not match a blower in terms of power improvement, but it is common to see as great a gain in changing the cam with a supercharged engine as it is changing the cam in a normally aspirated engine.

How does the camshaft affect the performance of a supercharged or turbocharged engine? And how does the addition of a blower or turbo affect performance relative to the camshaft?

Essentially, boost is the resistance to flow. It is common in blown applications to go to a better head and see a drop in boost (even with the same pulleys) but see a substantial increase in horsepower. Basically, the head change made it easier for the engine to breathe. On turbocharged and supercharged engines, we see similar improvements when the proper camshaft is selected. Clearly, if you force air into the engine, you make more power and operate at a higher RPM. However, if you tune the valve events for the forced-induction system and the correct RPM, everything is just that much better; both power and airflow will increase.

Generally speaking, you need more duration in a normally aspirated application than a supercharged or turbocharged engine operating at the same RPM, if you are selecting the cam for peak power or a specific, smaller operating window.

What are the attributes that make a good blower cam, i.e., overlap, lobe separation, etc.?

A blower grind does not need overlap to provide a signal from the exhaust to the intake, so these cams typically have less overlap. However, as soon as you open the intake, air will start flowing into the combustion chambers. While it might not always be the case in a normally aspirated engine, blowers would love an infinitely fast camshaft profile if it were stable. Going to the most aggressive profile that is stable in the intended RPM window will make the best power.

Because charge is lost through the exhaust when both valves are open, blower cams typically have a few degrees of wider lobe separation. This is most important when the blower is operating near the airflow limit. If you have extra blower capacity, a little extra overlap is less of an issue. With centrifugal superchargers, we tend to run smaller intake profiles to maximize low-speed torque, but couple them with larger exhaust profiles to reduce exhaust pumping loss at higher RPM.

With positive-displacement superchargers [Roots-type, Lysholm-type, etc.], low-speed torque is generally not a problem. With those applications, we can run larger camshafts that do not need to "cheat" the exhaust side as much.

So, generally speaking, with centrifugal blowers, we try to make torque with the camshaft and power with the blower. And with the positive-displacement blowers, we let the blower give us the torque and we make sure we give it enough camshaft to run at high engine speed.

What about lift and duration?

It's hard to make a general statement, because each application is different, but we jokingly like to say, "As much duration as you need and all the lift the engine will take without throwing parts through the valve covers."

Seriously, the guidelines discussed above will serve you well with street blowers. With LS engines, keep in mind that a positive-displacement blower tends to make the camshaft act "smaller" at idle, due to reversion not making [its way] backward through the blower. So, you get less of a negative effect of the camshaft in the mid-240 range [degrees of duration]. Also, with a good centrifugal system, you can make surprising power with a "small" performance grind that may only be in the low 230s at .050 inch on the intake side.

The most important thing is speaking with a technical representative from your cam company to make sure he understands your engine specifications and

Cam Talk (continued)

performance goals. You don't want to guess. Make sure the cam is tailored to your engine.

Does Comp Cams have a "standard" blower cam?

We have a number of blower grinds for various applications. Our LS-R cam series has several that are appropriate for supercharged engines. It's best, however, to speak with someone before ordering a camshaft.

How does a camshaft for a turbocharged engine differ from a supercharged engine?

They are very different. The pressure drop across the combustion chamber (comparing intake manifold pressure to the pressure in the exhaust headers) is very great, but it can be all over the board with a turbocharged engine. Some of the newer turbo systems

have mild backpressure, but some may have three times the amount of backpressure than boost. In some ways, turbo systems are like normally aspirated engines with great cylinder heads. Regardless, there are very different things going on with the valve timing points in a turbo engine. Again, speak to your camshaft rep and spell out all of the turbo system's specs to select the best grind.

How important is the cylinder head with a camshaft and forced induction?

Of course, airflow absolutely matters, but it's true that a blower or turbo will make just about any cylinder head perform better. That said, matching the cam means knowing how the heads flow, as you can use less duration with a better-flowing head.

An important note about the above samples: They are meant to provide an illustrated comparison and shouldn't be considered recommendations for any LS forced-induction engines. Factors determining the "perfect" camshaft grind include the size of the supercharger or turbo compressor; the displacement of the engine; cylinder-head changes over stock; and even the type of performance expected—i.e. street, street/strip, or dedicated racing.

Ignition and Ignition Controller

The production-style coil-near-plug ignition system is surprisingly good for even moderately high boost pressure—up to about 12 to 15 pounds. As boost pressure increases, a higher-energy spark system is

required because the higher pressure can effectively blow out the spark before it can jump the gap on the spark plug (much like trying to light a match in the wind). A few aftermarket companies, including MSD Ignition and ACCEL, offer replacement coil packs that provide greater energy than GM's factory units. That greater energy helps light the mixture under pressure, while also ensuring a more complete burn.

On racing engines, where high boost and high RPM define the engine's primary operating parameters (those making approximately 1,500 hp and more) the sequentially triggered individual-coil system has neither the energy nor speed to deliver adequate and dependable ignition control, even when using hotter aftermarket coils. The alternative is converting the engine from

the production-style crank-triggered system to a conventional distributor-based system that is also linked to a high-energy coil.

Fortunately, the tools for the conversion are already on the market, thanks to circle track series' that require distributor-driven ignition systems. To support them, GM Performance Parts offers a conversion kit (PN 88958679) that happens to be perfect for force-inducted racing engines. The kit provides the distributor-mounting fixture for the front of the engine, as well as the distributor drive gear that is attached to the camshaft. From there, a standard distributor and coil are used.

"It's the only way to ensure adequate spark energy, with the cylinder pressure and speed that the engine achieves so quickly," says experienced LS engine builder Brian Thomson.

The production-style individual-coil system works very well for even heavily modified engine making up to 1,000 hp or more. Aftermarket coils, such as these from MSD Ignition, provide more energy that is helpful on engines with higher boost levels.

ACCEL is another source for hotter-than-stock ignition coils. The greater energy helps the flame of the spark withstand boost pressure that wants to blow it out, much like blowing out a match.

When the individual-coil system reaches its limit, the only alternative is conventional distributor-driven ignition system. GM Performance Parts offers the conversion kit, which mounts to the front of the engine, under PN 88958679. A conventional distributor, such as the front-mount type for a Ford Windsor small-block, is used with it.

"The factory coil system is very good for even 1,000-hp combinations, but at this level, something stronger is needed."

Thomson used the distributor conversion system on the 2,000-hp, twin-turbo LS engine project on page 129.

Intake Manifold

In a general sense, the intake manifold doesn't have as great an impact on the output of a forced-induction engine, as the boost pressure largely overrides a manifold's plenum volume and runner design. That said, the intake should offer low restriction and a straight path to the combustion chambers.

For vehicles used primarily on the street, a production-style intake manifold with greater plenum volume helps maintain low-end torque for greater low-speed drivability on the street, when the engine isn't under boost. Bolt-on supercharger and turbo kits—even those used on modified, purpose-built short-block assemblies—perform very well on the street and drag strip with production intake manifolds, including factory-style intakes from aftermarket companies, such as F.A.S.T.

Vehicles designed primarily for drag racing, where the engine will spend most of its time at higher RPM, benefit from a carbureted-type "spider" aluminum manifold that has shorter, direct, and straight intake runners. These manifolds are readily available from several aftermarket companies, as well as GM Performance Parts. Using one with a high-boost turbo or supercharger system requires an adapter and/or elbow on top of the manifold, as well as an intake tube, to feed the manifold. These are generally custom-built parts, as the engines that employ such induction systems are typically custom built.

When selecting a spider-type intake manifold, be sure to match it with the cylinder-head intake-port design. The manifolds are designed to match the cathedral-port and different rectangular-port configurations of LS heads. Also, adapter plates are needed (perhaps requiring custom fabrication in some cases) when using any intake manifold with a tall-deck cylinder block, as the heads are pushed out farther

It's not that the intake manifold isn't important on a force-inducted LS engine, but because of the pressurized delivery of air, it's less of a factor in the ultimate performance of the engine. The factory intake manifolds work well with superchargers and turbochargers, so replacing them with aftermarket manifolds isn't necessary for most applications.

than on an engine with a standard-deck block.

For safety reasons, an aluminum or sheetmetal intake should also be considered for racing-oriented engine combinations that will see 20 pounds of boost or more. Rather

The use of a carbureted-style aluminum intake manifold comes with racing applications that will see very high boost pressure and require custom plumbing to route large-diameter tubing through the engine compartment.

This photo shows a typical racing setup that uses a carbureted-style intake with an elbow designed to accept the injection system's throttle body. The aluminum intake also provides a measure of safety for high-boost engines, as the cast aluminum is less likely to shatter than the brittle nylon material of a production intake.

This impressive-looking tunnel-ram-style intake has a fatal flaw for high-boost forced induction: As air rushes through the front of the manifold under pressure, it packs into the rear intake runners, leaving the front runners relatively starved. A better solution would be to introduce the air at the top of the manifold, where the airflow would be better spread among the runners.

than being cast as a single part, the nylon/plastic production-style intake manifolds are generally comprised of multiple pieces that are assembled with adhesive bonding agents. They weren't designed for the extreme pressure that comes with high boost and inadvertently discovering the pressure point at which the components separate or the brittle nylon material shatters is not something a racer wants to discover on the starting line.

Most off-the-shelf aluminum manifolds for LS engines are of the carbureted/spider style, although Holley offers an aluminum, production-style manifold (PN 300-111) for LS1/LS6 engines.

Throttle Body

The throttle body must be compatible with the engine-control module, particularly when using a GM controller that is calibrated for either a cable-operated or electronic throttle. For most street/strip combinations of up to 1,000 hp, or so, a production GM throttle body, such as LS7's large, 90-mm unit, works and flows just fine.

It is possible to adapt an electronically controlled throttle to a vehicle originally equipped with a conventional cable throttle and vice versa, but modifications are required, including changing the engine controller and pedal assembly, and is generally not worth the time. If the vehicle was originally equipped with a cable throttle, use a larger, cable-actuated throttle body if necessary; and if the vehicle came with an electronic throttle, continue using the same type.

Fortunately, GM cable-operated and electronic throttle bodies are generally interchangeable on intake manifolds, so a cable throttle body can be used on an LS7 intake manifold, allowing for example, this

Cable-operated throttle bodies are manufactured in a number of very large sizes to suit high-power racing engines, but options for engines with electronically controlled throttles are limited. Some companies offered ported and modified versions of production throttle bodies, but their effectiveness is limited, as they simply don't offer a significantly larger flow path for the air charge.

The 90-mm electronic throttle body found on LS7 and LS9 engines (they are of similar diameters, but not the same part), is sufficient for 6.2-liter and smaller engines, making up to approximately 1,000 hp. With larger-displacement engines, the airflow requirements are greater and the 90-mm unit runs out of breath around the 750- to 800-hp level.

high-flow intake to be used in a fourth-generation F-body with a cable-operated throttle system.

Dedicated race cars should use a cable throttle for maximum driver control. In fact, for safety reasons, many sanctioning bodies require it.

Also, the airflow requirements of a 1,500- to 2,000-hp engine can't be met with current production-based electronic throttle bodies.

Electronic Throttle Bodies and Blow-Off Valves

Some builders have reported a condition with supercharged LS engines that use electronically controlled throttle bodies where excessive boost pressure pushes on the throttle blade after it is closed—such as when the driver takes his foot off the gas—forcing unwanted air into the engine. At the least, it can cause stumbling and other drivability issues, but it could also lead to engine damage if the excessive airflow causes a lean condition.

The problem can be due to an inadequate supercharger blow-off valve (in many cases, the issue has been reported with Eaton-type Roots superchargers) that doesn't bleed off enough boost pressure when the throttle closes. It can also be due to a throttle body with a throttle blade spring that doesn't have sufficient strength to keep the blade closed. Or it could be a combination of both issues.

Some enthusiasts have had success swapping the throttle body with a strong factory unit, such as the LS3 unit from the C6 Corvette; however, it requires additional tuning to match the throttle body with the engine controller. A stronger or larger bypass valve is another solution.

Real-World Project: Building a 2,000-hp Twin-Turbo LS Engine

In an experiment backed by GM Performance Parts, Detroit-area engine builder Thomson Automotive decided to push GM Performance Parts' LSX block to see whether it lived up to the advertised claim of supporting 2,000 hp. Thomson did it with some custom parts and a couple huge turbochargers.

Because of projects like this one and a symbiotic relationship with GM Performance Parts, Thomson is rapidly becoming one of the country's foremost experts in high-horsepower LS engine development. The turbo LSX project was launched in 2007, when the LSX program was in its infancy and parts for it were being custom built.

GM Performance Parts was eager for an independent party to verify its claims for the LSX platform, so it donated the cylinder block, as well as a set of prototype LSX racing heads.

"One of the keys to the success of the LSX block is the additional cylinder head bolt provisions," says Brian Thomson, president of Thomson Automotive. "Production LS blocks have four head bolts per cylinder, but the LSX blocks accommodate six bolts per cylinder. It makes a huge difference in clamping power and, frankly, with the amount of boost this engine makes, it wouldn't survive without that added clamping power."

Those prototype heads were all the more necessary, too, because when the project started, they were just about the only six-bolt heads Thomson could locate. Today, GM Performance Parts and a couple other aftermarket manufacturers offer ready-built, six-bolt heads.

So, Thomson had the block and heads secured, but the rest of the assembly was still up for debate, including the displacement. A previous experiment with a boosted, 454-ci LS engine brought about

Based on the LSX cylinder block and using a smaller, 400-inch displacement, this Thomson Automotive-built twin-turbo engine consistently delivers more than 2,000 earth-shaking horsepower—with nearly 30 pounds of boost.

concerns of crankshaft flex, so the decision was made to go a little conservative on the stroke.

"We planned to rev the engine pretty high and throw a lot of boost at it, so we felt we could overcome the displacement deficit without too much trouble," says Thomson. "What we gave up in cubic inches, we'd hopefully make up in longevity and durability."

Thomson's caution paid off. The engine has made nearly 2,050 hp on the dyno—more than 5 hp generated for every cubic inch of displacement —and has survived approximately *150* full-load dyno pulls without so much as an oil leak.

"We've never lost a head gasket or had any real issues with it," Thomson says. "We inspected the bottom end numerous times and it all looked great. We replaced some bearings for good measure after so many dyno pulls, but the engine has been very reliable."

Basic Parts

When you first look at the twin-

turbo LSX engine, it looks as if a couple Caterpillar loaders were robbed of their turbochargers. A pair of 88-mm Turbonetics turbochargers dominate the assembly, along with a custom intake system that looks somewhat like a Mad Max version of a tunnel ram. There's also a front-mounted distributor in place of the typical LS-engine coil packs. Here's an overview of the basic parts and why they were selected.

Rotating Assembly: A Callies 3.750-inch-stroke forged crankshaft is connected to a set of GRP forged-aluminum connecting rods. The pistons are from Diamond and in order to keep the compression ratio at a boost-friendly 9:1, they feature large, 50-cc dishes.

"You could pretty much drink coffee out of them," says Thomson about the custom pistons.

The rotating assembly is housed in a tall-deck version of the LSX cylinder block. Its 9.70-inch deck height enabled the racing-style connecting rods to swing freely, without

the need for internal block clearancing. The bores measure 4.125 inches. With the 3.750-inch stroke, that makes the displacement just a hair less than 401 ci.

Cylinder Heads: As mentioned earlier, the heads are prototype LSX racing heads that were ported by Utah-based Chapman Racing Heads. They're filled with 2.200-inch titanium intake valves and 1.600-inch Ferrea Super Alloy exhaust valves. The intake port design is patterned after the high-RPM flow characteristics of the C5R head, but the chamber volume is a tight 45.6 cc—hence the need for the deeply dished pistons to keep down the compression ratio.

Camshaft and Valvetrain: A custom grind from Bullet Racing Cams was used, with comparatively mild .714/.721-inch lift and 266/268-degrees duration specs. Lobe separation is 113 degrees, which is appropriate for a forced-induction engine. The rest of the valvetrain is pretty standard stuff, including Comp Cams springs, titanium retainers, and keepers, along with 1.8:1-ratio roller rocker arms.

Intake System: During Thomson's experiment with a force-fed 454-ci LS engine, it used a custom, CNC-carved tall runner intake system with a conventional front-mounted throttle body. It found unequal distribution among the cylinders when the boost was turned up (it was blowing past the front cylinders and getting crammed in the rear cylinders), so it redesigned the intake. It now features a pair of ACCEL/DFI 2,100-cfm throttle bodies mounted on top of the intake, with a custom sheetmetal air box on top of it. Three-inch tubing from the turbos feeds the air box.

Turbochargers: Two 88-mm Turbonetics compressors are used and

Underpinning the twin-turbo project is GM Performance Parts' LSX cylinder block. Its iron casting makes it very durable for forced-induction combinations, while delivering the added benefit of great affordability; it retails for less than $2,000. It also is designed for six-bolt-per-cylinder-head clamping, tremendously reduces the chance for head gasket problems under high boost.

Coated pistons from Diamond feature soup-bowl-like 50-cc dishes in order to keep the engine's compression ratio down to a turbo-friendly 9.0:1. With the capability of more than 25 pounds of boost, any more "squeeze" in the cylinder could cause fragment-inducing detonation.

blow through a custom-built intercooling system. They're fed exhaust pressure from custom headers designed by GM Performance Parts to fit a specific project vehicle (more on that later). A pair of Turbonetics wastegates are also part of the system. Through the intercooler, the

A Callies internally balanced, 4340-forged-steel crankshaft complements the LSX block's 4.125-inch bores with a 3.750-inch stroke, for a grand total of 401 ci.

This super-strong and lightweight connecting rod from GRP was selected for the project. It's a forged-aluminum rod whose strength is matched by good shock-absorption qualities, which is a must for the hard hit that comes with the boost the engine generates.

turbos deliver about 25 pounds of boost, with a maximum of 27 pounds recorded on some dyno pulls.

Ignition System: With the engine capable of generating more than 25 pounds of boost at high RPM, the production-style individual coil ignition system would not be effective or reliable in delivering the required spark energy, so it was replaced with a conventional distributor system. The engine uses the GM front-mount distributor kit described earlier, along with an ACCEL dual-sync distributor and high-energy ignition coil.

Additional Details: Other engine

details include 160-pound Bosch injectors, custom valve covers, a Wagner racing-style water pump, and a dry-sump oiling system that uses a Moroso five-stage oil pump. One of the pump's stages is used to draw oil out of the turbos to prevent unnecessary buildup that could lead to blown seals or worse.

Dyno Details

Thomson handled the engine parts and assembly, but leaned on ACCEL/DFI's Joe Alameddine to help with the engine control system. It was a coordinated effort that was both challenging and rewarding. Alameddine experimented with a prototype version of ACCEL's Gen 8 control system, a standalone system that enabled him to batch-fire the injectors (it also handles production-style sequential firing). It was also designed to support tuning of forced-induction engines generating up to 40 pounds of boost. Thomson's turbo engine would make about 25 pounds, so it was well within the controller's limits (see Chapter 7 for more details).

"It's a great tool for completely custom engine combinations like this one," said Alameddine. "We designed it to support the wildest racing engine configuration, but it is also great for street/strip engines with more conventional combinations."

Capabilities notwithstanding, Alameddine spent many hours "sneaking up" on the turbo engine's tune. It wasn't a simple, "plug-and-play" operation. The fuel trim was kept safely flat and both RPM and boost were initially limited, as dyno pull after dyno pull revealed what the engine was capable of handling.

The engine recorded its best performance of 2,048 hp at 7,140 rpm

Bullet Racing Cams supplied the .714/.721-inch-lift, 266/268-degree roller camshaft. The lobe separation angle is 113 degrees. The specs are consistent with the airflow needs of a forced-induction engine, as the relatively wide lobe-separation angle promotes greater power at higher RPM, where boost can start to fall off. Because this engine uses a front-mounted distributor rather than the typical LS crank trigger, the camshaft required the addition of a distributor drive gear and fuel-pump lobe. It's available from GM Performance Parts in a kit that also includes the distributor mounting bracket. The PN is 88958679.

The boost generated by the turbo-chargers is pushed into this custom plenum atop the engine. Air is funneled through it and a pair of 2,100-cfm ACCEL/DFI throttle bodies before flowing down into a tunnel-ram-type intake. The entire intake system was custom fabricated, with the lower tunnel-ram section CNC-milled by GM and the upper plenum and intake tubes built by Thomson Automotive.

The cylinder heads are prototype LSX racing heads, but they're based on the same six-bolts-per-cylinder design as GM Performance Parts' recently introduced LSX street head. The CNC-ported combustion chambers of the heads displace only 45.6 cc—a tight displacement that drove the deep-dish design of the pistons.

Here's the front-mount distributor that replaces the production-style crank-trigger ignition. It's a GM part designed for motorsport classes that don't allow crank-triggered engines. The distributor is an ACCEL dual-sync unit, PN 77201.

Two of these mid-sized, 88-mm HP-88 turbochargers from Turbonetics are used on the engine. Each features ceramic ball bearings for greater wear and heat resistance, as well as Turbonetics' 3.50-inch turbine wheel. Alone, each turbo supports about 1,200 hp, but when used in pairs, the sky's the limit.

The elaborate exhaust system design and routing was custom built by Mike Copeland's team at the GM Performance Division. In fact, much of it was redesigned to fit in an Impala SS project car (see Chapter 1); so much of the work seen here was re-done later in the project.

and a neck-straining 1,507 ft-lbs of torque at the same RPM level. And while the engine makes big power even at lower revs (about 700 hp at 4,000 rpm), the power comes on like a sledgehammer from about 5,000 rpm onward. In fact, power jumps from about 980 hp at 4,800 rpm to nearly 1,400 hp at 6,400 rpm.

Similarly, torque leaps from the merely super-strong 906 ft-lbs at 4,800 rpm to nearly 1,700 ft-lbs at 6,400. That's almost an 800-ft-lbs jump— nearly *90-percent* more torque—in the time it takes the tach to swing only 1,600 rpm higher. Talk about driveline shock.

Thomson says there was even

more power to be extracted from the engine, but the dyno sessions ceased when GM Performance Parts asked to put the engine in a 1996 Impala SS that had been constructed especially for it.

"There was definitely more power to be found in it," says Thomson. "All we needed was more time with it."

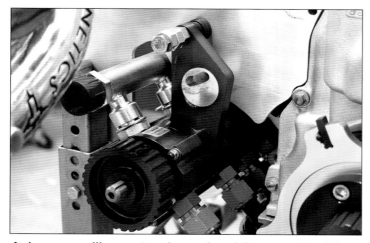

A dry-sump oiling system is used and the pump for it is a five-stage unit from Moroso. One of the stages is used to suck oil out of the turbochargers to reduce potentially damaging buildup.

ACCDEL/DFI also supplied the engine-management system, in the form of its recently introduced Thruster EFI. It supports up to 40 pounds of boost and offers dual-wideband-tuning capability.

ACCEL/DFI's Joe Alameddine performed the tuning magic, directing the engine to batch fire the injectors for greater performance consistency under high boost and high RPM. Conventional sequential firing can lose its precision under the extreme conditions this engine would encounter.

The twin-turbo LSX puts down more than 2,000 hp and more than 1,500 ft-lbs of torque. The engine has survived about 200 dyno pulls without a problem and, according to everyone involved in the project (including Thomson Automotive, ACCEL/DFI, and the engineers at GM Performance Parts), there is more power to be found with this radical combination.

FORCED-INDUCTION SUPPORT AND AUXILIARY COMPONENTS

Maximizing the performance of a supercharged or turbocharged vehicle includes more than the power adder itself. A number of supporting components in the powertrain and chassis require upgrades or attention to not only realize the full horsepower potential of the forced-induction system, but to ensure long-term durability by supporting the greater load imposed by the blower or turbo.

Headers and Exhaust System

Simply put, a bolt-on blower or turbo kit won't deliver as much power when breathing through the stock exhaust system. Obviously, the stock exhaust system is designed to minimize the sound level across the RPM band, but supercharged engines perform better with the least restrictions. Turbocharged systems, on the other hand, need a little backpressure for optimal performance, but not an excessive amount. Also, the very nature of how turbochargers are installed in the exhaust stream requires changes to the exhaust system.

The elements of the exhaust system discussed here include the

Because of the long length of the fully welded stock system, it is much easier to start the project with the car on a lift. Although it is technically possible to remove the stock system without a lift, the access and leverage needed to unhook some of the hangers makes the job infinitely easier with a lift. The most difficult aspect of the job requires a pry bar to remove the muffler hangers. They're very hard to see and even harder to remove without considerable leverage.

exhaust manifolds and exhaust system after the catalytic converter, but the decisions for upgrading them aren't necessarily as obvious as they seem. Installing headers with a cat-back exhaust system (one that bolts on after the catalytic converter to ensure emissions compliance) is often the best way to maximize exhaust flow, but not all headers

provide a commensurate return on investment.

On most LS-powered exhaust systems, the cast-iron exhaust manifolds flow quite well, with the merge-style manifolds of the LS7 and LS9 engines being particularly good. Adding conventional "shorty" headers (those with shorter runners that bolt up within the stock exhaust

Aftermarket exhaust headers and high-flow catalytic converters help make the most of the power gains offered by a super-charger system (turbo systems typically require a custom exhaust or come with specific exhaust manifolds). Long-tube headers generally are the most effective, but they may not be street legal in all areas. Ideally, the headers would be installed prior to or at the same time as the supercharger system, so that tuning and chassis dyno testing is more accurate.

system) may provide only a marginal airflow increase over the stock manifolds. Long-tube headers provide unquestionably greater flow than stock manifolds and shorty headers, but they also require additional system changes, including the possibility of new catalytic converters, due to the repositioning of the header outlets. Also, long-tube headers may not be legal in all areas.

The header option for turbocharged vehicles is mostly negated by the fact that they require either thick, cast-iron manifolds when the turbos are mounted directly to them, or one-off fabricated manifolds to accommodate a custom mounting position of the turbochargers.

Fortunately, superchargers and turbo systems don't necessarily increase the sound level of the engine by themselves, so adding a typical cat-back exhaust system does not adversely affect the sound quality of the vehicle. In fact, with a Roots-type or twin-screw blower, it may even be quieter at idle and low speeds. Of course, a lower-restriction exhaust system will be louder at higher RPM and wide-open throttle, but that would be the case for a non-blown vehicle, too.

The bottom line is a blower or turbo system should be complemented by a lower-restriction exhaust system to realize more power on the street. The cat-back system should be the priority over headers, too. There are countless aftermarket cat-back exhaust systems for all LS-powered vehicles, so finding one isn't a problem. Bolt-on headers, however, can be an issue for some vehicles, as they are not available for all LS-powered vehicles. The majority of the popular models have headers available, however.

For the enthusiast having a forced-induction system installed

The mufflers of many LS-powered vehicles are connected to the chassis via a "dog bone"-shaped connector. It must be pried off to enable removal of the exhaust system. This one looks wet because it was sprayed with WD-40 prior to removal to help slip it off the metal hanger that's welded to the chassis.

by a professional tuning shop, it is ultimately more cost effective and time effective to have the exhaust system installed as part of the entire project.

Real-World Project: Installing a Cat-Back Exhaust System

The installation of a bolt-on cat-back exhaust system is relatively easy, but can require the assistance of professionals or at least professional tools. Later-model LS-powered vehicles, such as the Pontiac G8 GT/GXP (and its Holden/Vauxhall cousins) and Chevy Camaro, are equipped from the factory with very large, completely welded exhaust systems. On the fifth-generation Camaro, for example, the exhaust system after the catalytic converter comes out of

When all of the hangers have been disconnected and the flow tubes unbolted from the converters (there's also a small cross member to remove), the exhaust system comes out of the car as a single, very long and heavy assembly. It's a two-person job to maneuver the very long 9.25-foot exhaust system down and away from the car. Fortunately, the Corsa system (and other aftermarket kits) are comprised of several, easier-to-install components.

Because this project car had an automatic transmission and GM's cylinder-deactivating Active Fuel Management feature, the exhaust system included a pair of additional resonators that aren't part of the kit for manual-transmission cars. The resonators are necessary to accommodate the four-cylinder exhaust note when half of the cylinders temporarily shut down. Note, too, how a transmission jack is used to hold the resonators in the correct position while they're being bolted to the converter flow tubes.

The new mufflers slip into the corners of the rear bumper. To follow the contours of the bumper of the Camaro, they're mounted at an odd angle, so they must be rotated carefully to ensure the tips are positioned through the outlet holes in the bumper.

Here's the finished installation. The less-restrictive exhaust reduces backpressure to help the force-inducted engine make more power. Another benefit is, generally, reduced mass over the stock exhaust system. That helps offset the added weight of a super-charger system or a pair of tur-bochargers and their heavy, cast-iron exhaust manifolds.

With the exhaust system in place, the fasteners are tightened completely. During the installation, they were only lightly torqued to allow easy adjustment and re-positioning. The last part of the exhaust installation involves the re-installation of the underbody cross member. The Corsa kit included a set of spacers to accommodate the resonators' thicker profile.

the car as a single component that is more than 9 feet long. It was replaced with a Corsa system comprised of multiple (and more manageable) components.

Although the basic procedures involved with this exhaust swap are easily handled by the do-it-yourselfer, the length of the stock system, along with the leverage required to remove hard-to-reach muffler hangers, means the job should almost certainly be done with the vehicle on a lift. There just isn't enough room to maneuver with the jack stands and ramps found in most home garages.

As mentioned in the previous section, taking the cost and labor for a cat-back exhaust system into consideration when committing to an entire blower/turbo installation at a professional shop is probably the best option for most enthusiasts. The following is the installation of a Corsa cat-back exhaust system on a 2010 Camaro SS, which is similar to the Pontiac G8 and Holden Commodore. And, in general, the steps outlined are similar for most bolt-on exhaust systems on most LS-powered vehicles.

Here is a stock muffler (left) next to one from the Corsa system (right). The unique noise-canceling design that's a signature of Corsa was just what we wanted for our project, because it's very quiet at idle and low speeds, but definitely has a louder, sportier sound when the revs are up. Best of all, there's no drone on the highway.

Generally speaking, the factory electric cooling fans and radiator of most LS-powered vehicles are adequate for most bolt-on blower and turbo kits of low- to moderate-boost levels. However, the variable fan controller found on LS3-powered C6 Corvettes is a popular conversion for those factory fan systems, as it allows the fan speed to be "tuned" through the engine controller software to optimize the speed.

A replacement thermostat that opens at a lower temperature than the stock unit helps reduce overall engine temperature, which is very desirable with forced induction in order to stave off detonation. This SLP Performance Parts thermostat for LS1 and LS6 engines, for example, opens at 160 degrees rather than the stock part's 195-degree threshold.

Even engine oil can affect the performance of a force-inducted engine. Synthetic oil has a higher abrasion resistance and greater thermal properties than conventional oil, standing up better to the heat produced by a supercharged or turbocharged engine.

Cooling System

Along with boost comes heat that promotes detonation and saps horsepower. So, the cooling system of a force-inducted car is a crucial component in ensuring consistent, long-term performance. The radiator and cooling fan(s) are the items to address, as the stock water pump is adequate for street-based vehicles with supercharger and turbo systems.

For most LS-powered vehicles, the standard radiator provides sufficient cooling capacity for bolt-on blower kits and mild-boost turbo systems. For all street vehicles with forced-induction systems that exceed 10 pounds of boost, larger-capacity radiators should be considered.

The electric cooling-fan assembly on performance-oriented vehicles, such as fourth-generation F-cars, Corvettes, G8/Commodores, and fifth-generation Camaros is also adequate for most street-based vehicles. Earlier truck-based LS vehicles, such as pickups, SUVs, and the TrailBlazer SS, benefit from cooling-fan assemblies that convert engine-driven fans into more controllable electric-fan systems. Popular swaps include the efficient fans from C6 Corvettes and the twin-fan arrangement from LS1-powered fourth-generation F-cars, particularly TrailBlazers.

A number of aftermarket sources offer electric fan conversion kits that include all of the necessary parts and wire harnesses. Such a conversion requires a tuning adjustment in the engine controller to not only activate the fans, but prevent the "Check Engine" light from illuminating.

Transmissions

The Tremec 6-speed manual transmissions that have been offered with select production vehicles, such as the F-car, Corvette, and GTO/Monaro, hold up well to bolt-on supercharger and turbocharger kits on cars primarily driven on the street. Vehicles that see considerable time on the drag strip or road course benefit from upgrades to strengthen internal components, such as swapping the shift forks and synchronizer keys with heavier-duty parts.

Additionally, higher-capacity, dual-friction clutches work well to prevent slippage and should be considered at the time of the supercharger installation, particularly if the vehicle has more than about 40,000 miles on the odometer. A stronger flywheel is also a wise consideration on high-power vehicles, as stock ones can break under high load.

When it comes to automatic transmissions, the stock Hydra-Matic automatic transmissions, which came equipped on the vast majority of LS-powered vehicles, can quickly strain the far edge of their capability envelope when a blower or turbo is added to the powertrain. Those transmissions are manufactured and electronically controlled to perform within a limited performance range and the 100-plus horsepower that is added to the drivetrain with a turbocharger or supercharger quickly exceeds the automatic transmission's torque capacity. The lifespan of the transmission diminishes even quicker if the vehicle is regularly drag raced.

A number of performance transmission companies offer upgraded versions and kits for GM's electronically controlled transmissions. As with manual transmissions, the majority of upgrades include replacing internal components with stronger, heavier-duty components. Indiana-based RPM Transmissions offers a range of upgrade options for the popular 4L60/4L65 transmissions and 6-speeds that include stronger clutch packs, hardened output shafts, and other strengthened components.

Along with strengthening the transmission (manual or automatic) to stand up to forced induction, another consideration when upgrading the transmission is altering the gearing to better match the power delivery of the supercharger or turbocharger. The same goes for the torque converter in automatic transmission vehicles. This is more of a concern for supercharged vehicles, where additional power is being made at even the lowest RPM levels. Stock transmissions, particularly GM's automatics, have relatively "short" (numerically low) first gears

Vehicles with automatic transmissions are particularly prone to the effects of the added torque delivered by a supercharged or turbocharged engine combination. The transmission's torque rating can be quickly exceeded with even a low-boost bolt-on kit. Transmission upgrades should be seriously considered, especially if the vehicle is intended to see more than occasional trips to the drag strip. GM Performance Parts offers a number of brand-new, performance-enhanced transmissions that carry the Supermatic label, including versions of the 4L60 and 4L80. Other options include having the stock transmission professionally upgraded by one of a number of specialty transmission companies, such as RPM Transmissions.

By channeling torque through all four wheels, the 4L60 transmission of the all-wheel-drive TrailBlazer SS has proven especially vulnerable to failure when the extra load of a blower or turbo system is introduced. That's mostly due to tuners who eliminate the "torque management" feature that briefly closes the throttle between shifts. On these AWD vehicles, that puts an inordinate strain on the powertrain. Typically, the transmission starts slipping between the 1-2 shifts or won't hold the gears, especially fourth gear. Any enthusiast contemplating a supercharger or turbo system for a Trailblazer SS should factor in the cost of an upgraded transmission, or make sure to leave the torque management alone.

Many LS-powered vehicles feature independent rear axles, such as the Cadillac CTS-V (shown), fifth-generation Camaro, Pontiac G8/Holden Commodare, and the GTO/Monaro. The axles in those cars stand up reasonably well with a force-inducted engine when street tires are used, but can be stressed to the breaking point when used with slicks at a drag strip. Heavier-duty axle components and suspension are available from companies such as BMR Fabrication.

One of the simplest, yet most effective, changes that can benefit LS vehicles with independent rear axles is a swap of the major suspension bushing to higher-durometer (stiffer) parts. The bushings from Specter Werkes/Sports helped reduce the road-course lap times on this 2010 Camaro SS by more than 1 second, but more importantly, they virtually eliminated wheel hop in straight-line acceleration. It must be noted that the car was not supercharged or turbocharged, but the dramatic improvement in wheel hop at launch is absolutely necessary for a vehicle that is force-inducted.

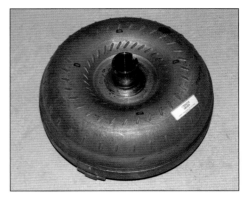

Whether retaining the stock transmission or investing in a new/modified one, a replacement torque converter should be considered. It is difficult to generalize about the necessary stall speed, because each vehicle and its equipment is different, so you should contact a reputable converter company, such as Yank Performance Converters to get a recommendation of the most appropriate size and stall speed.

that provide energetic launches in stock form, but are overkill with a power adder. A taller first gear (and equally matched gear pack) provides smoother, more controlled launches on the street and strip.

As for torque converters, there's not enough room in this chapter to give advice on selecting the most appropriate one. Your best bet is contact the tech department of a trusted, recommended performance converter manufacturer and discuss the type of power adder, along with the vehicle's intended use, to receive a professional recommendation.

Axle Upgrades

The rear axle on full-size pickups and SUVs are strong enough for most bolt-on blower and turbo kits, but those of other LS-powered vehicles are on the edge of their maximum load capacity when used with forced induction.

Generally speaking, the stock solid (Salisbury-type) rear axle of fourth-generation F-cars, TrailBlazers, SSRs, etc., should hold up to most street use and mild to moderate drag racing. More regular racing and the use of slicks or drag radial-type street tires hastens the demise of a stock axle, as the high load that comes with strong traction is usually the culprit of a broken axle. In a very real sense, the axle in a car with street tires that spends more time spinning its tires than yanking its way to 1.2-second 60-foot times lasts longer.

Stronger axle shafts and differential units are the cure for most vehicles, while replacing the stock axle assembly with a stronger, racing-style assembly from aftermarket manufacturers such as Strange or Currie Enterprises is recommended for higher-powered vehicles and those expected to spend more time at the race track. Convenient, direct-swap kits are offered for popular applications, such as the fourth-generation F-car (see "Real-World Project: F-Car Axle Swap").

Independent Axle Options

Although surprisingly robust in stock form, the basic design of an independent rear axle system is inherently weaker than a solid axle when it comes to the strains of drag racing and very high power on the street. For owners of a GTO/Monaro, G8/Commodore, Cadillac CTS, and fifth-generation Camaro, there's a well-established aftermarket industry catering to GM's independently sprung rear-drive cars. Stronger CV shafts, axle stubs, driveshafts, differential units, and more are available, along with chassis and suspension components designed to quell wheel hop and other launch issues. Florida-based BMR Fabrication has one of the largest selections of these parts.

Solid Axle Conversion

On vehicles intended for regular use on the drag strip, the replacement of a factory independent axle, such as the one found on the Pontiac GTO, G8, and fifth-generation Camaro, with a solid axle is a wise

consideration. Regardless of the strength of the differential or axle shafts, an independent-rear-suspension design simply doesn't offer the strength required for the load put upon it by repeated full-throttle launches, especially the hard-biting launches that come with using racing slicks or drag radials.

Currently, there aren't any direct-swap solid-axle conversions kits to recommend, but several GTO racers have adapted kits for fourth-generation F-cars. Similar adaptations can be applied to the G8, Camaro, and even Cadillac CTS.

Real-World Project: F-Car Axle Swap

In LS vehicles with solid rear axles, primarily fourth-generation F-cars and trucks, those axles may not stand up to the torque from a high-boost, high-horsepower engine combination. The F-body axle, for example, is a relatively mild 10-bolt/7.5-inch design that is only slightly stronger than similar axles used on countless low-power sedans of the 1980s.

Indeed, for most serious street vehicles and race cars, GM axles aren't always the first choice. Nine times out of 10, there's a Ford-derived 9-inch tucked between the rear wheels. Of course, most high-performance 9-inch rear ends these days share only the design of the Ford axle—all the parts are newly manufactured. The 9-inch design has proven to be extremely durable, but there is another strong, performance-minded axle option in the Dana 60 design.

As with most new 9-inch axles, the late-model Dana 60 is completely manufactured by another company. In this case it's Strange Engineering, called the S60. With the popularity and proven track record of the 9-inch, it is logical to ask, "Why venture into uncharted territory with the Dana 60?" For one thing, it is extremely durable. Strange Engineering says the larger, 9.75-inch Dana 60 is about equal in strength to a Ford 9-inch, but offers that strength at a lower cost. Certainly, cost is a factor for most enthusiasts, so strength for less cash is an enticing combination.

Strange's S60 Dana rear end housing is a perfect fit for a super-charged fourth-gen Camaro Z28. With beefier 35-spline axles and a huge 9¾-inch ring gear, the Strange Dana-style S60 is designed for the rigors of the racetrack, making it an ideal street/strip option. It offers comparable strength to the Ford 9-inch, but its conventional design makes it a lower-cost option.

The S60 housing is not a refurbished junkyard Mopar part; it's an all-new part that is cast with suspension mounts for the F-car.

Here's the stock, 7.5-inch 10-bolt axle out of our fourth-generation Camaro project car. While it served well for moderate increases in power and torque, it wouldn't stand up to the forces put to it by a new supercharger combination. The aftermarket suspension parts attached to it will be transferred to the new axle.

One of the details that makes this swap so easy is the pre-installed spring perches for the F-car suspension. This custom-ordered combination came with the axle tubes and end housings installed. We had to paint the tubes, however.

The axles are Strange's own induction-hardened, 35-spline S/T units. They are super strong and designed for street and strip duty. The axle also features a Power-Lok locking differential and a set of 3.73 gears.

The installation process began with the removal and transfer of necessary components from the stock axle to the S60. Some of the bolt holes on the aftermarket suspension parts required minor "hogging out" to bolt to the S60.

With the axle in place, the brakes and supporting hardware were swapped onto it.

Strange says the S60 axle weighs only about 25 pounds more than a comparably built aftermarket 12-bolt setup. And while the individual components for the axle can be purchased separately, Strange offers the S60 in a complete, bolt-it-in combination with 35-spline axles for many GM vehicles, including the fourth-generation F-car. The following is the installation of an S60 axle assembly into a fourth-generation Camaro. For

this project, the complete package included the S60 case and axle tubes with spring perches already welded to them. Because almost no two enthusiasts' combinations are alike, here's a rundown of what the project axle assembly included:

- S60 housing
- 3-inch axle tubes and end housings for late-model F-cars (with spring perches installed)

After the parts were transferred to the new axle, it was simply a matter of lifting it into place. This is where a shop with a lift and a jack comes in handy, because the axle is very heavy and awkward to maneuver. The fit of the S60 axle was perfect. All the suspension components bolted right back up without a problem.

Because the housings of the stock axle and the S60 were different lengths, a new, shorter driveshaft was required. A custom metal-matrix shaft was ordered and installed.

- Power-Lok locking differential
- 3.73-ratio ring-and-pinion
- 35-spline S/T induction-hardened axles
- Aluminum rear-end cover

Because Strange's custom S60 case is designed specifically for this application (it's not a cleaned-up, old Mopar part), the F-car's suspension components bolt right up to it. The only considerable detail to work out

with the axle swap was the drive-shaft. Because the S60's pinion is longer than the 10-bolt's, a shorter driveshaft was required. So, after careful measurements were taken with the axle installed, a custom metal-matrix shaft from Strange was ordered to fit. It bolted up without a hitch and the Camaro project car was again mobile—and ready to withstand the stress of a high-boost blower engine.

Auxiliary Instruments

Keeping tabs on a force-inducted engine usually requires instruments that aren't found in a vehicle's standard gauge cluster. That means adding auxiliary gauges and it's a process that's been done as long as hot rodders began experimenting with power adders in the 1940s and 1950s.

A quick scan of any performance parts catalog or Web site reveals dozens of different instruments, all seemingly vital to monitoring engine performance. But when it comes down to it, there are four gauges that are more important than the rest when used with super-charged and turbocharged engines.

Boost Gauge: A simple instrument to install by tapping into a vacuum source on the engine (usually by inserting a "T" fitting where a vacuum hose is located on the intake

The final step of the project was the re-installation of the torque arm cross member and torque arm. Now, the car's rear end is ready for the torque of a super-charged engine.

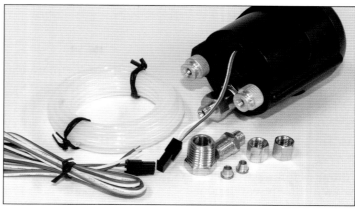

A-pillar gauge pods are popular for mounting auxiliary instruments, but the finish quality—including fitment and color match—on some parts is simply not good and detracts from the factory appearance of the interior. It is worth checking out other people's installed pods and asking around for notes on the best-quality parts.

This lineup includes the four main instruments suited to supercharged and turbocharged vehicles. From left to right, they include a boost guage, air/fuel ratio meter, pyrometer (for turbocharged engines), and a fuel-pressure gauge.

manifold), it delivers a reading of positive manifold pressure when the supercharger or turbocharger is generating boost. For most bolt-on supercharger and turbo systems, a gauge with a maximum range of 15 to 20 pounds of boost is adequate. Higher-boost gauges are available in 30- and 60-pound ranges.

Fuel Pressure Gauge: More important than the boost gauge is the fuel pressure gauge, which can provide a glimpse of inadequate fuel pressure and give the driver the opportunity to shut off the engine before a lean-out condition causes engine damage. An electric gauge is preferred for the higher fuel pressure of the electronically controlled injection systems found on LS engines. Because of the obvious safety concerns of tapping into the fuel system to draw the pressure reading, high quality fittings and lines (including braided steel) must be used. Typically, the fuel system is tapped at the Schrader valve on the fuel rail or the fuel pressure regulator.

Air/Fuel Ratio Gauge: Like the fuel pressure gauge, an air/fuel ratio (AFR) gauge can indicate a poten-tially damaging lean condition, but it is also helpful for monitoring the mixture to optimize tuning across the RPM band. Installation is fairly simple: It simply connects to the wiring of the oxygen sensors, whether factory-style narrowband or wideband sensors. It is possible to split the connection so at the flick of a switch, the AFR from each cylinder bank is read separately. Or, for the ultimate in engine minding, a pair of AFR gauges can be used to simultaneously monitor each cylinder bank.

Pyrometer (exhaust-gas temperature gauge): The pyrometer is more useful with turbocharged engines, where the exhaust temperatures can be extremely high. Excessively high exhaust temperature can indicate a lean fuel condition, restricted engine air supply or damaged turbocharger. Installation involves connecting the gauge to a thermocouple that is mounted on the exhaust manifold, ahead of the turbocharger. Pyrometers are typically offered with maximum ranges of 1,200 to 2,400 degrees F. Lower-range gauges should suffice for most low- and moderate-boost turbo engines.

A look at hardware of a typical aftermarket gauge shows they are relatively uncomplicated in what it takes to install them. The larger task involves installing the necessary sensor or sender on the engine or exhaust system to drive the gauge's readout.

ACCEL
www.accel-ignition.com

ACCEL/DFI
www.accel-dfi.com

Air Flow Research
www.airflowresearch.com

AiResearch Industrial Division
www.airflowresearch.com

Alternative Auto Performance
www.alternativeauto.com

Alternative Auto Performance
www.alternativeauto.com

A'PEXi
www.apexi-usa.com

APS Performance
www.airpowersystems.com

Big Stuff 3's
www.bigstuff3.com

Bill Miller Engineering
www.bmeltd.com

Blower Drive Service
www.blowerdriveservice.com

BMR Fabrication
www.bmrfabrication.com

Callies Dragonslayer
www.callies.com

Carputing, LLC
www.carputing.com

Cometic Gasket
www.cometic.com

Comp Cams
www.compcams.com

Diamond
www.diamondracing.net

Dynojet
www.dynojet.com

Edelbrock
www.edelbrock.com

Exedy
www.exedyusa.com

F.A.S.T.
www.fuelairspark.com

Fastlane, Inc.
www.fastlaneincorporated.com

GM Performance Parts
www.gmperformanceparts.com

Harold Martin
www.haroldmartin.com

Harrop Engineering
www.harrop.com.au

HP Tuners
www.hptuners.com

JE Pistons
www.jepistons.com

Katech Performance
www.katecheng.com

Katech Performance
www.katechengines.com

Kenne Bell
www.kennebell.net

Lingenfelter Performance Engineering
www.lingenfelter.com

Livernois Motorsports
www.livernoismotorsports.com

Magna Charger
www.magnacharger.com

Magnuson
www.magnusonproducts.com

Martin Motorsports
www.haroldmartin.com

MSD Ignition
www.msdignition.com

Mustang Dynamometer
www.mustangdyne.com

Northern Tool and Equipment
www2.northerntool.com

Oliver
www.oliverconnectingrods.com

Powerdyne
www.powerdyne.com

Pratt & Miller
www.prattmiller.com

ProCharger
www.procharger.com

Pro-Filer
www.profilerperformance.com

Quaife
www.quaife.co.uk

Racing Head Service
www.rhsheads.com

RPM Transmissions
www.rpmtransmissions.com

SLP Performance
www.slponline.com

Snow Performance
www.snowperformance.net

Specter Werkes Sports
www.spectergtr.com

Squires Turbo Systems
www.ststurbo.com

Stenod Performance
www.stenodperformance.com

Strange Engineering
www.strangeengineering.net

Swain Tech
www.swaintech.com

T&D Machine Products
www.tdmach.com

Thomson Automotive
www.thomsonautomotive.com

TiAL
www.tialsport.com

Total Seal
www.totalseal.com

Trick Flow
www.trickflow.com

Turbonetics
www.turboneticsinc.com

Turbo Technology
www.turbotechnologyinc.com

Ultimate Performance and Racing
www.upandracing.com

Vortech
www.vortechsuperchargers.com

Whipple Industries
www.whipplesuperchargers.com

World Products
www.worldcastings.com

Yank Performance Converters
www.converters.com